D1512079

JENNINGS SCHOLAR LECTURES

1970–71

THE 1970-1971 JENNINGS SCHOLAR LECTURES

REPORT ON A PROGRAM FOR OUTSTANDING TEACHERS
SPONSORED BY THE
MARTHA HOLDEN JENNINGS FOUNDATION

The Educational Research Council
of America
Cleveland

TABLE OF CONTENTS

Bowling Green State University Series:

INTRODUCTION

The significant role of the elementary and secondary teacher emphasizes the importance of opportunities for continued professional growth and development of these teachers. One of the major objectives of the Martha Holden Jennings Foundation is to improve the quality of elementary and secondary education. The trustees of the Foundation believe that the quality of education can be improved by providing valuable experiences for teachers. With the assistance of the Educational Research Council of America the preliminary planning and administration of the first Jennings Scholar Program was initiated in 1963.

The Jennings Scholar concept is based on recognizing a certain percentage of outstanding teachers in each school system. Instead of sending these teachers to universities and colleges, the program brings them outstanding scholars from universities in the United States and Europe, from government, and from business and industry for a series of lectures and discussions. It is a plan that is intriguing in its simplicity but far-reaching in its effectiveness.

The first group of approximately three hundred 1963 Jennings Scholars was honored at a luncheon in the Sheraton-Cleveland Hotel at the conclusion of the first Jennings Scholar lecture series in May of 1964. Each one received a plaque, a small monetary award and a bound copy of the lectures. All of these were in recognition of the honor of being chosen an outstanding teacher. A series of Awards Luncheons has been held in subsequent years and in each instance invitations have been extended to groups of Jennings Scholars to attend.

Selection of Jennings Scholars has been commissioned to participating Superintendents in each geographic area. Criteria have been suggested by a Superintendent's Advisory Committee, in order that maximum benefit accrue to the teaching profession by identifying and honoring the best and most competent teachers. In addition it is desirable to recognize these exceptional teachers because they exert such favorable influence on their students.

Dr. George Baird, president of the Educational Research Council, has said, "To my knowledge the Jennings Scholar Program is the first of its kind in the United States for effectively recognizing and stimulating superior teachers in a community. It brings outstanding national figures from many campuses to teachers in each area where the programs have been conducted."

The Jennings Scholars themselves have expressed the greatest appreciation for the opportunity that has been theirs. The following brief quote is representative of the feeling of the participating Jennings Scholars: "It has been an exciting and rewarding experience."

ABOUT THE MARTHA HOLDEN
JENNINGS FOUNDATION

The Martha Holden Jennings Foundation was established in 1959 by Martha Holden Jennings (widow of Andrew R.) of Cleveland, Ohio. It was the hope of Mrs. Jennings, who died in 1962, that her personal Foundation would provide greater recognition to the teaching profession at the elementary and secondary levels and also encourage teachers to specialize in areas beyond the normal curriculum of these levels.

The Foundation was established as a non-profit, charitable Ohio Corporation, with the proviso that a substantial part of the activities be carried on within the State of Ohio.

The broad purpose of the Foundation, as stated in the Articles of Incorporation, is defined thus: "to foster the development of individual capabilities of young people to the maximum possible extent through improving the quality of teaching in secular primary and secondary schools and by furnishing incentives with respect thereto, by such means as the Trustees from time to time shall determine."

It was in keeping with this broad purpose that the Foundation — in cooperation with the Educational Research Council of America — initiated the Jennings Scholar Program to honor outstanding classroom teachers and has extended its scope in each succeeding year.

BIOGRAPHICAL NOTES ON MARTHA HOLDEN JENNINGS

During her lifetime, Mrs. Andrew R. Jennings was deeply interested in education, the fine arts, culture and other humanitarian endeavors. This interest dated back through the two decades when she and her husband lived in Europe, where Mr. Jennings guided the growth and development of the International Business Machines Corporation. Upon her return to Cleveland in 1930 she continued to support her interests.

The growth of the Cleveland Museum of Art and of the University Circle area as a cultural and educational center, both of which she witnessed for over thirty years from her residence in the Wade Park Manor, appealed to her greatly, and prompted her to make substantial bequests to the Museum and to the University Circle Development Foundation in her will.

Her foresight and good judgment in making investments during her widowhood enabled her to provide other generous bequests, including a gift to Case Institute of Technology for expanding and improving its Computer Center, which has been named the Andrew R. and Martha H. Jennings Computer Center.

She maintained constant interest in medicine through association with the staff at the Cleveland Clinic and took great pleasure in informing them several years ago that she would provide the necessary funds for an educational building, which was dedicated on November 14, 1964. The gift resulted in an enlargement of the Clinic programs, involving training for interns and residents, and postgraduate specialized training to enable practicing doctors to keep abreast of new developments and techniques.

In 1959, Mrs. Jennings undertook to establish a personal Foundation which she envisioned as being a means to provide greater accomplishment on the part of our youth and their teachers. In part, she hoped it would bring greater recognition to the teaching profession at the elementary and secondary levels, and that it would encourage teaching activity in specialized fields and extend the horizon beyond the normal curriculum.

STATEMENT BY ARTHUR S. HOLDEN, JR.

One of the first and most gratifying projects of the Martha Holden Jennings Foundation has been the Jennings Scholar Program. It is designed to honor and reward outstanding teachers. This year, Programs were held in the Athens and Bowling Green areas. In the 1969–70 academic year, there were Programs in the Cleveland and Kent areas and, in 1971–72, we will have Programs in the Columbus and Dayton areas. We are more than pleased with the manner in which the Ohio University and Bowling Green State University Departments of Education conducted this year's Programs, with advice and assistance from the Foundation staff. In the future, our long-range plans are to support two Programs in the state each year. There will, therefore, be a two-year interval before the Program will return to any one location.

This bound volume of 1970–71 Jennings Scholar Lectures provides a permanent record of each lecture given in the two centers which operated this year. A review of attendance at the lectures produces a very favorable indication of teacher interest, in that the vast majority of this year's teachers have a record of perfect attendance. The balance of the teachers have, for the most part, missed only one or possibly two lectures. Such a record provides significant evidence of teacher interest and appreciation.

The most significant outcome of the Lecture Series is difficult to measure —namely, the effects which the lectures have on the minds and outlooks of the more than 4,000 outstanding teachers who have heard these lectures as Jennings Scholars in the past eight years. Perhaps equally important are the effects on the minds and outlooks of the thousands of young people whom the Jennings Scholar teachers have served.

Arthur S. Holden, Jr.
President
Martha Holden Jennings Foundation

July 1, 1971

THE MARTHA HOLDEN JENNINGS

SCHOLAR LECTURES

at

OHIO UNIVERSITY

1970—1971

Dr. Nicholas Nyaradi

Dr. Nicholas Nyaradi, Director, School of International Studies at Bradley University, presented the Jennings Scholar Lecture on September 26, 1970, in the John C. Baker Center, Ohio University.

Born and educated in Hungary, Dr. Nyaradi came to the United States in 1949 and became an American citizen in 1955. He received two doctor's degrees from the Royal Hungarian University of Budapest—one in political sciences and one in jurisprudence. Dr. Nyaradi was an attorney for 13 years and the legal advisor and executive director of one of the largest banks in Hungary.

Having participated in the anti-Nazi underground movement in Hungary during World War II, he was asked to accept a position in Hungary's postwar coalition government. He was first the Under-Secretary of the Treasury and then the Minister of Finance of the Republic of Hungary until 1948, when, because of increasing Soviet pressure, he and his wife were forced to flee their native country.

Since coming to the United States, Dr. Nyaradi has written several articles for leading newspapers and magazines, among them the Saturday Evening Post, Fortune Magazine, and the Scripps-Howard newspapers. His book *My Ringside Seat in Moscow* was not only acclaimed one of the best books ever published on Russia but was also commended as an outstanding antisubversive document. Several of Dr. Nyaradi's articles and speeches have been inserted into the Congressional Record.

Dr. Nyaradi has a unique and profound knowledge of the Soviet Union. He spent seven months in Moscow negotiating a Russian reparation claim against Hungary. During these conferences he came to know personally many Soviet leaders. He is also well acquainted with many leading personalities in the United States, in Europe, and in the Middle East.

Besides this vast background of international experiences, Dr. Nyaradi has established himself as an educational and civic leader in the United States. For his work in connection with Hungarian relief activities, he received a diploma of appreciation from the American Red Cross signed by its honorary chairman, President Eisenhower. Dr. Nyaradi is also a consultant for various government agencies and congressional committees.

His name is listed in *Who's Who in America, Who's Who in American Education,* and *International Who's Who.* The Freedoms Foundation at Valley Forge recently awarded him the George Washington Honorary Medal for his lectures throughout the country.

DISSENT OR DISORDER

Last year for me was the year of the consultant, because I had been appointed to more such jobs than at any time before in my life. First of all, I accepted an appointment to become a consultant of the National Schools Committee on Economic Education, which is a New-York based, nationwide, non-profit organization, the goal of which is to teach our public school teachers how to teach the basic aspects of our American economic system to their students in the classrooms.

Then—being the director and founder of the School of International Studies at Bradley University—I am not only a university professor but also a college administrator. In this capacity, I am greatly concerned about and involved in this present wave of dissent and disorder which sweeps the country. (As a matter of fact, just last week at our first Deans' Council meeting of the present academic year, I suggested to my fellow deans that, in view of the forthcoming confrontations, we had better appropriate to ourselves some combat pay because our jobs are getting considerably more dangerous every day.) This is also the reason why I have stored some bottled water and canned food in my office. I even have a cot there where I can spend the night if and when I am surrounded by fist-shaking and fire-bomb-throwing mobs.

Just because of my involvement in this wave of dissent and disorder, I decided to appoint myself as a consultant to the SDS. Now do not worry, my fellow teachers: The initials of my organization stand for "Students Disgusted with Socialism."

Then finally, a year and a half ago, the Administration appointed me as a consultant to the United States Department of State on European and Soviet affairs. You can imagine how greatly pleased and honored I was that as a naturalized American citizen and a former diplomat and cabinet member of my native country of Hungary, I was asked now by my adopted country to accept this appointment.

My fellow teachers, if you want to know exactly what the role of a consultant is, let me tell you that in my native city of Budapest, there was a district where the people were very unhappy indeed. The reason for their unhappiness was that within the district lived a viscious, old black tomcat which was the worst fighter in the history of the feline nation. Whenever he was out on his nightly rampages, he beat up every single dog and cat which crossed his way, and he did not even refrain from attacking human beings. So finally the neighbors got so uptight with the extracurricular activities of the cat, that one of them watched when he jumped in his backyard and threw at the cat a big pot of boiling hot water. The cat took off in terrible pain and collapsed in the back yard of his owner, who rushed him immediately to the veterinary hospital.

After this, blessed silence and quiet settled over the neighborhood.

Everybody could sleep; everybody was happy, as there was no more meowing and yelling and screaming.

Then about a month later the whole ruckus started again. So the angry neighbors called the owner of the cat and asked him what was the matter. They thought that the career of the cat had finally come to an end. Then the owner apologetically answered, "Well, you see the cat really is not in business any more, but has become a consultant."

One of the fringe benefits of my present work with the Department of State is that from time to time I am overseas in order to do some research and to participate in meetings and conferences. This was also the case during the last three weeks, when I traveled extensively in Europe, mostly in the Mediterranean area. I returned just four days ago from this trip. It was quite exciting because I was in Europe during the time of the hijacking of five airliners by the Arab commandos and, believe me, it was no fun whatsoever to take off from a European airport under the cloud of this terrorism.

The passengers were searched, baggage was opened, and constant bomb scares grounded planes all over the continent. When we took off, the captain left the seat belt sign on for about two hours after we had left Italy. We were already way out over the Atlantic when I asked the crew the reason for this unusual precaution. They told me that most of the Arab terrorist hijackers attack the cockpit about thirty minutes after takeoff in order to prevent the airliner from getting too far out on the Atlantic, and to give them the possibility to turn around and land in one of the so called "airports" in the Jordanian desert. The reason why they keep the seatbelt sign on is that the crew can see if there is some suspicious movement throughout the cabin. If there is, the captain of the airliner is under the order to put the plane immediately in a deep dive and sudden bank in order to throw the would-be hijacker off balance. (As you know, no hijacker is a good hijacker unless he stands firmly on his two hind legs.)

At the same time, however, the airlines are worried that, by such a sudden banking or diving movement of the plane, the passengers may fly against the ceiling of the cabin, so they have to be tied down until the danger of the hijacking is over.

Just last week when we started our classes at Bradley University, I sensed that people really did not understand the very dangerous crisis they had in Jordan. Last week, I gave my classes a brief, to-the-point explanation of what is going on now in the Middle East and how the United States is involved in this critical confrontation. When I finished my presentation, one of my students came up to me and said, "Doctor, I am completely confused. I just do not understand who is with whom and who is against whom."

I said to her, "My dear, did you not read the newspapers?" She answered, "You see, I generally do not read newspapers."

I was somewhat taken aback, so I asked her, "Could you please tell me what you are majoring in?"

She answered, "I am majoring in education."

After this, I really got worried. I saw here a very fine student of the College of Education at Bradley University who will go into the most important profession in the world, teaching. She seemingly was so bogged down by the technical aspects of education, with the ideas of how to teach, with the finances of high school organization, with the role of the superintendent and the school psychologist, that she did not have the time to look at what might well become the most critical aspect of the future.

As I saw this, I decided to begin this address to you, my fellow teachers, with a very brief explanation of what is at stake today and how our future is affected by this international tension and what a completely unknown role dissent and disorder presently play today in our international difficulties.

Until now the difficulty in the Middle-Eastern situation was a confrontation between the Israelis on one side and the Arab countries on the other over the possession of what was called for centuries Palestine. When the Jewish state was founded in 1948, when Israel became an independent country after the British had resigned their role to govern and to administer this particular area, the hostility between the Arabs and the Israelis exploded into an open war.

Since this time there have been three wars in the area: in 1948, in 1956, and the last one in 1967. Basically what is behind this is on one side the deep conviction of the Jewish people to have a homeland after it was destroyed some 2000 years ago by the legions of the Roman empire, and after which the Jewish people lived in dispersion—called the diaspora—all over the world. They were subjected to persecution, to discrimination, to killing—like when the Nazi monsters exterminated some six million Jews in their concentration camps. Their conviction is that after all this horrible experience, they are entitled to live in freedom, in independence, and in security in an area that they regard as the homeland of their ancestors.

On the other side, the Arabs retorted to this that the Jewish people lost their claim, their right to this area, 2000 years ago, when the Israeli state ceased to exist. The country then came later—some 1500 years ago—under Arab-Moslem domination, and therefore, the Arabs say that the Jewish claim based on the biblical justification of Moses and his people occupying the Promised Land has about as much validity as if the Indians today reclaimed the Island of Manhattan, which their ancestors sold three centuries ago (for $24.) to the Dutch settlers. (Between you and me, I think that they overpaid the Indians. I personally do not feel that Manhattan Island was worth $24.)

Here you can see the basic confrontation and the great difficulty in reaching some kind of agreement. The situation in the Middle East was then complicated by the fact that the two nuclear super-powers of the world, the United States on one side and the Soviet Union on the other, got directly involved in the Middle-Eastern conflict.

The United States supported Israel, not only because of humanitarian reasons, not only because we have a large number of fine Jewish citizens in this country, who are, of course, interested in the land of their brethren, but, also because it is its primary interest to keep a free and independent Israeli state alive in the Middle East.

The reason for this is very simple. First of all, in the whole Middle Eastern area today, Israel is the only country which is still friendly towards us. Israel is the only country which has a Western type democratic system resembling very much our own. Israel is the last stronghold of American presence in the Eastern Mediterranean which is especially enhanced by the fact that our main alliance, the North Atlantic Treaty Organization, is anchored in the Mediterranean through the participation of Italy, Greece, and Turkey, which are all Mediterranean countries.

If Israel were destroyed and if American influence lost its last foothold in the Eastern Mediterranean, then the Mediterranean would become a Russian lake. NATO, the North Atlantic Treaty Organization, would be virtually destroyed, and its southern flank would dangle in the air.

There is one other thing which is extremely interesting, and this is that the Middle East is the largest oil-producing area of the world. Two of the countries there, Iran, the former Persia, and Saudi Arabia, which are outside of the conflict today, are still producing a great amount of oil, which goes to Western Europe and to Japan, our two main allies. Now if American influence were eliminated from the Mediterranean, we could see that there would be such an increased pressure in this area that the oil supplies of Western Europe and Japan—which depend up to 90 per cent on Middle-Eastern oil deliveries—would be greatly jeopardized. Russia would have a strangle-hold on the jugular vein of the economics of our most important allies. This is the reason why the United States is supporting Israel, as our goal in that area is to create a just peace in which each of the parties could live within internationally secured bounderies.

On the other side, the Russian intervention in that area was not motivated by the same reasons. Russia for the last 300 years wanted to get herself a foothold in the Eastern Mediterranean, which we call "The Crossroads of the World." This was the reason why Russia gave 10 billion dollars' worth of military and economic aid to the Arab countries, which are determined to destroy Israel as an independent and free nation. To this already complicated situation, a new complication was added recently, with the appearance of the so-called "Palestinian guerillas" or "commandos" on the scene. These people are Arabs who were displaced mostly by their own will from the territories where they lived after the Jewish state was established. These people are fanatical, they do not accept any kind of compromise, as they think that the only solution is to push the Jews into the Mediterranean. These are the people who are located today in the country of Jordan, where they made an all-out attempt during the last two weeks, not only through the hijacking of five Western planes to which they caused 62 million dollars' damage, but at the time of this meeting they are still holding 38 American citizens as hostages. These people were directly engaged in trying to topple the rule of King Hussein of Jordan, who is among the most moderate Arab leaders with whom there is still a possibility to arrange between the Jews and the Arabs some kind of acceptable compromise.

If King Hussein had been toppled by the Palestinian guerillas, the whole Middle-Eastern situation would have exploded within 48 hours in an over-all war.

Until now Russia has invested tremendous amounts of money in the President of Egypt—the United Arab Republic as it is officially called—Abdul Gamal Nasser, who was the hero of the Arab world. How-ever, the successful hijacking and the subsequent destruction of four big Western jets had increased greatly the prestige and the influence of the so-called Palestinian commandos in the Arab world. They were beginning to turn away from Nasser, and they were beginning to look towards those guerillas whose commander is an Arab physician by the name of George Habash, who openly admits his admiration for and his affiliation with Mao Tse-tung, the leader of Communist China, which, of course, Russia does not like. Because if the Arab world would suddenly swing away from Nasser—in whom Russia has invested 10 billion dollars—and would instead turn towards the Palestinian guerillas, the result would be that a wide door would be opened in the Middle East for Chinese influence. And this is basically the blueprint of this extremely dangerous and complicated situation in the Middle East today.

However, my fellow teachers, there is something even more dangerous in this connection, in spite of the fact that during the last few days some of the explosiveness of the confrontation between King Hussein and the Pales-tinian guerillas was diffused. The situation is that it continues to be con-stantly on the brink of explosion. It is like a powder keg. The fuse which was lighted just two weeks ago and which could have led easily to the explosion of this whole situation, for the time being at least, has been extin-guished. However, the powder keg is still there.

I would like to remind you all of the following historical fact: In 1914, when World War I broke out, this was preceded by a constant bickering and quibbling between the small nations on the Balkan Peninsula of Europe—nations which were at each other's throats and nations which felt an open hostility towards the Austrian Empire. In June of 1914, as a conse-quence of this basically secondary problem, the heir to the Austrian throne, Franz Ferdinand, was murdered. One month later, however, this event erupted into World War I, which ended with a casualty figure of 15 million dead.

In the late 30's another potential powder keg was created by the rivalry between Poland and Nazi Germany over the possession of the port city of Danzig. Finally on September, 1939, Adolf Hitler's Nazi army invaded Poland, an invasion which became the beginning of World War II, when another potential potential powder keg exploded into a conflict which ended with 20 million dead.

We have today a similar situation when a basically secondary problem —which, of course, is very important to the Israelis and to the Arabs but

9

to the world is still only a secondary problem—over a relatively small area of Palestine threatens to become just as much of a powder keg for World War III as was the Balkan question or the Danzig problem before World War I and World War II.

This is the reason why Americans should be aware of these extremely complicated factors. One shot fired carelessly somewhere in the Jordanian desert might very well result in what President Nixon called in his July 1970 press conference: "a confrontation between the super powers of the world, the United States and Russia," because of their backing of the two opposing parties.

I am sure that you all have noticed and recognized the great effort which President Nixon exerted in order to maintain some semblance of peace in the Middle East. This was not only in line with America's traditional intention to avoid armed confrontations, but it was also the consequence of the feelings of the American people.

There was a report out of Washington last week that the President told a visiting Senator that the American people just do not have the heart to go into a war in the Middle East. Therefore we have here an extremely dangerous situation; namely, that the mind of the American people is conditioned so strongly against the war in Viet Nam that this feeling is being transferred to a possible American involvement in the Middle East. We were told so often not to be the policemen of the world in Southeast Asia, so people think, "Why on earth should we now get involved in a war which concerns only the Arabs and Israelis?"

This is, of course, extremely dangerous because primary American interests are at stake in the Middle East exactly as our desire to stop communist agression in Southeast Asia was also in the interests of the American people.

Maybe I should quote you such an "authority" on this problem as my son, John, who is now 20 years old, a junior at Bradley University, and a cadet-lieutenant in the Air Force ROTC. He just signed up a week ago as he took the oath as a future Air Force officer. When he came home from the swearing-in ceremony, he told me, "Dad, I really hate war. But if one day I would have to go to war in order to defend you, Mom, and my little sister, I would still much rather fly my jet fighter over the Mekong River Delta than over the Mississippi River Delta."

This remark might explain to some people why four American presidents, Mr. Eisenhower, Mr. Kennedy, Mr. Johnson, and now Mr. Nixon felt that we cannot leave communist aggression unchecked in this particular area of the world. Perhaps this decision makes more sense after I quoted the simple words of a young native-born American, John Nyaradi, cadet-Lieutenant in the ROTC of Bradley University.

In this connection now we have to examine very closely the role of dissent and disruption. This dissent and disruption, which really did not seem to bother too many Americans, has projected an increasingly bad image of the United States to the people in the world today. Not only do people abroad begin to question whether the United States is able to stand up for its commitments, but they are beginning to question even whether we are really willing to fulfill our promises. People are beginning to question whether this image of a "house divided," which we are now projecting all over the world doesn't mean that the United States' power, determination, and courage as a leading country in the free world was jeopardized to such an extent that the United States is really falling apart. The leading countries of the Communist world, the Soviet Union and the People's Republic of China—meaning Russia and Mainland China—are watching very carefully what they believe are *signs* of a gradual American withdrawal from important positions.

In international affairs there is no such thing as a vacuum. If a vacuum is created by one power, immediately another will begin to move in. The great danger of the dissent and disorder in our country is that it projects an image of weakness, an image of division, an image of reluctance to stand up against aggression if our government cannot count anymore on the support of the people.

Look only at the difficult task which Mr. Nixon has to face as compared to the situation of 66 or 67 years ago. Please remember that during the administration of President Theodore Roosevelt in the early years of the 20th century, Morocco was a very insecure place to live in. There were constant robberies, gangs roamed the highways, there were killings, murders, and kidnappings. (As a matter of fact, 60 to 70 years ago, Morocco was almost as bad a place as today is in Central Park in New York after sunset.)

At that time a naturalized American citizen of Greek descent whose name was Perdicaris, was traveling in Morocco when he was captured by a gang whose leader was a gangster chieftan by the name of Raisuli. (Our documents sometimes refer to him as Rasul Ali, but I think the name was Raisuli.)

Raisuli notified the American consulate general in Tangiers that he was holding this American citizen captive as a hostage for ransom, and unless the United States paid $100,000 in gold, he would kill Perdicaris.

The consulate-general dutifully reported this fact to the State Department, and the Secretary of State, John Hayes, immediately went to President Roosevelt, reporting this incident. President Roosevelt's answer was to place the "Great White Fleet" on immediate standby alert, ordering it to be ready to immediately sail to Morocco if necessary. Then, on the order of President Roosevelt, Secretary Hayes sent the shortest cable known in the diplomatic history of the world to Morocco. This is verbatum the text of the cable: "Perdicaris alive, or Raisuli dead" Within 24 hours the American citizen was freed—safe, sound, and unharmed.

Ladies and gentlemen, the reason why we can't stand up for our fellow citizens who in this very moment are held as hostages in the desert of Jordan by gangsters and by criminals, is not that President Nixon has less courage, has less determination than Teddy Roosevelt had. Unfortunately our country today is divided. Unfortunately today our country is infected by a thought which blurs our vision, and by which the people cannot see that a great power sometimes reaches a period of its existence when it has to either stand up for its rights or perish.

In this connection you might also have noticed a very interesting change in the attitude of some of our distinguished lawmakers in Washington. There were a large number of senators and representatives who favored our immediate withdrawal from Viet Nam; who said that the United States cannot be the policeman of the world, and they were even willing to place restrictions upon President Nixon in his role as commander-in-chief. But, lo and behold, these same distinguished lawmakers today are suddenly arguing that President Nixon should take an extremely forceful stand in the Mediterranean, and one of them, as a matter of fact, even urged that we should confront the Russians with an ultimatum to withdraw immediately from there or we would shoot them up with our long-range rockets.

It is a very interesting sight to see that some of these distinguished people who told us that we cannot be the policeman of the world when it came to Viet Nam, now tell us that we should be the policeman of the world when it comes to the otherwise justified defense and protection of Israel.

Inevitably, as a private American citizen, I had to come to the conclusion that this very interesting change in their attitude can be due only to politicking. We know that these fine lawmakers have quite a number of outstanding Jewish voters in their constituency—but there are very few Vietnamese who can actually vote in the United States elections.

Here you can see the extremely tragic picture of confusion—the confusion of the American mind which was due to a great extent to this dissent and disorder which started on the campuses of this country among our students in higher education and which is now spreading to secondary education. How did this all come about?

Fellow teachers, let me convey to you as a college professor and as an American university administrator, my sincere opinion that in spite of what we see around the campuses of our country, in spite of what we see in the deplorable costumes and habits among students of this great university where we are meeting today; in spite of the mysterious letters on the walls: "GIK," which means "Grass is King"; in spite of all of this, the overwhelming majority of our students are honest, good willing, straight-forward American young men and women. The only trouble with them is that they are extremely idealistic, and their idealism actually borders on naiveté. They walk constantly with their eyes fixed on cloud nine in the sky and they do not see the rocks on the road over which they are walking. We have a proverb in my native Hungary according to which "the road leading towards hell is paved with good intentions."

The second fact about these nice American young women and men is the situation that, contrary to all of the information you have received, these people in their great majority are abysmally ignorant. They do not know the situation in the world. They do not know the situation in the country. They do not know the causes, reasons, and facts because of the propaganda they are getting. Their lack of knowledge makes young people easy prey of a very small but extremely determined group which stands behind all of this and which fosters all of the disorder, all the militancy in this country.

How do they do that? This determined small militant minority in the background picks out some completely uncontroversial, even noble issues, for instance "Peace." Then they attach themselves to these issues just as the barnacles do to the hull of a ship, and then they can be carried an awfully long way towards their goal. These issues are as sacrosanct and uncontroversial as is motherhood or was—until recently—the flag before the rascals started to burn it on the street corners and on the campuses. Their main issue is "peace." There is nothing less controversial in the world than peace. All of us Americans want peace, we work for peace, we are for peace, and those who—like myself—believe in God, even pray for peace. However, these good willing, honest, naive and ignorant young people do not know that peace is not a one-way street. In order to achieve peace, it is not enough that we should want peace on this side of the street, but the other guy across the street should have the same ideas, too. Let us suppose that tomorrow morning I would have to go through a wild-animal-infested jungle. Then as a good Presbyterian I definitely would take my Bible in my pocket. But you know what? I would also have a six shooter in my belt—just in case the tiger cannot read or is not a Presbyterian!

These young people say that they want to destroy the Establishment. Well, what is the Establishment they want to destroy? The Establishment is the constitutional form of government under which we live. The Establishment is America's military might. The Establishment is our American economic system. And if they destroy this, whom are they going to help? Only those countries which are the trouble-makers in the world, the Soviet Union and Red China, which are bent on world domination and against whom the only remaining roadblock is the constitutional, military, and economic power of the United States of America.

It is frightening to watch the ignorance of these young people, who all agree that the American economic system, which they call "capitalism" should be destroyed. They do not give a hoot about the fact that it is because of this economic system that we Americans have become the world's best fed, best housed, best dressed, best taken-care-of people in the history of the human race. It is because of this economic system that we Americans, who are 6 per cent of the population in the world, can have today 62 per cent of all the automobiles in the world and 42 per cent of all the telephones in the world—even if they are on strike from time to time. Yet these people simply disregard all this and constantly mutter about the necessity of introducing some kind of Marxist socialism, a communist type of economy, into the United States.

If they weren't as ignorant as they are, all they would have to do is look 90 miles south of the border to Cuba, where Fidel Castro has introduced this type of economic system. I am asking you, my fellow teachers, how many American students know the fact that the people in Cuba live under the strictest system of rationing which exists in the whole world today? According to this, each and every Cuban today can buy each month four pounds of rice, two pounds of meat, a half-pound of butter, and one bottle of beer. So if the Cuban worker decides to drink his bottle of beer on the first day of the month, then for the rest of the month he is out of Schlitz and out of beer.

But in order to appreciate the American free economy, you don't have to compare it with a relatively primitive system such as Cuba has today. You can go to the showplace among the communist and socialist nations, the Soviet Union, where today—after 52 years of existence of this system—a Russian citizen can already buy himself a car. Of course it is not much of a car by our standards, because it is only a small, 32-horsepower, 4-cylinder contraption. As a matter of fact, it looks like a sardine can on wheels, and it also sounds like a sardine can on wheels—but you can drive it. The only thing you have to do to get this car is place your name on the waiting list and wait for five years. After this you will have to have the equivalent of $7,500 in cash to buy this car.

What is the reason for this? The explanation is very simple. Last year Detroit turned out nine million passenger car units. At the same time, Russia's passenger production was 275,000 cars. Obviously you have here the explanation of simple mathematics.

But, my fellow teachers, if our young people do not know these facts, if we the teachers of America do not teach them these facts, how on earth shall we be able to prevent these otherwise innocent, young men and women from becoming the victims of the militants and the provocators?

What do the provokers want? They say that they want to destroy our constitutional form of government, which they call "participatory democracy." However, if our young people knew that here in the United States we have an absolutely unique system of government, by which each and every individual or group can find a remedy to all of its grievances, then they would understand that in our country you do not have to destroy anything. If we want it, there is always the possibility of changing the Establishment, or even throwing the Establishment out of the window —provided that you have 51 per cent of the people behind you.

It is extremely important that we convey adequate knowledge to our young people. Please remember that the Greek word "democracy"— "demos" meaning people, "kratia" meaning rule, "demos-kratia" the rule of the people—does not mean only the privilege to participate, it does not mean only the right to guide and to lead. Democracy also means the obligation to learn; democracy means also the duty to know. How will the young people make up their minds, how will they reach important decisions for the future of this country and the future of the world if they do not know the issues which are involved?

The small minority of troublemakers are called sometimes the "activists," then again "militants," "radicals," and "extremists." I do not think that these names fit these people. What these people really are I am sorry to tell you: They are neo-Nazis, neo-Fascists, and neo-Communists. What this militant small group wants to do is exactly the same thing which Adolph Hitler did in Germany, which Benito Mussolini did in Italy and which Lenin, Trotski, and Stalin did in Russia: namely, to establish the

14

rule of the minority over the overwhelming majority of the people.

Fellow teachers, when I told you the symptoms of our present disease, then I gave you the diagnosis—which you call the anatomy of dissent. I would not be a good doctor if I did not try to give you the cure for the malady.

The immediate cure is that we have to stop the permissiveness which has taken hold in our country. Political permissiveness, permissiveness in our courts, the permissiveness of weak-kneed school administrators, who will have to put steel in their backbones. We have to stand up to the trouble making in our schools no matter from which corner the trouble making comes.

Last week when I had my first meeting with several hundred students who are enrolled in my various classes in the School of International Studies of Bradley University, I told them the following: "I, as an American citizen and an American educator, have my right to be here to teach you and to express freely my views. You as American citizens and American students are here to get an education for which you have paid and also have a right to express your views exactly as freely as I express mine. Please remember that this country did not become the leading nation in the history of mankind because it was a country of yes-men. This country developed into what it is today because of constant debate and constant discussion of ideas, philosophies, and politics. So, therefore, if you follow in the footsteps of your ancestors and you dissent, you have not only my permission but you have my blessings to do so. However, if one day you get the mistaken idea of trying to prevent me from entering this classroom to teach your fellow students to study, then, I will call the police—so help me, Lord—and have you all thrown into jail."

We have to maintain the goodwill, the generosity, the understanding of the American people towards our schools and institutions of higher learning, but we cannot do this until we bring to an end the age of permissiveness. Dissent, yes! Disorder, no! It is the duty of all of us in the educational profession to see to it that this is done.

On the other side, however, I would not be a good doctor if I did not believe in the age-old American adage that "one ounce of prevention is worth a pound of cure." Therefore, I feel very strongly that in the field of primary and secondary education you have a great opportunity and a great responsibility. It is your duty and your privilege to give an education to the students who study under you by which they should be able to understand problems they will have to face in the future.

We would be able to improve our primary and secondary educational system by giving our students a thorough, non-political, non-ideological, and absolutely objective and factual education in some vitally important fields. We would teach the operation and the blessings of our constitutional system of government and the principles and unparalled opportunities of our American economic system.

I feel that, especially in view of the fact that even today only some 40 per cent of our students go on to higher education, it is vitally important that the 60 per cent who end their formal education with you giving them their high school diplomas should get all this knowledge which will be their guiding light when they become voters, when they are called to serve in our armed forces, or when they are asked to pay their taxes. And for those 40 per cent of the students who go on to college, this basic knowledge which they will have gained in the public schools will help them to diffuse the often hostile propaganda they might encounter in the universities and also to stand up more effectively to the troublemakers.

In this connection I can give you an example. After the tragic events at Kent State, the students of Bradley University decided to hold a candlelight parade from the campus to the courthouse plaza through downtown Peoria. They received the necessary permission, but the police told them to avoid the main business street of the city, where the big plate windows might have been inviting targets for rock throwing. So 1500 of the 6000 students of Bradley University started with candles in hand in a parade from the campus.

When they came to the police line where the patrol cars were lined up, the policemen directed the students to the alternate route to the courthouse plaza. At this very moment the troublemakers went to work. Shouts were heard in the crowd. "Kill the pigs." "Burn the police cars." "Let's break through."

Seeing this, the members of the student government, including my own boy, from whom I heard the story, virtually threw themselves between the police and their fellow students, begging them to take the route for which they had permission. The students followed their advice and all 1500 followed this alternate route. What happened? The 15 revolutionaries looked around and saw suddenly that the students whom they had almost succeeded in getting into a bloody confrontation were not there. Then they began to yell obscenities and suddenly ran away. This is the way to handle this type of disorder.

Ladies and gentlemen, the Foundation on behalf of which I am privileged to speak to you and I have developed something for the teachers of Ohio. Last spring we finished a brief, six-piece film series which gives some guidance to teachers in the field of what to know about America's role in the world, about our constitutional system of government, about our American economy. These films are available to you, now and they will be available all over this state. We also hope that we will be able to organize several workshops through which I hope I will be able to collaborate as an educational aide in conveying this factual and nonpolitical information to their students. I sincerely hope and honestly feel that this work, the first of such ventures in this country in which the Foundation and I are now engaged, will be successful.

Besides this I also have a large number of invitations to participate in such workshops with individual school systems. I hope that the material we will develop in this connection can also be added to the work of the Foundation so perhaps we shall see here the beginning of a very worthwhile program.

The greatest trouble we have in this country is the wave of negativism which invades us. Everybody is against something in this country. On one side you have the anti-whites; then you have the anti-blacks. You have the anti-communists, the anti-socialists, and the anti-anti-communists. You see the anti-capitalists, the anti-Protestants, the anti-Jews, the anti-Catholics, the anti-everything people. Please remember, my fellow teachers, that never in the history of mankind was a cause won by being merely "anti." If we want to survive, we have to become strongly and positively *pro-American, pro-freedom, pro-God.*

I am not here to urge you to join me in any "anti-communist crusade" or a "campaign of hatred." What we need so desperately in our country is not to hate more those who oppose us, but to love more and appreciate more our own traditions, our own institutions, our own heritage, which we are so appallingly taking for granted.

My fellow teachers, although it is late, but I hope not too late, I would like to ask you to pick up the ball and start running with it. But if you feel that there is absolutely nothing that you as an individual or that you as a member of your school system can do about it, if you believe that the only thing you can do is to go ahead with teaching as usual, then at least I would like you to meditate for a second over the word and the spirit of an old Hungarian adage which was my own guiding light during the last 25 very difficult years of my life. This is how it sounds in an English translation: "You should work as if you would live forever and you should pray as if you would die tomorrow."

And if you ask me how come that I, who am a newcomer around here, am giving you this very harsh, this very rude, some of you might even call it controversial address, let me tell you that I have a vested interest in America.

When my wife and I stood 15 years ago in the Federal courtroom taking our oath for American citizenship, I asked myself a question: "How should I ever be able to repay this country for the privileges I am receiving here today? Freedom instead of slavery in my native Hungary, opportunity instead of oppression in my native Hungary, life instead of death in my native Hungary. How can I, with my European background, repay all of this?" And I came up with the answer. The only thing that I can give is knowledge, understanding, comparison, and, before and above all, appreciation. Ever since, I have only two overwhelming feelings left in my heart: The one is deep humility, and the other is everlasting gratitude for being permitted to be a citizen of this much maligned country. Thank you very much.

Dr. George Z. F. Bereday

Dr. George Z. F. Bereday, professor of comparative education at Teachers College, Columbia University, presented the Jennings Scholar Lecture on November 7, 1970, at Bowling Green State University. He has been on the faculty at Columbia since 1955.

His professional experiences also include: associate of the Russian Institute, member of the Faculty of the School of International Affairs, exchange professor at Moscow University, Fulbright professor at Tokyo University, visiting professor at the University of Hawaii, and director of the Japanese-American Teacher Program.

Dr. Bereday has been a member of cultural missions to the U.S.S.R., Finland, and Japan and was chief of the STAG Mission to Western Europe in 1970. All of these missions were sponsored by the Department of State.

Dr. Bereday has degrees from the University of London and from Oxford and Harvard Universities. He has language proficiency in Polish, his native tongue, English, French, German, Russian, Italian, Spanish, and Japanese.

Among the books he has edited are *The Making of Citizens, Essays on World Education,* and *Studies from the Center of Education in Industrial Nations.* His articles are published in several professional periodicals.

TOWARDS INDIVIDUALIZATION
OF INSTRUCTION

There is a story about an American colonel who rode into the ruins of the Coliseum in Rome after the war. He looked around, rubbed his hands, and said to an Italian guide, "Our bombers have sure done a good job!" And when the Italian guide said to him, "Oh no, no, Colonel! That was done a long time ago, by quite some different people," the Colonel replied, "Oh, well, in my country when we have ruins, we take them out of the way."

This little story is a good introduction to some of the old problems that we have had in American education, and old problems sometimes live on and stay with us. Ten years ago we lived through what experts in education called "the decade of infamy"; ten years ago many people seemed to attack the enterprise of education from all sides on the ground that we in school who were entrusted with the job of taking care of the intellectual life of the young people, have failed to teach the young children enough about the Coliseum, have failed to teach our colonels enough about the times of old, about the Western heritage. Since we are all teachers, since we don't have to defend ourselves from anybody right this minute, we can, in the privacy of this room, say that in an enterprise such as ours, with 30 million young people we process every year, when the diverse profession of one million persons attacks the problem of schooling the young, here and there we still raise Colonels who don't learn enough about the Coliseum. We bookish people, we teachers, we men of the word, would like all people to become men of the word. In the recesses of our hearts, even though we may pride ourselves on being practical and having common sense, we are longing for the book, and would like to invest our young people with that same kind of longing, and we get chagrined when our students don't perform—when they don't learn enough about the Coliseum.

The problem is still with us. The problem continues to trouble us at all levels. One of my predecessors, Professor George Counts, recalls a story on the subject. He was endowed with a photographic memory and could remember every student he ever taught. One day as he was getting off a train in suburban New York, he ran into a young woman with two children. "I know you!" he exclaimed, "You were my student at Columbia four years ago. You used to sit in the third row in the first chair from the left. I think I remember your name. Your name is Mrs. Adams." "That's right," replied the young woman. "And who are you?" Stories of that kind do happen and we teachers who always want to do better, who always look for new hills to conquer, are aware of this kind of bitter failure.

And yet, there is a profound wisdom and historical truth in the American colonel saying, "In this country when we have ruins we take them out of the way." It is, on an American prairie, on an unsettled piece of flat land, that a story of Western civilization has come to its perfect conclusion. It is here that Europeans and people of many other origins have found the way to grow together and thrive. It is here that a country has come into being, where change is normal, where innovation is a household word, where growth charts are the indices of progress, where we don't talk so much about good children and bad children but about fast learners and slow learners. It is here that movement has been enthroned as the central concern of the country. A journey through it is a joyful discovery of unprecedented creativity.

One gets out of an automobile in Lincoln, Nebraska, and one expects to see a pavement as gray and drab as only pavements can be. But someone thought of inserting into that pavement alternative black slab stones, and all of a sudden one is walking on a mosaic in Pompeii. One parks a car in a parking lot in San Diego, California, and one faces a side of a building, as drab as only sides of a building can be. But someone thought of painting on that side a full scale Mexican mural, and all of a sudden one is in a museum. One gets into an elevator in Hartford, Connecticut, and soft music greets one and a voice says, "Don't forget to push the floor button!" And further north in New England where English influences are strong, somebody perfected an alarm clock that not only wakes one with music, not only puts on the electric light, and not only turns on the coffee pot, but also says, "If I were you I would have tea!"

Stories of creativity, of change, of innovation, of charming wit, are everywhere in the United States. And with this in mind, with this close to our hearts, we must ask ourselves the question, "Where do we go from here?" From year to year, in meetings of this kind, we must prepare ourselves to be conditioned to being willing to forsake the known and to embrace the unknown. Man must always look upon himself as climbing up the hill and never as standing on top of a hill. If one psychologically feels that one stands on the top of a hill of one's profession or personal work, then every step forward must head down. One must never view oneself professionally or personally as being on a pinnacle. One must always climb. Here today we must ask ourselves the question, "What is the next peak?"

We have done well in our educational system as far as it goes. We have brought forth to the world the principle that it is important to educate every man. We have brought to the world the principle that every human being, however humble, is educable. In Poland, my native country, we had, before the war, a Minister of Interior who was an ex-general. One day he took a drive through the countryside and discovered that the fences were extremely shabby, bedraggled. At once the government issued a regulation, and four different kinds of paint were issued. Within six months every fence in Poland was painted one of the assigned colors. We in America are the one nation in the world that has chosen not to place its faith in the minds and the hearts and the tastes of our ministers and our generals. We put forward the proposition that in this country the educational system must do the best for everyone and get the best out of everyone. Ours has been a proposition that all human beings are infinitely educable and can make up their minds for themselves. In the fulfillment of this task, we have opened the schools wide.

In the fulfillment of this task, we have started a grassroot society. We have come to recognize that if we sit here in Ohio, or in any other place, and wait until a government program or a program from a central group of our best thinkers comes down to us, two, three, four hundred years from now we shall still be waiting for our turn to come. The quintessence of development of a new society into a thriving society is to start grassroot movement so we prepare common people, ordinary people, everybody, to take instant action. We bring them into the schools, we teach them the things that we think they should know, but more importantly still we set them on the run. They come in walking and they come out running. They are supposed to come out running. If they come in walking and come out walking, we as American teachers have not done our job.

We also played what might be perhaps inelegantly described as a number game. We were the first country in the world, and we are still the first country in the world, to educate the masses of the people. In fact, we are in this in a very small ball park because if one takes us, Japan, the Soviet Union, and one or two countries of Western Europe, that is all there is to this ball park. It is only in those countries that education proceeds at a pace we are used to. It is only in these countries that we can talk about common experiences. Beyond that is the third world. They don't belong to our ball park; they don't belong to our number game.

It is in these countries, during the last 15 years and while the number of school places in the world has doubled, that illiteracy increased from 50 to 60 percent. There are now more people who cannot read and write than there were ten years ago. With all the advances of technology and all the foreign aid that the rich countries want to give and will give, by the end of the century, there still will be illiteracy. At that time we are going to be living in houses supported by a warm cushion of air and traveling to our work on small self-propelled disks, and talking to people through two-way television. And still in the year 2000, one out of four human beings will not know how to read and write. We are in a separate ball park—the favored countries, the developed countries, the rich countries.

Our number game was to open the gate wide, bring as many people in as fast as we could, do the most we could. It did not matter if the half-educated taught the uneducated. The important thing was to get the ball rolling. This is our strength, and we talk continuously about this marvelous achievement of taking a majority of all the citizens and hoping that something will happen to them in the school even if they learn nothing from formal instruction. A chance remark in a cafeteria, a chance book picked up from the shelves, a chance encounter with a stimulating teacher will hook them, will set them on fire. If I had the time, I would like to take the count among you in this room to find out how many in the recesses of their childhood remember being hooked by one good teacher.

23

The numerical expansion of the educational system was our strength. We would always answer people who said that we do not teach enough in school: "Maybe we don't teach enough in school, but we teach many more people." What does it mean when the English congratulate themselves on the fact that they yearly graduate 20,000 high school graduates who are beautifully educated. We have 20,000 National Merit Scholarship winners alone! The very *best* of our people equal *all* of the people that are graduated in England. We rightly pride ourselves on this universal attendance.

But we can pride ourselves on it no longer. Today, for the first time, in 1970, the schools of Japan graduated as large a proportion of youngsters from their high schools as we graduated from ours. Today, for the first time in the history of the world, we are not alone. Three or four countries are close to doing the same things as we do, and some of them do it better. If we wish once again to be pioneers, we must address ourselves to what lies ahead.

Now that the lesson has been learned at least by a few countries, where do we go from here? What do we do for our children in order once again to make them into pioneers? In order once again to tower above others, we must be prepared to pay the painful price of making mistakes first, but of giving the world in the end a lively, dynamic educational system willing to move forward.

What happens to our children when they come into schools and are grouped into units of 30 people with a trained teacher attempting to get through to them? What happens in a school when we deal with groups of people? How do we reach individual children? What happens to individual children when they come into the schools? Jack and Jill go into the first grade the first day of school. Jack has played marbles on the street corner, so he knows that two and two are four. Jill is a nice little girl, sugar and spice and all things nice. She didn't play marbles on the street corner so she doesn't know how much two and two are. Jack and Jill come back home from the first day in school. The mother asks, "How was school?" Jack says, "Great! The teacher thinks I have a good head for numbers." Jill thinly says, "O.K." Twelve years later Jack takes calculus, and Jill says, "I have no head for figures." (Except the subtraction of her husband's bank account). Some place along the line, early in the school pace, early in the school process, earlier than we know it, a process on individual hooking on learning begins.

Need I say it—we know it. Some place very early in life, earlier than we know it, people commit themselves to this or that because of a chance remark or a chance statement or a chance success. You must have heard about K. K. Moore, the sociologist from Rutgers University who has developed a talking typewriter. Two-year-old children are being put into a little glass booth. There is a typewriter in that glass booth. Two-year-olds are very dexterous with manual skills. It takes them but a little time to discover that this instrument has keys and they can be depressed. It takes them but a week to learn all the letters and, by pressing the digits on the

24

typewriter, to conjure on a screen connected with this typewriter, a talking sound—a letter. Every time they press an A an A comes on the screen. Every time they press a C, a C comes on. It takes but a week for two-year-olds to discover the letters of the alphabet, to name them correctly, to find them on the typewriter, to press them, to realize themselves through it. Then the typewriter gets locked, and they cannot move it this way any more. The only way they can depress the keys of the typewriter is to press the letters in a correct sequence so that they make up words. This is the great intellectual hurdle that the children face.

My little five-year-old son can spell all of the letters, just as all the children in the E. K. Moore's experiments can. You write C-A-T on the blackboard and you ask him, "What's that?" and he will say the letters separately: "C-A-T." You draw a picture of a cat on it and you say, "C-A-T is cat," and the next time you draw C-A-T he will draw a cat and say, "That's a cat." But if you erase the C and put an R in its place, it's now R-A-T. You ask him, "What's that?", and he will draw a picture of a cat and say, "That's cat." That is to say, he knows letters, but he doesn't know the basic human intellectual truth that letters put together make up words.

When the typewriter gets locked in E. K. Moore's experiments, the children take several weeks before they discover the new system. They press the keys at random and nothing happens until by chance they press the C-A-T sequence. Then a cat flashes on the screen and, as letters appear, a voice says, "C-A-T is cat." If the child does it often enough to imprint in himself the notion that there is a system to it, he discovers he can read at the age of two. E. K. Moore reports the fantastic excitement that occurs when youngsters discover this principle. Some of you may have seen the film "The Miracle Worker" about the life of Helen Keller, the famous blind person. There, too, is depicted the moment when she discovered the meaning of words.

This basic initial discovery that letters make up words apparently can occur at the age of two instead of at the age of six. Last week I was reading new documents from USSR. They have just revised their entire school system by shifting the curriculum one year downward. The senior year of the kindergarten became the first grade, the first grade became the second grade, and so on. They shifted the whole school system, as only the Russians can dare, in one sweep, downward. This is one more recognition that the comprehension of young people now that they're exposed to media, to television, to fast-moving events, has been greatly upgraded.

This recognition is helping us to look again at the urgent business of illiteracy. If we compared an American group of youngsters with an Indian and a Polish group, we would find that after the first year of literacy training the Americans would score perhaps 75 percent success, the Indians would have 50 percent success, and the Poles only 25 percent success. They would have the same ability range, the same random collection of children, and yet the school success would be so different because the Polish children would be first generation literates, because their parents, and their grandparents, and their great-grandparents, were illiterate. The Indian children would also be first year literates, but they have a marvelous oral tradition they pass on from generation to generation—stories and legends of their country. The American children alone are third-/or fourth-generation literate. And where people leave off as parents, there people start off as children, and there is a cumulative sense of literacy about young people in schools for several generations which makes an earlier comprehension possible and individualized teaching more rewarding.

I am mentioning all of these rather disjointed facts simply to stress again the fact which you are very familiar with—namely, that the human young mind is a mystery; that the human young mind, that mystery, gets hooked on the enterprise of learning by accidental means; and that each individual gets hold of his own personal pattern. A youngster opens his eyes and he sees only shadows. His head is bobbing uncertainly, and he begins to hear the sounds and see the face of the mother leaning over him. Right away he begins to learn on his own.

We now know, for instance, that there is no longer such a thing as equality of opportunity. There is no such thing as lining children up and firing a gun and making them dash through the school system and take hurdle after hurdle. There is no such thing because each privileged youngster once opened his eyes and saw the shadows and heard literate speech and heard great issues discussed and experienced the professional type of life and culture surrounding him. By the time he is six, when we fire the gun of equal opportunity, he is much further along than some other child in whose home there is only one book—a telephone book which they use to prop up Junior when he cannot reach the dinner table. By the time the gun is fired at six, the child who did not have the literate culture surrounding him is already left behind.

We no longer can talk about equality of opportunity; we must talk about compensatory education; we must talk about giving more to those who don't have, in order to be able to equalize the chances of each performance. At that early moment, when a child begins his entry into culture, he's a mystery, he is indefinable; it is to the programming of that mind that we must now address ourselves. It is to the programming of children who are less individually capable of wending their way through the maze of educational system that we must devote ourselves.

Is 30 the right class size? I don't know. Do you know? Is 50 the right class size? I don't know. Is 12 the right class size? I don't know. There is no right class size. If you have a superb mathematics teacher who really teaches beautifully through a talk and chalk lecture, why couldn't he be heard by three million children? What is there against his being introduced on a television screen to all the children of the age group of the country? Maybe three million is the right class size for a lecture, and 30 or 50 is a wasteful thing. Or maybe Mark Hopkins on one side of the log facing the student is the only right class size. Or maybe not one—maybe two is best. If we have a one-to one- ratio between teacher and student, the teacher is on top of the student all of the time. Maybe it should be two so that the student can get out from under the teacher half the time and breathe and be free and do things on his own.

These answers will never come unless they are tackled on a grassroot level in colleges of education and schools across the country. We professors insist on little term papers; we murder our students in hundreds of courses by demanding that they write little essays and term papers, often without seeming relevance to the performance of these people in a professional capacity. How many term papers does a working classroom teacher have to write in the course of his professional performance? None! But we train our people to do these things because we hope that the teacher of tomorrow is going to be a researcher as well as a teacher. We hope that the teacher of tomorrow will forever experiment in the classroom by matching control groups on one side and on the other and trying to put things together from the differences between them.

How beautiful it would be if the educational system worked like the legal system! In the legal system, everything any prominent lawyer ever said in court since 1875 has been printed and is bound in leather volumes. How beautiful it would be if there were an Education Record like the Law Record! A phone in a classroom would ring, and an irate mother, Mrs. Brown, is on the other end of the phone. She says to the teacher, "Miss Jones, you don't wipe my Johnny's nose right." How beautiful it would be if Miss Jones could reply, "Oh but Mrs. Brown, the Pennsylvania Education Record, 1963, backed by Maryland's Education Record, 1970, clearly indicates there is no better way of wiping your son's nose!"

This is what happens in the law courts every day. How beautiful it would be if we in our profession had an Education Record, bound volumes, year after year, state by state, school system by school system, in which working classroom teachers could put on record their performance, their particular experiments. They could finally use in these reports the training in writing term papers we have given them and justify the hope we attach to our insistence on them.

I do not want to overdo my insistence on individualization. We know that human beings are alike. I do not want to talk as if everybody were infinitely different from everybody else. Every human being is a totally different mix, but in many fundamentals human beings are all the same. There are two sides to human beings, so there must be two sides to their schools. Sometimes people speak of educational programs as if they were carrots. They say "It is the pleasurable things that make people move. Show people pleasure, reward them pleasurably for their learning—praise them, and they will learn." But we know that carrots are only one kind of incentive. Carrots move people forward, but they make of them good educated men or simply cleverer rascals. The proper education mix is the carrot and the stick—excitement and discipline. You show the donkey the carrot and you push him with the stick. If you show the donkey the carrot only and do not show him the stick—the first carrot he will eat, the second he will eat, and after the third one he will be so full he will just waggle his tail at you. If you only hit the donkey with the stick, after the third blow he will sit down squarely on the ground and nothing on earth will move him. But education is that delicate balance of things where you show the donkey the carrots and you nudge him with the stick. Fundamentally, under the matrix of individuality, human beings are alike and respond in similar ways to outside stimuli.

In all of our children we all hope for intellectual fulfillment. Even more in the first instance we want to avoid one great threat that is posed to them, the presence of hunger. But once hunger is satisfied, we want to achieve the greatest gift, the only one that life holds out for us—the right to self-dignity. The avoidance of hunger and the pursuit of self-dignity are the two steps, the vocational and the intellectual, of any education.

We must also put ourselves in a frame of mind of trying to look at the young people and trying to discover by experimental method, by looking at thousands of children going through the system, by looking at different people and the different ways they relate to learning, the answers to these questions: What are the things that we can truly teach in groups? What are the things that would be wasteful to do over and over individually? What are the things that are individual, from which we have to withdraw, which the system damages rather than helps? What are the things that free the human soul?

Every year the youngsters go to school on the first day, and their eyes shine. They think to themselves, "Maybe things will break for me this year." But threee months later, too often their eyes are glazed over. The school has done its job. I call true education thawing out the glazed eyes, because that's what it is—in terms of really opening up the sense of fulfillment in children.

Let me give you one simple example: A long time ago, about 1960, as a professor of education I became worried about the fact that I hadn't taught in school. Teaching theory without having had actual practice is a fraudulent job. So I traveled down to Brooklyn, which is the Board of Education's locale in my city, in order to obtain a teacher's license to be able to teach in primary or secondary schools. This is a story in itself, with which I won't trouble you. Let me just say that I was denied that license and, being extremely chagrined by this, I complained about it one day in a lecture in New Jersey, across the Hudson River. A school principal after hearing my lecture came to me and said, "Do you really want to teach?" I said, "Yes." "How much do you want to be paid?" I said, "Nothing, I am paid at Columbia." "Well," he said, "We can hire you as a consultant. There's only one catch—there must be a certified teacher supervising your teaching. Don't you have a doctoral student in my school?" "Yes, as a matter of fact, I do have a doctoral student teaching social studies in the seventh grade." "Fine," he said. "We shall make him your supervisor." Thus for a year every morning I traveled across the river to teach the eighth grade social studies while my doctoral student supervised me.

I also made a bet with the principal that by a simple device of my teaching methods referred to often as "body English"—the method of bulging eyes and waving hands—I would simply prove that the 150 students he had assigned to slow classes were not slow. This was a school that was bent on access to universities, and everything was done according to a standard achievement test. Some perfectly normal children were pulled into the slow classes because they did not perform to the highest standards. I said to the principal, "The key is not in their minds, the key is not in the tests, the key is in creative teaching. Let us see if with my kind of teaching you can reach 10 percent of these children and have to reclassify them.

I was very fortunate at the end of the year 20 percent were reclassified. One of the humble lessons I learned was that half of my students who returned their evaluation sheets thought I was God, and the other half thought I was a gas bag. The proportion holds true in primary and secondary schools as well as in college, because there are people to whom my kind of teaching is not useful. There are people who need a quiet teacher, a gentle teacher, to whom the kind of teaching I use would be threatening personally, who would turn me off with the feeling, "What on earth is he trying to put across?" But I remember the hundreds of hours I spent planning and boning up on the presentation before going into the classroom in order to be able to hook those people that my teaching did suit. I was looking for people that I could hook to school success.

One lesson I gave—my first victory—was a unit on the geography of Canada, prepared for eight hours. I was in front of the blackboard, the map was up, and I was saying to the children," Isn't it just the most fascinating thing to think that 90 percent of the entire population of Canada lives within 100 miles of the southern frontier! "Ugh,"—that's how interesting it was.

I was going out of my mind trying to get the youngsters interested and alert. I tried again: "Have any of you seen a Prussian officer with a monocle?" Oh well, they were born after Eric von Stromheim, so nobody had seen one. Finally I said, "Has anybody ever heard about Homer?" One girl said she was watching a serial on television called Ulysses and that was the story about Homer and, yes, she had heard about him. I said, "Do you remember a serial in which all of Ulysses' men visited an island of Cyclopes?" Yes, she remembered those horrible monsters with the one eye in the forehead and a lot of whiskers. "Well," I said, "look at the map of Canada; it's the face of the Cyclopes: the Hudson Bay right in the forehead and all the population at the bottom, all the whiskers.

She grew thoughtful. The next day she discovered that her mother was from New Brunswick. The next day she knew everything about Canada—population, cities, mineral resources, everything. She was my first victory. She was the first one retested on the achievement tests. One had found the key. She discovered that learning can be personally exciting. Look how chance, how random, how difficult that key was to find. But by individual probing of children, one finds a key to open the universe, an individual telephone line to Heaven through which they can communicate with infinity.

It is this business of individualization of instruction, the individualization of attention, the individualization of everything, that we need to work on. Sure there will be things that must be done *en masse*. What does the doctor do when he examines a patient? He takes the pulse and the temperature. Well, it is a perfectly known medical fact that when you teach an exciting lesson, the children's pulses quicken and their temperatures rise as they get excited. If we had them plugged to the wall with the dials in front of us to be able to gauge the level of excitement, of drowsiness, or what have you that our lecture entails, we would be able to deal better with groups of people before us. Sure a great deal of work remains to be done in groups. But over and beyond this in the recesses of individual people's minds, in these individual educational yearnings and throbbings, there some place is a key—a hook. It is the duty of the teachers to probe and to find these hooks in order to make people able to do better in the field of education.

Not very long ago I attended a Cottonwood County picnic in Minnesota, a county with the foundation of which my wife's family was associated. I was dragged to that picnic protestingly but was told it would be good for my soul and good for sociology. There came together a small group of old codgers, people who seem to have crawled out of their holes and crevices, kind of scared by all this traffic and all these problems they triggered all around them and yet yearning in their hearts for the warm annual fellowship of frankfurters and beans. There was one really old doctor among them—he must have been about 90 years old. He was making a speech, and he was very inaudible. Only snippets of the speech were coming through to me and he was saying, "Oh, it was so hard 75 years ago when we staked out Cottonwood County. There was nothing but a prairie. We dug our well, and we built our church and we built our school and we hung on!" Then his voice grew to a triumphant pitch and you could hear him loud and clear, "We broke the prairie!" he shouted. This old man seemed transformed and so full of that self-dignity I speak of, when he spoke so triumphantly, "We broke the prairie, we broke the prairie!" It was then that I really understood the nature of American life and education. They broke the prairie and so many of us have forgotten it and just live off it as if it were our right to walk on the tamed prairie. But all of us, because we are American, know deep down that we need our *own* prairie to break, that in order to keep nourishing the the genius of our nation we must forever populate and colonize new prairies. And the prairie for us teachers is in the schools, the unfinished business of our society. Through schools—that public device into which we take the children, separated from natural agents of education, the parents—we infuse the best we know into them through precept and example. It is in the schools that we must fulfill the mission of teaching individual people how to inch closer and closer to the vision of a perfect society.

Jesse Stuart

Jesse Stuart, Greenup County, Kentucky, author, lecturer and educator, presented the Jennings Scholar Lecture on November 21, 1970, in the John C. Baker Center, Ohio University.

Currently one of the world's most widely read living authors, Mr. Stuart was born on a farm in Greenup County, where his parents were tenant farmers. He began his education and teaching career in a one-room country school and wrote his first stories and poems while a pupil in Greenup High School.

He is a graduate of two universities and has honorary doctor's degrees from nine colleges and universities. He has taught in rural elementary schools and in high school, served as a high school principal and a county superintendent, taught in the University of Nevada and the American University in Cairo, Egypt, and lectured in colleges and universities around the world.

The author of 32 books, he is recognized as one of the outstanding poets of America; his short stories are used as models by teachers in the field; one of his novels, called a masterpiece of satire, has sold more than two million copies; one autobiographical book is a classic in the teaching field; and another, written after he suffered a major heart attack in 1954, is considered a masterpiece in the field of modern recuperative therapy.

Mr. Stuart's stories, poems, and excerpts from his longer works have been reprinted in hundreds of textbooks in this country and in dozens of other countries on every continent of the world. He is approved by educators as one of the most constructive modern authors.

Popular as a lecturer as well as a writer, Mr. Stuart has spoken to hundreds of groups of educators and students. He is in constant demand throughout the nation.

THIS IS THE WAY IT WAS

It is very nice to come here this morning and to speak to you fellow teachers, fellow high school principals, elementary principals, county school superintendents and city superintendents. You're school people, and we understand each other. I have one fault: I can't criticize schoolteachers I know sometimes they need it, but I can't do it. I think of the good they have done and their missionary zeal that's gone out to help change our country and to help our country and to help change the world. You don't know your power unless you've worked overseas and know what some of the American teachers can do. That's what I'm going to get into here this morning.

In a minute I'll tell you a little of my background. I'll tell you how it pays to be from a poor family in America. Of course we never stayed that way, but it counted for me in another part of the world. I got a telephone call one day asking me to teach in Cairo, and I though it was Cairo, Illinois. I couldn't imagine Cairo, Egypt. I said, "You mean Illinois?"

He said, "No, we mean Egypt."

I just couldn't get over it—somebody calling me to teach in Egypt! He said, "We tracked you and we know you and we want your wife, too. And we have a place for your daughter since she's entering college."

So I said, "Sure, I'll teach." I didn't discuss with anybody how much money we'd get. We were told, though, that we could live in Egypt on a dollar per head per day. Well, don't you ever be fooled like that. The Americans don't live like that. So we got prepared and went to Egypt. I had to arrive one month early to take indoctrination on how to teach school. We had to become temporary citizens before we could get paid; we had to believe that there is no Israel. That it was only a state of mind. You should have heard these discussions. They were terrific discussions and you just simply had to go along with your state. And I went along. It was the first time that I had ever lived in a dictatorial country. I started teaching there, and my first class I will never forget. No one had big classes. For less than 500 students in college, we had something very close to 100 on the faculty. But it's like in a war—you send up a group of men and you have to pull them back and rest them and let a fresh group go up. That's how it is to teach school over there. The students are interested in everything. You've never seen students like them. I had a class of 11 students in this school, and I'll never forget the Greeks. I've taught probably every race of mankind, from every kind of government, and every color of skin. But at the American University in Cairo, we have a composite group of the world. In this class of 11, I had one American. The rest were from different countries—Kuwait, Syria, Egypt—and Egyptian Greeks. I had three Greeks in this class, more of the Greek nationality than any other. I learned something about students. These three quarreled so I had to put

Argrire Klonosis, a blue-eyed, blond Greek over to my left, Marianthia Cormeou in the back of the room, and Kwiar Valsakis over to my right. (There's a story about Marianthia. I could give you a lecture on her!) One time she came to me and said, "Mr. Stuart, I'm afraid of Kwiar Valsakis."

I said, "Why are you? I'm not going to permit him to bother you."

"Well," she said, "I'm not afraid of him like that."

I said, "If he starts anything, I'll throw him out the window." Well, I couldn't have thrown Kwiar out the window, but I told her that.

She said, "I'm afraid of his mind."

Did you ever hear of a student being afraid of another student's mind? Now Kwiar Valsakis wrote a short story for me; he wrote an essay on why he wrote the short story; then he wrote an article on why he wrote the essay. Have you had students like this? They'd quarrel; and they never quarreled about money but about ideas. You know that's what caused the Greeks on the mainland a long time ago to fall apart. They didn't agree. They're individualists. My class would go out behind the school under a palm before I got there, set my class up, and go through the class. They would rehearse the class. They'd read what they were going to read. I tell this because it shows a great interest in education. Out of that group I believe today 10 hold Ph.D's. You have one right here on your faculty, so that's 11. And there's a story about her coming to this country and how she competed with 168 graduate students in a test when she was about 18 or 19 years old and had a perfect score in mathematics. She said she didn't know she knew any math. She was first on this exam. That's your Greeks again.

The Armenians were excellent students and so were those Moslem girls that just got out of the veil and got into a school room and were given a chance. They were terrific students. You'd ask them a question—they never held up their hands—but you'd ask them and they could quote the whole thing out of the textbook. Maybe they had read it one time. I had students like this. Maybe they were the best students I ever taught.

I walked across the campus one day. It was just a three and one-half acre campus right in the heart of Cairo. I don't know how much that land would be worth, but the Egyptian government has never taken that school. It's too valuable. I walked across and an American hollered at me, "Hey, there, Stuart!"

I looked around, and I didn't know the man.

He said, "I'm John Slocum."

Who is John Slocum? A cultural attache with the American embassy. He said, "I remember when I worked for Scribner's Magazine and you sent stories in, I accepted three stories. Publicity came in on you. You were from a very poor family out of the Kentucky hills."

I said, "True."

"Well," he said, can you do public speaking?"

I said, "I can try. I have given it some thought."

He said, "We need somebody in Egypt. We've got Russia to fight here, and we have never filled our USIS auditorium."

I said, "How many does it hold?"

He said, 300 people. We can't get a handful out. Russia is in the saddle in Egypt."

"Why," I said, "sure, I'll do my best to help you. I've got an idea."

Knowing the people over there and my students, I went down to my classes and told that I was going to speak at the USIS on a certain date.

"Now," I said, "I teach here. I give the grades. You need them, and I need you. I need your families."

These are big families, and they're tied. You talk about Scotch clans that my people are out of, they don't tie up like the Moslems. You ought to see a Moslem wedding and how many people come to it; one family would fill a whole auditorium. The American Government wanted me to tell the Egyptians how in America a man could start from nothing and go to school and rise up. The story of America—that's what John Slocum wanted.

So, I told them where I was born, and here's my story. I got up there, and the auditorium was packed. There was not standing room and the American embassy was surprised. They couldn't get over it. They didn't know how it worked, you know. There's power in the schoolroom and among teachers! I told them, how if I had been born in their country I would have been born in one of their villages, one of the poorest villages and into the poorest family. I told them about my dad, who had never been to a schoolhouse and couldn't read and write and my mother, who had gone to the second grade. I told how they had rented land not owned it and moved from farm to farm, those steep Kentucky hills, and made a living. Canned fruit. We raised everything we ate in the early days but salt, pepper, soda and baking powder on those Kentucky hills. We traded eggs for them and for our clothes. There's a long story in the bringing up. I played with no children. There was none close to me, but I learned a world around me. I went to a one-room school where one man taught 56 classes in six hours. Clavin Clark got $45 a month. I was always there first in the morning and was the last to leave. I loved that school. I never will forget when I could put my name on paper. I went home and I was elated and I told my dad, "Dad, I can do something you can't do!"

He said, "What's that, Jesse?" (He was embarrassed. His face got red). I told him I could write my name. My mother taught my dad, then, a memorized signature so he could sign a check. He worked on the railroad, and the highest he ever made in his life in one month was $102.50. I remember that and how elated he was to make that much. He always complained about bills, about making a living. My mother kept other people's children and other people that went to school. I counted up later. It totaled 110 years. No wonder Dad was always having it hard making a living! But we all joined in a family. They became one of us; they had to milk a cow, feed the hogs, feed the chickens, help get in wood, help get up water and I don't know what all. We had all our livestock named, and this pleased the Egyptians. That's a great world of livestock over there. They're great animal people. I told them later about going to this school 22 months and then going out and working for 25 cents, then 50 and 75. Then I went into Greenup, Kentucky, and got a job putting down the streets. I told these Egyptians, "If you ever come to my country (and some did) and ride over the streets of Greenup, Kentucky, you remember this speaker over here in Cairo, Egypt, helped put every bit of cement there. I don't know whether one of my books is going to be a monument to me or not but the concrete in Greenup, Kentucky, are a monument. They're good streets. I helped build them" They're lasting yet, and I helped build them before I was in high school.

Now I saw something in Greenup that interested me very much. I saw a high school and I wanted to go. Here they had smart looking, well-dressed, clean youngsters, laughing and talking. They didn't have any cement on their clothes or on their shoes and I went over to see the superintendent and said I wanted to get into high school.

He said, "Where did you go to school?"

I said, "Plum Grove."

He had never heard tell of Plum Grove. It was five miles from the high school, a one-room school. I wouldn't leave him and it was finally decided that I would take a common school examination. I had to make an average of 75—couldn't make below 60 on any subject. I took five subjects I had never had in grade school I made an average of 78, but in English composition, so help me, I made 59. Those three people who judged the papers gave me an extra point and let me enter high school. Now high school was great for me, and I loved football. My, what a wonderful game! You can hit a youth legally as hard as you want to, and there's nothing anyone can do about it. You can back him up when you tackle him. I was already trained. I ran to school, five miles there and five miles back, and I was in good shape, hard as a rock. I loved football, loved an English teacher, and loved the school. The English teacher in that school was 5'11" tall (I told the Egyptians) and this was good. I said she had black eyes and she had one that looked straight out and one that went around and around. You couldn't do anything Mrs. Hatton didn't see. She had three majors and was a graduate of the University of Missouri; and her husband had a Ph.D. and was over at that little school. We were fortunate to have people like this in that school. Mrs. Hatton asked us to write themes. She had degrees in journalism, music, and English. We could write anything we wanted to. She said, "You can write the best on what you know the best."

I wrote her a theme on a rooster. I didn't know that a rooster is a universal theme, did you? You go to Jerusalem and you'll hear them crowing at night; in Cairo they kept me awake when we first moved over there—chickens crowing in a city of four millions. Everywhere around the world you'll find chickens. Well, anyway, a hen had laid in a paw paw patch 22 eggs. I found the nest, told Mom, and she said, "Jesse, get the eggs before they spoil." I got 21 out and left one. She hatched a rooster and went to the woods and raised it. That young rooster came back, killed every one of our roosters with hens, and took the hens. They followed him—a good looking rooster. He went down to Collins', killed a rooster down there, took their hens, and they followed him up to our house. Went up to Daughtery's, killed their rooster, had them all in a big white oak tree. That tree is still standing in the backyard. I never saw such a tree—full of hens and one rooster. One night, with all those hens in there, an owl got in and got him. That hurt me. I wrote this sad theme about my rooster and called it "Nest Egg" 'cause I had left a nest egg in that nest. Mrs. Hatton read it and laughed till she cried. She marked me down and "A" right there in front of the class. That started me with an audience in writing right there in high school. I took 20 themes a week to Mrs. Hatton. I took "Nest Egg" with me when I went to college. At Lincoln Memorial University, Harrogate, Tennessee, they had different English teachers, and "Nest Egg" found every English teacher in my classes, and maybe in some others. It went on to Peabody College at Nashville and Vanderbilt University. Everywhere "Nest Egg" was turned in, it got an "A." "Nest Egg" made 28 "A's." Twenty-eight school teachers were right, too!

I got into World War II. You know you don't know whether or not you're coming back from a war, so I was looking over some old things and found "Nest Egg," re-typed it and sent it to "The Atlantic Monthly." The "Atlantic Monthly" accepted it. I'll never forget it. I got $200 for "Nest Egg." Then "Nest Egg" got into the Wall and Cargill's College Reader. And people used it—Harvard, Yale and Columbia. It's out of print now. What if they had known as they read this story of "Nest Egg" that a boy who had only 22 months in a country school with a teacher teaching all the grades in six hours, and one year in high school had written that story. Now it's the lead story in "The Jesse Stuart Reader." It's in textbooks and students are reading it all over the world. They certainly are in America, too. Well, that's how "Nest Egg" was born. I told them that over there, and they thought it was a dream and wonderful and wanted to crowd into my classes and wanted to come to America. But I finished my talk over there and told the rest of the story about how I went to college on $29.30 and went three years and two summers to Lincoln Memorial University. I received two one dollar bills from home, worked half a day, went to school half a day, and washed pots and pans after each meal. Then I told them about how I went from teaching school back to Peabody College during the summers and attended Vanderbilt University on $130. I told them I had the equivalent in hours to have a Ph.D, and I had spent in America less than $500 for my education. I told them that America gave me a chance. That story is great over there. They rise up, they thirst for it, it's what they want. But in America I think my story has sort of slipped. There's another way of doing it in America now. Youth are paid and they get all kinds of money in scholarships. At Lincoln Memorial University, I did 43 themes, wrote pieces that made magazines like "Esquire," "Harper's," "The Atlantic Monthly," and had short stories in "Colliers," the old "North American Review." And you know they told me at Lincoln

Memorial that I couldn't write a short story! Now my teacher was the best friend I ever had, but he did the plotting; there was a little plot at the end of his stories. I thought a short story was a slice of life, a big broad slice of life, with color. I got that from Greenup High School. A book of short stores by de Maupassant, the French writer, was in our library. That one book influenced my life. One teacher can influence the life, and one book can. I told the Egyptians this when my speech was over. My, they rushed in and I had a hard time getting out of the USIA Auditorium.

They said, "This is America." My speech was a hit in Egypt.

John Slocum had been right, and I found out later that John Slocum hadn't been any failure himself. If I were to tell you how many million dollars that man had! I was out with him one time and he said, "Jesse, I've got a New England conscience, and I have to make a contribution to America before I can give up life." He gave back to America five times what he made, and his wife could have given more. The two could endow a university or build one. And they were out doing their bit for the United States Government; they were battling for it too. So they sent me out to speak. They sent me down to Alexandria. They sent me to Luxor. They sent me all over Cairo, to their universities, colleges, clubs. I found only one man that ever heard me speak in Alexandria. They sent me down on the train and I stayed at the old Cecil Hotel. That night when I went in, there were two people to meet me, a blind man and his wife. He was a Coptic Christian; his wife was an Italian Catholic. They interviewed me and asked me what I was going to talk about. I said, "I think I'll talk on American free enterprise and what it's done for America."

He said, "Oh don't do that. It's out. It'll ruin you."

I said, "What shall I talk about?"

He said, "Tell them where you were born." He didn't know anything about my talk at Cairo. He said, "Tell them about what you eat for breakfast, about going to school, about American high school bands, about the American wheat fields, about the leaves on the trees, how they turn golden in the autumn. Tell them about America. Give them some other kind of culture besides this Russian culture."

I changed all my notes, changed clothes, and did it in 40 some minutes. Now the gentleman here heard the speech. I spoke two hours and 20 minutes. He testified that my speech caused him to go back to college in this country, and he is now a schoolteacher. He's in this audience.

When I got back to Cairo, the youth met me at the gate. I was one of them. They backed me, and I tell you, you couldn't deface a school building. Some student would have hurt you. You couldn't break a window, you couldn't mark a wall, because a school to them in Egypt is learning and light. Learning is light and God. That's the way they feel toward education. I went down one time to Port Said to speak. I spoke to a little group and they were all on my side. They were with me all the way. When I got through, I was shaking hands with everybody. It was like long ago when they had these revivals out under the trees and had a big sermon, and after it was over, everybody was shaking hands and talking about how great it was. Well, this is the way that meeting was over there in Egypt. They were very friendly people and they went through circles, around and around. After a while the runner came in and said, "We've won! We've won! We've won!"

I said, "Won what?"

He said, "We've beaten Russia tonight. Russia only had 43 at their meeting. We had 87 here."

Now that's the way they fought right down to the wire for Egypt; we battled for it, and I loved it. It was competition. It's like a ball game; it's like rivalry. I like rivalry. That competition, that's what makes this country. Competition. What do you have up there at Columbus today? You have a great ball game and so we have it all the way around, and competition is great.

Then my wife—women always know something before men—said, "Jesse, they're going to do something with you."

A man who had heard me speak at Alexandria said, "The State Department ought to use you." And the State Department did. We had no more than got home when they asked me to take a trip for the United States State Department. The group I worked with was the USIA in this country. It's USIS overseas, both the same thing. It's called the Right Arm of the State Department. Now the American State Department makes mistakes, but they're not as foolish as you think, although there are some people who will lead you to believe they are. They're a little bit smarter than I am. Especially, financially. I don't believe I ever worked as hard for anybody as I worked for the State Department. After this much work, I went in debt $11,000, after taxes, and ended up in the hospital. But that's all beside the point. I went out and gave it for America. The first think they asked me when they briefed me in Washington, D.C., was if I lost my head—if I had an uncontrollable temper.

I said, "Nope, I'm pretty level-headed."

"Well," they said, "you write poems and do all this writing. We thought you might be emotional and go overboard."

"No," I said, "I'm not going to go overboard. I've taught school and have been superintendent of county schools and city school systems, I've taught in big city high schools and universities."

They asked me to take my wife and pay her expenses. Now that's for a reason. In the Moslem countries where I worked—and the State Department considered me very good—the men never take their wives out. The wives will be in the home with a group of children, and maybe a man will have four wives, sort of a harem. They're behind the walls while the men all associate together, and sit up at a street cafe and drink coffee. And they might be smoking something that we disagree with over here. You see a lot of that over there. They don't pay too much attention to it. My wife, Naomi, went with me and I paid her way. She's a schoolteacher, and she helped in the elementary schools. I went under dual professions, teaching and writing, but it was mostly teaching all the way. They wanted to know about American schools. They wanted to know how we did it. The first country we went to was Iran. It was one of the two countries where we had an interpreter who protected us and went with us. There was no need to protect us. The only country I found where we needed protection was the United States. Over in Iran you can go anywhere and you won't be bothered; but you can't go anywhere in New York and a lot of other American cities. That's what bothered us when we came back here. I was scared to death in some of the American cities after being over there. I was in nearly all the capitals of the Near and Middle East and the Orient.

In Iran, one of the things they had of interest to elementary teachers was a system the French picked. I never saw anything like it. They showed us their textbooks. I couldn't read them in their language, but they had one of these for little fellows just starting in school. I asked my wife what to do, and she said, "Throw them out, and get the American systems." And you know they threw them out and got American systems in Iran. Iran is probably the way our people came. They are Aryans that filled Europe. They came that way, and I think they are our people. And they are very close to us in a lot of ways. But the Greeks had something to teach them. After what they did to Greece, they went back and paid the Persians off. There was a man named Alexander the Great who went back there and burned Persepolis, their ancient capital. Right where the Greeks crossed we were all coming up from Shiraz, the city of poets where I'd spoken a number of times. My wife was the only woman in the car with five men. The car got stuck right at the exact place where Alexander had crossed taking his army to burn Persepolis. It stuck in the sand in a gap. We were worried; we were out there in nowhere. No water. That's a dry country, and we hadn't thought to carry water. They all got to quarreling among themselves. I sat back and I was the only man who didn't try to drive the car out. I knew their attitude toward women, and I said, "Would you let my wife try to start that car?" They hesitated. Finally, they agreed. They couldn't get it started. And do you know she was lucky enough to start that car the first time! She drove it out through the sand and pulled it over to the side and told them to take it over on dry ground and the hard road. They couldn't get over a woman doing something. If you knew Iran, and knew something like that, it's terrific. It's a Moslem country and women are held back. But not an American woman!

There is only one country in the world that's got a city of poets, and it's Iran. They don't need poetry. They need science. They need practicality and know-how in education, but people chant poetry all over that country. They can't read and write, but they can memorize books of poems and chant them. When they cut wheat they chant poetry. Oh, I loved that country!

I don't know how much good we did, but I think quite a bit. The Americans are the ones that have pure water in Shiraz, in this city of poets. We don't have a city of poets in America. Now here's what I liked about it. The writers over there get big mausoleums. They're great poets, and they have two who equal Shakespeare. And they don't have a single mausoleum for a politician or a state leader. Not a one. They're for the writers and teachers, so there's something good about the Iranians.

We came down from there and I went over to Egypt again and I lectured for one week. One place was the University of Alexandria, where the good Dr. Luke in our Bible once taught medicine. I felt it a privilege and an honor to stand on the ground where he had once taught and lectured. After the first lecture during the question period, the British were after me. There were two English teachers and a Scotsman. Here's what they attacked me on. Right in front of all the Egyptians (they just ate it up, they loved it) —an American over there was trying to defend America and the British after him, because the British had mandated Egypt 75 years. And the British are not fools; they're brilliant. They talked about the colleges and universities we had. Now about the schools, I said, "Would you trade your Oxford for our Harvard?" They would not. I said, "Will you trade it with Yale thrown in?"

"Yes." They would trade Oxford with me.

Then I went on to Cambridge, I had Columbia, New York State University with all its different branches—I believe 23—and I had New York. I had spoken at several of these schools and I happened to know them, and then I brought in Ohio State. I brought up schools, and after a while England had traded out. They didn't have anything left. Then I said, "Now who's got the schools?" Boy, the Egyptians stood up. I just traded them out on the platform. So we won that round. And you know we have got the schools. We've got them for the world. Look at what Ohio has. Ben Webb and I used to sit and discuss the good schools in Ohio. Kentucky has good schools. We don't have as many as you have in Ohio, but we don't have near as many people either.

All of the students wanted to come to America. If you want to see an exodus of the American youth who think Ameria's not got it, let them exchange with the Europeans, let them exchange with the Egyptian students, let them exchange with the students of the Near East, the Orient. They'll be for America, don't you believe they won't. Now that would be a good exchange.

Let's trade.

There's a matter of horse sense in teaching and getting around in the other countries like in Egypt. I got a big banquet thrown for me, the first American educator to get out. And the American embassy couldn't touch the department of schools in Egypt. They wouldn't look at the American Embassy. They gave me a banquet and they said, "Do you have some people you want to invite?"

I said, "There are some people in the Amrican Embassy that I'd like to invite."

They said, "all right, if you invite them, we'll have them." And they came. They had made it.

John Slocum said to me—he had criticized school teachers, "Jesse, how do you pull this?"

I said, "John, did you ever hear of a thing when we talked about school teachers and teaching? These are schoolteachers. Teachers are teachers the world over. They're the ones having it."

I had spoken to the teachers at the banquet. I had never had a nicer banquet. It was the first and only country that ever had a banquet for me, and it was great. The embassy asked them to sign a paper and give all their addresses. I wanted to write them, and I did. When I got through, John Slocum said, "It's a stroke of genuis what you've done for the embassy."

I said, "I didn't do it for the embassy at all. But you can have their names and addresses."

He took them.

From there, my wife and I went to Greece. If you haven't been to Greece, go. It's one place in the world where you will feel that you own the place. You'll feel as free in Greece as you feel in America. You've never seen people like them, and I must say the best students I've ever taught have been Greeks. They think on the whole, not parts. Go to Greece and see what they've built. They're up with the sunlight and air and where they can see water. This is again beside the point. We used to talk about what race of people has given more to mankind. The big argument comes up between the Hebrews and the Greeks. Now you decide. Who has given more? I've decided on the Greeks. A lot of people in America haven't. The deeper religious people will not have this at all. Look what the Greeks gave to us. Now what's the matter with Greece with all these brilliant minds? The thing that is the matter is what I had in my class with three Greek students. They can't get along. They've got all these opinions; they're individualists. You have never seen people like Greeks. I went over to Petras and spoke. They introduced me as the man who came down from the hills. Well, the man who came down from the hills was a Greek Orthodox priest, who led the Greeks in an uprising against the Turks. And then the world went in to help the Greeks, because of the learning and the culture they had given to the world.

They introduced me, and I walked down this aisle and around and around, and they followed and we talked. I lectured this way. They said we agreed. We are tied in the head and we are tied in the heart. Our Western civilization started from "The Rocks," the Parthenon in Greece. Think of that little rock up there, what the Greeks have done, what they've given to the world.

I left Petras to lecture at the University of Athens. It had not opened. I left Greece, so I never got to lecture there. You know why? They all got into it. Now can you imagine an American university, Ohio State, not opening because the Board of Trustees got into a ruckus? Now can you imagine that at this University right here? But where the Americans and the Greeks worked wonders, we go back. We ought to pay our debts. The American teacher among Greeks (and they just are wonderful) make the schools run on time. You know why? We've got a thing in America we call politics. You know how you play it and how you get things, even in schools. Super-

42

intendents are diplomats, or should be. Teachers should be diplomats. Well, over there they are. I could give you a lecture on this if I had time this morning. But I'll cut it down. I've written I don't know how much on it. I love that country!

I went to Lebanon. Lebanon is in trouble you know with this war. They've tried to stay out of it. They're pro-West in Lebanon. There's not even a little town—not even Bilboo where I've not spoken in Lebanon. That's in the Bible. I lectured in every little town in Lebanon for the U.S. State Department, but it wasn't working like I thought it was working. I knew they were clannish, they're tied, and they're oh, so pro-educational. Look at the Lebanese that come to this country. They're out for learning and light, and they are good students, too. The American University in Beirut is a great university. It's equivalent to Yale (I'd say better) and it's considered America's greatest university outside this continent. At one time leaders of 67 foreign countries were graduates of the American University in Beirut. I said there one time at a lecture, "Where are my people?" None had called me. We are akin to the Lebanese people. Here's how we're akin. My wife's sister married Russell Zachem, pure Lebanese. That's how much akin we are to the Lebanese. That evening the telephone rang in my hotel room and it was our relatives calling. It ended up in I don't know how many more talks, and the thing got so big that the State Department had to take over the publicity. One of the Zachems told me that he'd never marry an American girl. He'd fallen in love with one once, but she was Canadian. They were both in the same school in the University of Syracuse. I said, "Why?"

Well, he was sort of a cranky Zachem and he was a medical doctor, He said, "They're not affectionate like my people."

Now these Lebanese are the most affectionate people I've ever seen. They eat the richest food I've ever eaten, and they get to be a pretty good size. No one can figure out their economy. They've got good schools. They could all speak like the Americans do. All could speak good English, but when I shook hands with every one of them, their hands were as hard as could be—even calloused. The Lebanese will work. The Lebanese are bright. I made that statement about the Greeks. For 44 straight years the Greeks have made the best grades at the American University in Cairo, Egypt. The Armenians have been second, so I wasn't talking through my hat.

The Armenians are without homes, and the Greeks were put out of their Egyptian homes. They helped make Egypt. They told me in Egypt that the Greeks were not citizens, because they have just been there 2300 years. And I told them about America, what made up America. All kinds of people had made it up from every country in the world. I don't care what color the skin is, what the religion is, what your politics is, there is something about a person that comes up if you're an American. You've got something, you're an American. There are no people in the world like Americans. They act like they know it all and they'll go in and take a chance where others won't and they'll take over things and they're always inquisitive and asking questions. They're always getting involved and always getting arrested in so many countries.

Now from Lebanon we went to West Pakistan. When we got there, there were all kinds of things against our government. Papers had headlines against us, the United States was a reprobate, and I don't know what all. I told my wife, "We're in the wrong pew this time." We stayed in the hotel in Karachi. After a while we got to sticking our heads out of the windows. When someone came and got us, we said, "Is it safe out?"

They said, "Sure, it's safe."

We went out. I lectured there, and they came out and said, "We love you people, but we just don't like some things your country does."

I said, "I'm from that country and I'm over here to represent that country. You've got an awful lot of your people over there in America and you helped make what we've got."

Then we went up to Lahore. There's more in Lahore than in any other city in West Pakistan; that's Rudyard Kipling's old home town. I said, "How would you people like to go out and speak when the frost is on the ground, speak to an acre of people in college, without a shed over them, without a wall?" I spoke to that group. Frost out there. We nearly froze to death. I just found a little coal and had some wood that wouldn't burn very well at the little place where we stayed.

I spoke to a women's college there, and Dr. Gray was the head of it. She actually came from Arkansas, but she couldn't tell it. You know why? You remember that trouble they had when Eisenhower was President? She told them she was from Memphis, Tennessee. A little later, she couldn't have told them she was from Memphis, Tennessee. So she had to change the place again. I'm just telling you how these things worked. They got all excited. Except for the East Pakistanis, these people in West Pakistan were the poorest that I've ever seen. Yet they wanted to pass the hat and take up money for me to bring back to help Appalachia. Anyone on food stamps in Appalachia was rich beside one of these people. That's how our publicity gets over there. They cried for us when I told them I was from Appalachia. My ancestors all came from there. I said that we were poor, but we haven't stayed too poor and I said we could make it if we got out and worked. Some of us do and some of us couldn't. Then I gave this talk. All of the schoolteachers came in, all of the writers, all of the industrialists—what few they had—and I lectured on American literature. A man got to a live microphone, and he said, "Mr. Stuart, go back to America and talk to the iron clad society that you have in America, that doesn't have any culture, and ask them why a man in Detroit, Michigan, working in the automobile industry can make 100 times as much as one Pakistani working on a farm."

I listened to that as he was getting the people all riled up. I had given a pretty good talk, I thought. They were all for me. At that time they could all turn quickly, and I asked for the microphone when he got through for a rebuttal. I said, "Sure, they make this money in Michigan. I know because I've got relatives up there making cars." (Don't you tell them that I didn't

44

have) "Out of this big salary they make, did you ever hear of taxes? Over in America some of these people who make this big money pay 92 percent taxes." (Well, I think a few do—Jack Benny and a few more.) I said, "Here's how the money that they make is postmarked: 'For help for West Pakistan.' You get it, that tax money."

Boy, listen, did they turn to me. I had them all, got them all on my side. We went one more place, up to Preshawr. It is up against the Khyber Pass. That's where Alexander stayed. That's as far as he got. The Western civilization met the Orient at the Khyber Pass. There's an awful lot of blue-eyed people up there. They look at a Greek coin of Alexander's time. They've got people on both sides. They take them and compare them to the Pakistani up there. They look alike. And there's a lot of Greek blood left up there in that area. The Greeks have been soldiers. Who's ever conquered them man for man? Up there the gun is the law. They don't have courts. They don't have judges. The gun's the law. They make their guns, too. They can pick up any gun here and make a replica of it.

I lectured for Preshawr University, and they came in and stacked their rifles like you do in the Army or the Navy. Their President was the kindest old man I have ever seen at a school. He was the kind who spoke softly, was sweet and easy-going, and I knew he never carried a gun. But when he stooped over and his coat came down, I saw a .45. I lectured there I don't know how many times and nearly got shot myself.

I went to take a picture of a man coming down the hill leading seven women. The women had big bales of hay on their shoulders. He didn't have any, but he had a gun to protect them, and he pulled the gun right quick. I dropped the camera. When I got in the embassy car, a Pakistani said, "He wouldn't have shot you."

I said, "Well, I know better. He would have shot me. I'm from an area where they shoot people. That man had blood in his eyes. He would have shot me."

He said, "No, he wouldn't." That man in the embassy car had a gun that was as long as my arms.

So it's a wild place up there. They said, "Mr. Stuart, do you have any answers in the way of education for this area? Can we get away from the gun?"

I said, "You sure can. You can get away from it. Did you know that my grandfather grew up in an area like this? In Kentucky, the gun was the law. The strongest won out because the law was too weak to handle that situation. It was the old clan problem—the clan wars. And there is something that has helped us no end in Kentucky. We used to have the feuds and the fights but anymore we take them out in a game."

They said, "What kind of game?"

I said, "Basketball."

Did you know they applied to the American Embassy to get coaches in there? And who's going to referee one of those games? There's your problem—the referees!

From West Pakistan we flew over to East Pakistan, and my wife had to

45

leave me there. Her parents had been killed in a car wreck. She came home. Before we came home we worked with the Peace Corps up in the Northern part of East Pakistan. We landed in a pasture field, worked out there, and do you know the big problem they had with the schools? The students didn't want to go four years to college. They wanted two years. I was with them three days. I don't know how that ever came out. But we argued and we worked. One old man came to me and said, "Mr. Stuart, when can we catch up with your progress in America?"

I looked him over and I said, "Now I'm going to tell you, and don't you tell that I told you, but you work the way you are, trying to get these schools organized and get four years in college. If you work that way for ten years you'll be digging right on our heels.

They'll never catch us. They'll never catch our progress. We're 1000 years ahead. But if we go backwards we might meet somewhere back there.

Then I flew out of there, and what I needed the most in the world was a tooth pulled. I had an abscessed tooth from eating goat's meat in East Pakistan. I hit a bone and broke off a tooth. I needed a tooth pulled and a haircut. There was no place to get a haircut but sitting on a stool and letting someone take clippers and trim my head. I didn't want that kind of haircut.

I flew down to India. I know many of you have been there. Probably you've seen them pick up the dead who starved to death—500 in Calcutta alone every morning. From there I went to Burma. There are not many American schools there, but it is one of the most beautiful countries I've ever seen. And down to Thailand, another beautiful country. How beautiful that world is through there! From there I flew over Viet Nam and Cambodia and went into the Philippines.

It's a lesson in education for Americans to go to the Philippines. Methodist missionaries went there years ago, went up in the mountains, and converted to Chistianity and sent to school head hunters and their children. Today they have Ph.D.'s. They're schoolteachers, and one's a college president. The power of education. The Filipinos know it. They've got big families in the Philippines. There's always a girl who never marries but works on the side and send her brothers and sisters through school. That's the policy they've got over there. That's how much they're fighting for learning and light in the Philippines. I've never spoken to a Catholic university as big as the one at Cebu, and do you know, they offered me a teaching position there? I said, "Why is that? I've not known you people, and you've not known me," but I was from the United States Government. They have a problem of getting students in the university too young—about the seventh or eighth grade. I said, "For heaven's sake, put back the seventh and eighth grades. You've got to get more preparatory schools. Do like we do." I don't know whether they've done it or not because they've got a feeling in the Philippines against the United States, and you ought to know what it is. You see we mandated the Philippines, Alaska and the Hawaiian Islands. We let the Hawaiians vote to come into the United States, we let Alaska

46

vote, but we didn't let the Philippines vote. I think we would have had another area big enough for fives states. Do you know why we didn't let them vote? The Philippines are too far away. We would have had all kinds of problems protecting this area. But I think this country could and would have been a wonderful part of us—all five states in the Philippines. And what we could have done for them if they had been allowed to vote to become a part of us!

I thought it was the most beautiful country I had ever seen. I loved it. It's the land of the big snakes. Twenty-two feet long, so big they can't hibernate. They don't need to hibernate. The coldest day they had in years it was 88. And all these multicolored birds, all the species of lizards! Here was my world. When I was in Dumagette, at Silliman University, I stayed at a little Nisular Hotel. I got the only air-conditioned room they had out of seven rooms. I'd go to bed, turn off the lights, and then right quick 'Id turn the lights back on. The lizards would be all over the walls in my room. Chicken lizards. The chicken lizard is about as long as my arm. He's got a tail that he uses to hit a chicken and kill it, and there's chickens all over the Philippines. Cock fighting is a Sunday thing, like a basketball game. But this chicken lizard kills chickens and eats them. The Filipinos kill the chicken lizard and eat him, and they say he tastes like chicken. I left there quickly. I got the tooth pulled there, by the way. Don't anybody ever say anything to me against the Seventh Day Adventists. They've got the best hospitals in the world. It's where the embassy sent me with this abscessed tooth. I went in there expecting to see an American. I saw "No Smoking" signs everywhere. At that time I was smoking a little bit. I had to be careful with my cigar because I didn't want them to know even that I smoked. A little Filipino was the dentist, and he pulled that tooth. The United States gave me three days' rest in Hong Kong. I saw the schools and what they are doing over there and then went into Free China. If the Communist Chinese are as energetic as the Free Chinese and if they do have 800 million people—look out, World, if they ever start. These Free Chinese of Taiwan or Formosa, are the finest people and the most industrious. Formosa is two-fifths the size of West Virginia, and it's mountainous. They have 14 million people in Free China. They were paupers that fled Communism. They had nothing in 1946. If the United States hadn't helped them, they would have been goners. About six or eight years ago, they said, "Uncle Sam, we want no more help. We thank you. You have helped us. You have saved us, but now we save ourselves."

They had a balanced trade from that island. They were exporting rice. They're working people. I recall what I told the Moslems over in Lahore, West Pakistan. A Moslem girl, when I spoke at a girls' college, asked me, What has made the United States great? What has made it so wealthy? Don't you have one automobile in every home?"

I said, "No, we have more than one automobile in every home."

They couldn't get over it. They said, "What made it?"

I said, "Our women work." I told them that the women in America have a family, belong to a political party, help in two or three clubs, travel, and do everything. And I said, "I'll tell you something else about them. The women have got most of the wealth." You should have seen those Moslem women's smiles. They had just come to school out of the saddles out on the ground where they had herded cattle. The black eyes could almost look through a wall. They are really a handsome group of people.

They said, "What about the men? Why don't they have the wealth?"

I said, "The thing of it is in America, the men work so they die of heart attacks. And they just leave the wealth to the women."

It's true. So many of us go that way, you know. I barely missed death in a heart attack.

So I went from China into Korea. Tell me a place I've not been in Korea, a place I've not spoken. They're pro-education there. I'm glad my old school, Peabody College, set up for them schools to eradicate a bottleneck they had. They had the elementary schools and they had some of the colleges. If you doubt what I'm telling, get a World Almanac and check up on South Korea. Check on what they've done in education. Peabody College set this thing up. When they were freed from Japan, 22 per cent of the people could read and write. The Japanese were using them for industry. Now 97 and a fraction of a percent can read and write. That's in 24 years. Have we made such progress?

I came back home to this country. I had finished the longest trip a man had ever made for the United States Government. I came back to this country and I was puzzled at something. We had had 6 per cent of the earth's surface, 7 per cent of the earth's population or did have, and 57 per cent of the world's high school graduates. But now something is happening in my country. I came home, and 42 per cent of the national average had dropped out sometime between the first and twelfth grades. I talked to teachers. Kentucky had 44 per cent and West Virginia had 46 per cent. We were a little above the national average at that time, but I got to asking, "How could it be, how could it happen?" I'd ask schoolteachers, and they'd blame themselves and the school systems. I said, "We've got the best school systems in the world, the best trained teachers, as well trained nurses." (You can't beat the English, the Scotch and the Danish nurses).

You give the world and other countries our schoolteachers and you know we'll choke the United States down, because they're out there working like we used to work. Learning and light—they want it. They're working to get it. Look at Japan!

I have talked over my time, and I want to say a schoolteacher audience is wonderful. It's time for me to sit down. I could go on, but I have to stop.

Dr. Marcus Bach

Dr. Marcus Bach, Director of the Foundation for Spiritual Understanding, Palos Verdes, California, presented the Jennings Scholar Lecture, on December 12, 1970, in the John C. Baker Center, Ohio University.

Author and specialist in inter-cultural and inter-religious relations, Dr. Bach was for fourteen years on the staff of the School of Religion at the State University of Iowa, where he received his Ph.D. degree in 1942. Four other schools—Bradley University, Hillsdale, Carthage, and Elmhurst Colleges—awarded him honorary degrees. He has been the recipient of numerous citations in the field of writing and research.

Unlike most professors, Dr. Bach has had the opportunity of alternating his teaching program between a year on campus and a year in travel. "An excellent arrangement," he contends, "if you can work it." His research has taken him into many areas of the world, where he has lived among various religious and ethnic groups in an effort to "empathetically interpret their ways of life and subjectively enter into their experiences."

His work has brought him into association with many outstanding leaders, including the late Dr. Albert Schweitzer in Lambarene, Africa; Vinoba Bhave in India; and Buddhist leaders in southeast Asia. Two State Department assignments under the auspices of the Educational Division of Cultural Affairs took him to Pakistan, Cambodia, and the sub-continent.

Recently Dr. Bach helped establish the Foundation for Spiritual Understanding, which is designed to explore new approaches to the total circumference of concepts which unite humanity on deep feeling levels of response. He takes a new, bold look at the convictions men live by and interprets them against the discoveries of his years of intimate and unbiased research.

Dr. Bach is the author of numerous interpretive books including *The Will to Believe, Had You Been Born in Another Faith, God and the Soviets, Spiritual Breakthroughs for Our Time,* and *The Power of Perception.* His inspirational book, *The Wonderful Magic of Living,* brought out by Doubleday in January, 1968, was Dr. Bach's fifteenth publication.

WHAT IS RIGHT WITH THE WORLD

After choosing this topic, I got to wondering if there really *is* anything right with the world. The title sounded good, especially since it was stated not as a question but as a statement of fact. So perhaps we can explore the possibilities together.

Actually, to find something good may be a new departure for we are reminded on every hand that things are in a most deplorable state. If you were a benevolent dictator, if there is such a thing, where would you begin to set right that which you feel is most *wrong* with the world?

Yet the very thought of the title suggests convincingly that there is something inherently right, if we could only make the points and details of the rightness explicit.

I am reminded of a story told about a plumber who wrote to the United States Bureau of Standards about the advisability of using hydrochloric acid to clean drain pipes. He received a reply which said, "The efficacy of hydrochloric acid is indisputable, but the corrosive residue is incompatible with metallic permanence." Somewhat confused, he wrote back and asked, "Is it it okay to use or not?" Along came a second letter from the Bureau saying, "We cannot be responsible for the toxic and noxious residue and suggest you consider some satisfactory alternative." Still confused, he wrote back and asked, "Should I use it or shouldn't I?" The letter he got resolved things. It said, "Don't use hydrochloric acid. It eats the hell out of drain pipes."

I hope to be explicit about what is right with the world, though it may not always be that easy. As a general thesis on which to peg what I'd like to say, let me suggest that it is not through knowledge only but through experience that one comes into a proper relationship with life, and it is well we keep this in mind in our investigation of the world's rightness.

The collective state of mind around the world seems to be that things are in an unholy mess. You need not go to any so-called foreign country to hear the complaint; you can get the message just by listening to the man on the street or keeping an open ear on college campuses. In fact, you don't have to leave your own living room. Turn on the radio and TV and you will find it is almost sacrilegious or subversive these days to believe that God might conceivably be in His heaven, that there is something right with the world.

This is a rather interesting phenomenon when you stop to think about it. The wonder of electronics and radio and TV are still, to many of us, so wondrous, so fantastic in their creativity, that you would imagine we would stand in awe and say, "Isn't ours a great world!" I have long had the feeling that God, our creative Power behind the universe, is revealing Himself scientifically in our time as He once revealed Himself theologically in other days, and, unless we take cognizance of this fact, we will make the same distortion out of science that we have made out of theology. It is not by knowledge only but through experience that we come into a relationship with life.

Speaking of this world in which we live, this scientific world, reminds me of the first moon landing, the Apollo project on July 20, 1969. Mrs. Bach and I were watching this spectacular on the TV in our cabin in British Columbia. A young man watching it with us was smoking up one cigarette after another. He was, in fact, a chain smoker and he wanted, he said, very much to give up cigarettes and had tried unsuccessfully several times. Anyway, when the white-helmeted, hooded figure stepped down for the first time to etch his imprint on the lunar dust, this young man who sat with us ground his cigarette in the ash tray and said, "If they can do that, I can do this!" I don't know whether or not he really gave up smoking, but that a message from outer space can be transmitted so convincingly to us earthlings suggests to me a remarkable mystical rightness with the world for those who get the message.

By this time, flights on the 747 strato-cruisers are no longer news, but I always remember one experience connected with a trip I took coming from the Orient. I thrilled at the ease with which this jumbo jet took off and how effortlessly it carried its nearly 400 passengers through the ocean of space at 600-plus miles an hour. Concealed within the craft are some 40 miles of wiring, mazes of technical devices, networks of gears and gadgets all flawlessly synchronized to lift its occupants into a realization that there is something right with the world. It came gallantly as a seagull, and when we docked at the L.A. airport, I was met be a friend. He greeted me by saying, "Well, after your global tour I'm sure you'll agree that things are in a mess all around the world." That was his welcome.

We walked through the beautiful parlors of the air terminal, rode down the shining escalator, made our way through the mural-decorated corridor, onto the automatic walkway, picked up my bag, went out through doors that opened automatically when they saw us coming, and proceeded to my friend's shining sports car in the affluently crowded parking lot. He turned on the radio and the air conditioner. Not liking the radio program, he pressed another button, and a cassette brought us a command performance of the L.A. Philharmonic.

We drove to his home overlooking the city, the ocean, the surf, the sailboats, and the yachts. We went into his beautiful Monterey home, where he had music piped into every room and out into the patio where we sat. His beautiful wife came and served us refreshments, and as we sat relaxing near the swimming pool, my friend sighed and said, "This old world, what's it coming to?"

His wife interrupted. "Oh, now, just a minute!" she said. There was something in her words that plunged us into deep reflection. There came to us a sudden sense of recognition and realization that there was with us a *forgotten* world of self which, in this moment of quietude and sudden interpenetration, caused us to give at least a momentary thought to our blessings and to have a sense of gratitude and thankfulness.

Something happened in that particular moment, and I wonder if one of the purposes of meetings of this kind is perhaps to awaken in us this something *right* about the world that we often overlook or miss or feel its distortion in our day-by-day careers and our day-by-day routines. Because actually, as we sat there, we hadn't changed the big world, the world "outside." It was still there. But we had become cognizant of our inner world, which is always *here.* And it occurs to me that we cannot hope or seek to solve the trouble in the big world until we have made peace with the world within ourselves.

We cannot create a new consciousness in the world around us unless we discover a new consciousness within ourselves. We cannot correct corrupt conditions until we are strong enough not to be corrupted by the conditions we wish to correct. Society is a reflection of the individual, and the individual reflects society. A new methodology for thinking is necessary, and we dare no longer think of the world "out there" as being beyond our influence. We are continually being reminded to meet the world from a basis of power and strength. Now for a little while we began to wonder what might happen if we were to meet the world from the basis of gratitude.

Often when I am counseling students and they have told me all about their gripes and their hangups and their frustrations, I ask them, "What do you have to be *grateful* for?"

Recently I saw the documentary of James Cross, the English diplomat who was kidnapped by the Quebec Liberation Front. He recounted how he had been kept for 60 days in a darkened room without a sight of sunlight. He never slept at night but with the awareness that men with tommy guns sat over him. On a number of occasions they taped dynamite sticks to his head to intimidate him. James Cross said, "I learned something about the world in those 60 days. I learned most poignantly that we never appreciate the common everyday things of life until they are taken away from us."

There is a saying that if you really want to find out what's right with the world, imagine that everything you love and everything you have are suddenly taken away. And then imagine that you get them all back. The true meaning of life comes not only through knowledge, but through experience.

With this in mind, let me mention four points that I think represent a basic contemporary rightness with the world:

1. There is a rightness in the fact that the overall trend these days is from *exclusiveness* to *inclusiveness* in life.

2. There is a rightness in the fact that we have moved from a concept of infallibility to a sincere attitude of introspection.

3. There is a rightness about our determination to shift from a point of disrespect of nature to a respect for nature and nature's laws.

4. There is a rightness in our development and recognition of the coming of the new man for the new age.

A word on each of these points. The concept of *inclusiveness rather than exclusiveness* is very important to us who seek to teach or arouse or transmit an idea. As long as we stand apart or above people, excluding them from ourselves, we miss a basic rightness about the world. Surely we are beginning to recognize the inclusiveness of basic drives in people, basic desires and aspirations, basic spiritual and psychological quests coded in every individual. The emergence of this approach is fundamentally apparent and, to my way of thinking, fundamentally right. We are learning at long last that the more knowledge we bring into human relations, the greater all cultures and individuals become.

I recently spent some time among the aborigines in Australia. I feel I understood these emerging people better because of preparation I had among so-called "primitive cultures" in other parts of the world. The more knowledge you bring into a field, the greater the field becomes. The fault, the limitation may lie in you, not in the individual or group with whom you are dealing.

Think about this for a moment, and the meaning becomes clear. Up in Canada near our summer home is a mine that was closed and abandoned for many years. It was a gold mine originally and when all the gold had been removed, the mine was closed. Then men began looking for tungsten. The old mine was opened and tungsten was mined out of it. After it had yielded all that was profitable for the taking, the place was boarded up again. Then came the whole new field of uranium and precious metals. Back men went to the mine and they worked it again, astonished at what it had to yield. Now, the precious metals had been there during the tungsten craze, and the tungsten had been there during the days of the gold rush. Everything had been there all the time. That is the way it is with your life and mine. That is the way it is with cultures and people. It is only the knowledge that we bring into play that causes us to draw out the riches.

When I got into what the aborigines call the "Dreamtime" or "The Dreaming," I was fascinated how closely it related to depth meditation or the practices of the transcendentalists. Yet here are people who have no formal education, illiterate, so-called primitive people, who now because of *our* knowledge and insight are beginning to be recognized more and more.

Because of our growing knowledge in the parapsychological field, we now recognize the heightened sensitivity of the aborigines in their extrasensory perception. Pharmaceutical researchers are interesting themselves in the herbal lore of the aborigines, artists are taking another look at their creative expression, and so on. This, too, is what I mean by inclusiveness—that we no longer stand apart; that we recognize, as I have been saying, that the true meaning of life comes through experience; and experience reveals the deeper rightness of the world in which we live.

The second point. What do we mean by "introspection rather than infallibility"? I mean that we are living at a time when we dare to question, when we hold the quest for truth as valid as truth itself, when we are beginning to trust our own judgment, our own wisdom, and our own intuition. By this is certainly not meant a ruling out of the rational mind, but it means a re-examination of our sense of values and an updating of our integrity. Is there a symbolism of language out of which the meaning has gone? Are we insisting on passing along to oncoming generations concepts and ideas which we no longer believe in?

We are all facing a moment of truth. There comes a time in the life of every individual and every moment when the confrontation with truth takes place. There may seem to be confusion in Roman Catholicism at the moment, as a case in point, but there is also a recognition of clarification and coming to grips with the contemporary meaning in age-old faiths. Think for a moment of the impact of Teilhard do Chardi the Jesuit paleontologist who stirred the world with his *Phenomenon of Man.* Banished years ago because of his views on the evolution no less than on the future of man, he was reinstated within our time. Pope John brought him out of his exile and made it possible for his writings to be freely circulated.

Is this sudden trend toward introspection in *all* of life rather than humble acceptance of infallibility good or bad? Only time will tell. Let's not forget that we are often too closely involved with a period of transition to judge its total effect. We are too close to Vietnam. We are too close to outer space. We are too close to the scientific breakthroughs of our time to be able to judge their effect in the light of history.

There was at the University of Iowa a Chinese teacher who had an office next to mine. Someone once asked him for his appraisal of the significance of the Napoleonic Wars. The teacher said, "It is too soon to tell. We are still too close to them in time." We are too close to the periods of contemporary transition to tell whether everything is "good or bad," "true or false." All we know is that our seeming infallibility both in religion and in areas of the educational process are frequently severely tested and put on the spot.

It is a sharpening experience. We certainly know that. This simulsense approach, this "sensory-mix" that challenges both our methodology and our convictions, are good for us. Personally, I feel it is part of the rightness of our world, in which now, as always, the only changeless thing is change.

As for point three, I rather think we are all quite in agreement: There is something right with the world when we recognize we must work in harmony with nature rather than to oppose it and show it disrespect.

Just now one of our action words is "ecology." We are really excited about doing something for the "ecology." We have many new movements, new legislation, new champions, new slogans, new committees going all out for "ecology." We can only hope that something will be done that will be more than just cerebral intellection. Each one of us must begin to live in harmony with nature and nature's laws.

I recently read an article titled "What's Happened to the Ospreys?" On the face of it this sounds far out. Who cares about the ospreys? Where we spend our summers, up in Canada, we used to have hundreds of ospreys. We photographed these birds for years. I recorded their squawking cries, and we used to take visitors on a boat ride so they could watch the ospreys build their nests and hatch their young. Last year we saw only two nests. The ospreys are dying. The whale is becoming extinct. The koala are gone. The kiwi are gone. The bald eagel is just about gone. The rivers, the lakes are being polluted. The other day I saw an announcement that Waikiki beach in certain areas is now restricted and closed to bathers.

Viewed from one perspective, there is something definitely wrong with a world in which man is fighting nature and nature, in turn, is fighting man. But there is something tremendously right with a world in which the recognition of the need for cooperation has suddenly become a living issue. Roger Peterson, perhaps our greatest ornithologist, has said, "Birds are the litmus paper of our environment." As we see the birds go, so we see a foreshadowing of how and where man will go unless we do something.

But, again, there is something gloriously right with the world in this awakening. You and I, in the positions we hold, are in strategic situations to form and frame the minds of youth and to alert them to the challenge of working in harmony with nature all down the line, from personal living to environmental life. But the moment I say this, I realize that many youth are already more alert to this than you and I.

As to point four, the rightness which I suggested was apparent in the coming of the new man, the evidence of the emergence of a new individual with a new life-style, let me just say this: We *are* in a new age; life *is* a "whole new ball game," as the saying has it; we *can* no longer communicate only merely on a verbal basis and expect to reach the listening inner ear of those with whom we work. We must learn to communicate on a subconsciousness, a subliminal basis. What does this mean?

It means that what you project as your true self, as your inner self, as to what you truly hold to be right and true, is what is communicated to students. You who have some kind of senority in teaching know this. When I meet students who were in my classes years ago, fellows and girls who are now in career positions in the world, they are frank to say that what impressed them most was not what I said, not even what I presumed to teach, but what I projected of my deepest self to the onward going quest within them.

The new man is unbound in this quest for meaning. He takes all philosophy, all spiritual thought, all symbolism and imagery and mythology into consideration. He is, at heart, more interested in existence than in things that exist. My field, which is basically religious research, has proved that young people are unbound theologically, nationalistically, even moralistically in their common meaning of the term. They are hardly convinced, as many of us once were, of heaven and hell as locations, of life as beginning with the physical body, or of God being an anthropomorphic Deity in a far-away sky.

They are interested in synthesis. In synchronicity. In centroversion and the like. Centroversion has become a kind of mystique—a concept that within every organism is an innate tendency toward unity. There is also a growing belief among the new generation that the organism bears within itself the properties of well-being and perfection. Centroversion taps the compensatory processes which lead to healing, well-being, and perfection. In this respect, God is very much in the picture. God is an evocative word with the 'new man" and is rapidly becoming a greater reality than He has been in the past when He often *was* but a word.

Recently one of our contemporary thinkers suggested we make a distinction between that which is complex and that which is complicated. When we say a problem is complex, we mean that the organism or the situation is orderly but we do not quite understand it. Nonetheless, there is a pattern. When we say a thing is complicated, we infer there is no discernible pattern. Is it possible that we of the so-called Establishment often look upon life and society as being complex, while the oncoming generation considers it complicated? Perhaps if we could communicate with students against the background of this kind of understanding and then remember the importance of nonverbal communication on the level of "spiritual understanding," the rightness of the world in our particular time in history would become more clear.

Our meeting today, set as it is in the Christmas period, suggests that there is something right with the world far beyond the measure of the four points we have talked about. We find this rightness in the everyday, ordinary things of life. We find it in the sound of Christmas songs, in the sight of Christmas lights, in the touch of the Christmas spirit. We may lose it when we are caught in the crowds, but we find it in the quiet. We may miss it when we think of our own frenzied attempt to meet the coming of the 25th, but we find it when we stop to count our blessings.

We must begin with our own inner world; for, as we said at the beginning, before we can find a rightness in the world around us, we must find it in the world within. Then we reach a point something like this: We realize that all we need to do is to make this sense of something right collective and bring it into unification, so that in a little while, through us as good messengers, we will light other fires of rightness in other hearts and eventually create a better world—a better world which, in fact, we already have and often don't realize it. And that may be the one thing that is wrong with the world! We don't realize how right it is. Outside of that, everything is probably in good order and we are back where we began: It is not through knowledge alone, but through experience, that we come into a proper relationship with life.

Dr. Jose Delgado

Dr. Jose Delgado, Professor of Psychology at Yale University, presented the Jennings Scholar Lecture on January 16, 1971, in the John C. Baker Center, Ohio University.

Dr. Delgado was born in Ronda, Spain, and received his medical training at Madrid University, where he was Associate Professor of Physiology and Investigator of the Spanish National Research Council. In 1952 he came to Yale University. Dr. Delgado received the Ramon y Cajal Prize from the Spanish Government in 1952 and was a Guggenheim Fellow in 1963.

Dr. Delgado's research has centered on brain physiology and behavior, using rhesus monkeys and chimpanzees as subjects. His investigations are based on methods he has developed for the permanent implantation of electrode and chemitrode assemblies in the brain, which allow long-term electrical and chemical stimulation of specific cerebral areas in behaving subjects. Micro-circuitry recently developed in his laboratory permits multichannel remote control brain stimulation and recording in free animals and the study of social relations.

In addition to influencing autonomic, somatic, and motor behavior, brain stimulation modified psychological manifestations, including friendliness and aggressiveness. Intracerebral electrodes have also been used for diagnosis and surgical orientation in patients suffering from epilepsy and other neurological disorders, showing that mental activities such as memory, fear, pleasure, and pain can be induced, inhibited, or modified in free patients by radio stimulation of discrete cerebral areas.

The knowledge of brain physiology gained from such studies should facilitate creation of more intelligent techniques to educate human behavior and new approaches for the treatment of mental disturbances.

Dr. Delgado is on the editorial boards of various scientific publications, including the Journal of Nervous and Mental Disease, the International Journal of Neuropharmacology, and the International Review of Neurobiology. He has written more than 200 articles for scientific journals. His book, entitled *Physical Control of the Mind: Toward a Psychocivilized Society,* has been published by Harper and Row as Volume XLI in the *World Perspectives Series.*

EDUCATION AND PSYCHOGENESIS

The main quality that differentiates man from other animals is the complexity of his mental functions. Man's superior intelligence and resulting ability to communicate and plan for the future, create cultures, and use or destroy the surrounding environment are consequences of his unique cerebral development. Precisely because of his perceptivity, man has always endeavored to understand himself, to learn the properties of his mental functions, and to devise explanations for his own existence.

In the past, human beings were like spectators in the theater of Nature, each an outsider within his own physical form, perceiving the world through sensory inputs evaluated by the unreachable mechanisms of the mind. Early attempts to decipher biological secrets yielded misleading clues, postulating the existence of vital forces, locating the soul in the heart or pineal body, and underestimating the importance of the brain, which was considered merely a cooling device. Relations between mind and body have been debated by philosophers and scientists from Aristotelian times up to recent symposia (see Eccles, 1966; Scher, 1962). Until recently, mental functions have eluded scientific experimentation because brain activity could not be detected, measured, or modified by any known physical or chemical means. Studies were performed by simple observation: Human beings looked at other human beings, and tried to estimate the influence of sensory inputs on behavioral outputs. Even introspection was only an attempt to analyze the effects of information received from the environment on individual behavioral expression. The link between these inputs and outputs lies within the brain and involves neurological mechanisms prerequisite for any mental manifestations. Perhaps because these mechanisms have been unknown and unreachable, they have often been considered irrelevant for an understanding of the mind.

Even in psychology, the brain was referred to as a "black box," outside the realm of investigation. It was as if we were denied entrance to an automobile factory and had to remain outside, observing the delivery of steel, rubber, glass, and other raw materials, and the exit of smoke, refuse, and finished cars. As outsiders, it would be impossible for us to discover the number of elements involved or the sequence of their construction, and without familiarity with these processes, it would be impossible to predict or influence future production models. If we could place in the factory a net of agents equipped with cameras, microphones, tape recorders, and other sensors to transmit information to the outside, our understanding of its internal organization and prediction of activities would be greatly facilitated. If, in addition, our agents had the skill and power to influence the factory staff and workers, from the outside we could modify their behavior patterns and the products manufactured.

Modern techniques for brain exploration give us precisely these alternatives. In many laboratories throughout the world, mechanical, thermal, electrical, chemical, and other types of sensors are being placed inside the working brain for prolonged periods of time. With these sensors it is possible to detect the electrical discharges of single nervous cells or the synchronous pulsing of neuronal pools, and we can correlate physical phenomena with specific sensory stimulation of sounds or shapes, or with determined behavioral responses such as learning or problem solving. We can introduce microscopic amounts of chemicals into a brain structure—for example, catecholamines or amino acids into the limbic system—and, depending on the chosen substance and the selected neuronal structure, we can increase or decrease sleep, sex, appetite, and a variety of other functions. Memory is somehow related to a stereochemical synthesis of proteins. Richness or poverty of experience is manifested in the thickness of the cerebral cortex, in the submicroscopic structure of neuronal connections, and in the enzymatic composition of the brain. We can electrically stimulate the activity of specific cerebral structures to induce motor movements or emotional responses such as rage or placidity. In man, hallucinations, pleasure, hostility, friendliness, and other mental manifestations have been evoked by the direct application of electricity to specific areas of the central nervous system (Delgado, 1969a, 1969b; Sheer, 1961). Communication from the depth of the brain to a computer and back to the brain has been established by means of radio waves, circumventing normal sensory organs (Delgado *et al.*, 1970).

These and many other findings are being reported in today's scientific journals, demonstrating that a most significant revolution has already begun—the revolution of the human mind exploring and directing its own biological basis. This possibility to discover and manipulate the physiological mechanisms of mental activities is providing better understanding of what man is in terms of his emotional and intellectual capabilities and limitations, and it should give us tremendous power to influence the structuring of future minds. In addition, information about the neurological basis of human behavior constitutes a new frame of reference which should clarify fundamental questions concerning personal identity, consciousness, education, freedom and the purpose of human life.

THE PSYCHOGENESIS OF PERSONAL IDENTITY

One of the classical philosophical questions is: What is a human being? How is man like or unlike other things in the world, such as stones, trees, and animals? At the personal level, a host of related questions may be formulated: What am I? What are the building blocks of my personality? Where and how do they originate? How are my personality and mental activities preserved or modified through time and circumstances?

Attempts to answer the question What is a human being? usually assume that a stable entity exists with fixed properties that can be known and defined. This is not, however, the case because: (1) Human beings are not static but dynamic, and undergo considerable morphological and functional changes during the individual span of life. (2) Individual identity is not fixed and determined at birth but is dependent on and molded by the continuous stream of sensory inputs provided by the environment. (3) Man is a product of evolution and is still evolving in his physical and mental characteristics. (4) Any decision as to the moment when the fertilized egg, the fetus, or even the baby can be considered human is arbitrary and depends on the qualities deemed essential for our species. (5) Any estimation of the moment of earth history when ancestral apes evolved sufficiently to be considered humans is also an arbitrary question of definition. In the transition from ovum to infant or from ape to man, there are no sharp boundaries, but rather wide, overlapping zones of development.

In the past, understanding of what a human being is had a mainly philosophical value. Today the question has, in addition, important medical, social, and even political consequences because we are at the verge of acquiring the scientific technology to influence the structuring of future men decisively by means of purposeful manipulation of (a) genetic endowment, (b) neurophysiological mechanisms, and (c) information and experience provided through sensory inputs.

Human engineering has been considered desirable by some authorities (Skinner 1948, 1961) who would like to influence the natural evolution of man, while recognition of the risks involved has led others to propose a moratorium on this type of research. The individual characteristics of each person, including his ideological and emotional structure, are the result of two classical groups of factors: Nature and nurture, or genes and environment. To discuss which group is the more important would be inappropriate because both are essential; it is preferable to investigate the role of determined factors in specific human qualities.

The fecundation of the ovum by the male spermatozoa is the decisive step for genetic determination of a future individual. From thousands of possibilities, only one set is established by chance, according to the choice of partner, sexual drives, local chemistry of the female organs, swimming skills of the male cells, and a variety of unpredictable factors. The successfully mating cells carry a precise genetic plan comparable to an architectural drawing. We know, however, that blueprints are used only to direct the ordering of materials and the efforts of the builders, who must coordinate many elements during the construction of a house. In the absence of suitable materials, workers, and proper direction, the project will not be realized. We cannot identify drawings with a house. By themselves, they are useless pieces of paper that cannot provide shelter.

In the same manner, the fecundated germinal cells contain only a plan for a being—not a reality—lacking the physical form as well as arms, head, heart, and all of the functions that characterize man. The idea that a compressed homunculus with a complete, microscopic body was present in each male and female cell proved false. The genes are only a combination of amino acids which will direct the acceptance and organization of building materials provided from the outside (carbohydrates, fats, and proteins) in order to structure tissues and organs with a predetermined, functional specialization. Most of the genetic plans, which are the culmination of millions of years of evolution, will be misused and destroyed with the death of ova and spermatozoa. What a formidable waste of natural products and possibilities!

We must realize that even in a fly, the biological potential exists for it to develop into a human being. After all, we are the product of a long evolution, and our ancestors include monkeys, lizards, and butterflies. It is merely a question of considering different time scales. The spermatozoa and ova of a germinal cell have the potential to become human in months. Flies might possibily evolve into human beings in millions of years. The main difference, from our personal point of view, is that we are at the spermatozoic scale of time and can witness the appearance of our own children, while we cannot expect to live long enough to see a new human race evolving from existent flies and apes. At the cosmological scale of time, however, there is no hurry, and the stars will wait patiently with minor transformations while life appears, evolves, and disappears on the planet earth.

In the immediate reality of the human scale of time, we know that genetic determination is established by chance without the slightest intervention of the desires of the concerned individual, who at the moment of conception does not yet exist as a human being because his central nervous system and therefore his mental functions have not yet appeared. Even parents are totally ignorant and powerless to influence the choice of a genetic set for their children. From these facts, three conclusions may be drawn: (1) The individual does not participate in the determination of his own genetic structure. (2) The individual is therefore not responsible for the behavioral consequences of his genetic make-up. (3) Society (including parents) is not responsible, either, for the genetic structure of its members, because until now it has lacked means to intervene. The third conclusion may be modified in the near future because of (a) further unraveling of the genetic code, (b) the possibility of genetic surgery and genetic manipulation, (c) the increased efficiency of artifical insemination, (d) the success of genetic selection and (e) the practicality of sex selection in humans, based on the selective ability of "male" and "female" spermatozoas to swim and survive in the acidity or alkalinity of female sex organs. Preliminary findings in these areas allow the prediction that, in the next century, man will control the genetic selection of human beings. Tomorrow's question will not be: What is a human being? but Given a set of genetic characteristics, which should be selected and which suppressed in order to obtain a specified result? In other words: Which genes should be chosen to construct future men? Most people would be in favor of the elimination of genes known to cause illnesses such as mongoloidism or hemophelia. It would be difficult to decide about the color of the eyes or skin, and even more controversial to favor aggressive or submissive behavior.

Along with the risks, great benefits may be expected from man's ability to influence evolution. Genetic engineering need not lead to uniformity. The consequences of technology are related to the purpose of its use, which will be determined by man himself. The danger is not in knowing, but in the mental activity of the brain, which is the organ responsible for the interpretation of information and the elaboration of behavioral consequences and practical applications. It is up to us to decide whether the aim of genetic manipulation is uniformity or diversity. We already know that we can breed rather similar cows, specialized to produce milk or meat, and we may select races of bulls with greater strength or ferocity, or better adaptation to cold weather or meager pastures. In man also, the trend could be toward homogeneous or heterogeneous characteristics, toward increasing or decreasing the length of bones, the size of the brain, or its specific functional qualities. In the past, Nature was responsible—or perhaps still irresponsible—for the genetic determination of man. In the future, man will be to a great extent responsible; therefore he must clarify his conception of what human qualities should be favored. The genetic decision must be kept in mind, although it will not be faced immediately.

Our present task is to explore (a) the role and consequences of the set of genes given to an individual, and (b) the possibility to influence and direct the huge number of potentials in order to obtain a final anatomical and functional product. Genetic plans are rather flexible and have an impressive capacity for substitution and even improvisation. The general objectives are rigid: The future being should have one head, two eyes, two arms, one stomach, and a collection of other definitely prescribed organs. With a few exceptions, this plan is usually accomplished. The blueprint, however, lacks total precision, and elaboration of many details depends on the conjunction of the initial planning with the fortuity of environmental factors. To build a house, an architect decides on the basic structure and designs a roof, walls, floors, windows, and a set of rooms with different functions; the details of the final product as well as the sets of fixtures and decoration depend on later decisions influenced by the development of the house, workmanship of the builders, availability of items, taste of clients, and other unpredictable elements. Construction is a gradual process, and it would be difficult to determine the exact moment when the house actually exists. The traditional celebration when the roof is completed—with wine, food, a flag or tree, and a good luck toast—is only symbolic, because without inside walls, plumbing, or electricity, the building cannot yet provide any of its main functions.

The birth of a baby is certainly a dramatic event. Expectation during pregnancy is transformed through the anxiety and pain of labor into the appearance of a new human being. A satellite of the mother's body gains independent existence that is duly recognized in a birth certificate and joyfully celebrated by family and friends. Although the newborn is legally and emotionally accepted as a human being, we must realize that he does not walk, speak, or even understand. Intelligence, planning for the future, ethical sense, and many other mental activities uniquely ascribed to man cannot be detected at this moment. The newborn has only reflex activities which do not require the existence of a working cortex. The behavior of a normal baby is similar to that of deformed babies, born without brains. In both cases, the baby will cry, suck, digest, soil diapers, and exhibit defensive reactions and disorganized motor activity. At birth, mental functions have not yet appeared (Delgado, 1969a). We could therefore question the baby's humanness, or at least attempt to clarify our concept of this term. Shall we say that a newborn is not human because he is not reasonable, coordinated, or fertile? We know that the normal child will develop approximately according to the timetable of our species. He will crawl at six months, walk at one year, talk at two, reach the "age of reason" at seven, and mature sexually at twelve to fourteen. At birth, however, none of these abilities exists, and we can speak only of potentialities for future development that will appear slowly, contingent on the presence in the environment of specific elements whose roles in the integration of each individual can be identified and evaluated.

If a baby dies after only a few days of life, his potential will be blocked. He has never spoken or understood a word; he has never walked; he has never even recognized his own mother. He never will. We may ask whether there is much difference between the mental activities of this unfulfilled entity and the potential minds of the ova and spermatozoa, wasted by the millions. A newborn baby is nine months closer to becoming a human being than is a germinal cell, but has he attained humanness? Only after the brain gains information and experience is a frame of reference structured for evaluation of further sensory inputs.

Parents may be shocked by this statement. They may exclaim, "My nice baby, so tender and beautiful, so full of charm, expected with such love, the source of my deepest emotions, the reason of my life and efforts! How could anyone question his glorious humanity, the promise of his future? Emotionality or wishful expectation are not, however, substitutes for reality. Parents must be patient, because within a very short period of time, the normal baby will begin to exhibit signs of mental activity, exploring his crib and learning to coordinate his motor activities.

Physical birth represents the moment when messages from the outside world begin to affect the brain through the senses, influencing the anatomical, chemical, and functional patterning of the developing cerebral cells. Some impacts will have greater influence than others on future reactivity of the individual. Child psychiatrists agree that the first two to three years of life are the most decisive in the structuring of personality. The transition, however, is so gentle that we cannot determine when human qualities emerge. Some joyful events may be recorded at certain dates, such as the first smile, the first word, the first steps, but a human being is more than smiles, words, and steps. The birth of humanness is not a sudden event but a gradual appearance of mental activities, a progressive enrichment of knowledge, emotionality, and reactivity, a slow growth in skills and intelligence. For legal convenience, classifications have been established by physical age. In the United States, a baby is considered an appendix of his parents until the age of about three, and he can travel, lodge, and eat free of charge. At twelve, he is obliged to pay not half but full fare on airplanes. At sixteen in some states, he is allowed to drive a car. At 18 he can be drafted and at 21 he can vote. Humanness is a complex and multifactorial condition with many intervening elements of different origins, acquired at different times and supported by highly complex neurophysiological mechanisms. An "all or nothing" conception of the onset of humanness is not realistic. Attempts to define what a human being is may also be unrealistic and unnecessary. It seems preferable to understand the many paths open to man and to use intelligence to influence the choice of determinants which will result in the single path of individual mental structure.

The fact that in genetic planning there is capacity to learn, grow, and evolve, does not mean that the material to be learned or faculties to be developed are also in the genes. Clarification of this point is essential. The homunculus theory of a dormant microscopic man, waiting his call to duty in the depth of the germinal cell, proved incorrect. We know that the initial growth of the ovum constitutes a conglomeration of fast dividing cells without any remote similarity to man or any other creature, and devoid of any trace of the organs that will be formed. Another theory, explicitly expressed by some authors, has been that the germinal cell, or at least the viable fetus, possesses a microscopic soul, spirit, or mind which is the foundation and core of personal identity, dormant and hidden, awaiting only physical development of the body in order to demonstrate its individual specificity and functional characteristics.

This idea of a "spiritual homunculus" is unacceptable for several reasons: (a) In the absence of a brain, mental functions do not exist. (b) The brain of the newborn is still very immature; for example, the pyramidal tract, which is in charge of voluntary movements, does not complete its anatomical development until the child is about two years old. At birth, some cerebral structures, such as the hippocampus, which is somehow related to emotional responses, have only 10 per cent of their neuronal nets. (c) Although elemental nervous reflexes exist, the immature brain of the newborn does not have the functional capacity to think. (d) In the absence of information from the environment received through the sense organs, serious anatomical and physiological disturbances appear, and mental activities do not develop normally. Sensory stimulation is absolutely necessary for the physical and functional growth of the brain; genetic planning is not enough. (e) Even from the moral and theological point of view, a spiritual homunculus is not acceptable because a metaphysical entity (the soul) cannot have a material determination (the genetic code). In addition, if the mental qualities of an individual were predetermined by genes, he could not have moral responsibility for his own behavior.

We could think that, if not at conception at least at birth, the baby is a little physical homunculus because his body already has a shape and proportions comparable to those of an adult man. It is true that vital functions such as respiration and digestion are certainly dormant in the fetus and are prepared to perform efficiently if the baby is born somewhat prematurely. We cannot say the same, however, about a possible "mental homunculus," because, although the potential to learn and develop are there, mental functions are absent. For them to appear, it is necessary to have elements coming from outside the brain (perception of the environment) plus essential anatomical, chemical, and functional changes within the brain substance determined by the reception of sensory stimuli.

To be more precise about the respective roles of genes and sensory inputs in the integration and appearance of the mind, let us analyze one of the most important human characteristics: the use of language, the symbolic representation of reality essential for the handling of ideas. The ability to talk depends on (1) the specialized anatomical and functional structure of larynx muscles and vocal cords; (2) specialized anatomy and physiology of a cerebral area in the superior temporal convolution related to organization of acoustic information; (3) existence of a spoken language with words, meaning, symbols, and rules; (4) individual learning of the language by receiving acoustic stimuli from the environment through the senses. This experience will imprint chemical and functional changes in the structure of specific neurons.

Genetic determination is responsible for (1) and (2), which are unique for our species. The anatomy of the larynx, even in some of our close relatives such as the chimpanzee, is not sufficiently developed for the refined complexity of articulated sounds. An ape can never learn to pronounce human sounds, and patient efforts to teach chimpanzees have always failed. Several of these animals have been raised in scientists' homes along with their own children. While the children quickly assimilated language, the apes learned only a few simple words such as "mama" and "cup."

In order to talk, a suitable human larynx and a good brain are not enough. Genes do not carry the information or experience that make it possible to understand words and to talk. Individual learning and exposure to a suitable environment are necessary. Because genes direct the basic anatomical structuring of vocal cords and brain, they may influence the acoustic quality of the voice and also the learning capacity, but if the individual is not exposed to a language, he will never talk.

This point is crucial for our understanding of the acquisition of language, as well as the integration of many other mental activities: The brain per se is not enough to cause the emergence of the mind and its manifestations. Its role is to receive, store, evaluate, combine, modify, and express information originating in the outside. Basic brain structure, and therefore heredity, represents factors which filter and bias the input, circulation, and output of information. This is the behavioral impact of heredity.

The brain is not the Aristotelian "tabula rasa," where signs are printed as in wax. It is a highly reactive organ and has special symbolic codes of electrical spikes, chemical quanta, and spatial and temporal organization designed to handle information, the source of which is always extracerebral. Genes or neurons do not invent words spontaneously. Language is created slowly by the effort of many men through centuries.

Immaturity of the newborn brain is a great advantage because it is not committed to a determined functional set. At the beginning, the brain is empty. There are no motor formulas for movements, no behavioral patterns, no emotions, no experiences, no understanding, no ideologies—only an elemental group of reflexes to regulate body temperature, gastrointestinal activities, respiration, circulation, and other vegetative functions. The initial lack of ideological and behavioral commitment gives man a privileged situation, allowing him within a few years to learn and store in his neurons the cultural experience of milleniums of mankind's existence. In the case of language, an individual may in only 15 or 20 years master a wealth of words and concepts that were thousands of years in creation.

The selection of a mother tongue is of decisive importance for a child's destiny. Shall we select English, Chinese, or some other language? Since only a few can be learned by each individual, this choice has positive and negative aspects of acceptance and rejection, with the eventful consequences of immersion in an emotional, ideological, and behavioral set that constitutes the cultural parameters of a language. The baby whose personality is being shaped cannot be consulted about his preferences because his cerebral mechanisms of choice do not yet exist. He lacks not only experience and reason to choose, but also the means of intelligent expression. The decision is made, usually automatically, by his parents. If they are Arabs living in Egypt, the child will speak Arabic. As a result, specific languages are transmitted from parents to children in a rather spontaneous and natural way, although they determine in an authoritarian manner formation of an essential aspect of personality. This is not a criticism; it is only a statement of reality. It is natural that your son should speak your own language. In any case, you could not teach him one that you do not know.

A parent very concerned about the personal freedom of his child could try not to impose a single means of communication, but to teach him several idioms. However, there is still a limit in the learning capacity of the brain, and a choice—again by the parent and not the child—would still be necessary. We may favor a bilingual or multilingual education, but a child cannot learn 100 languages. Personal identity is, to a great extent, language bound. Individuals feel comfortable and communicate easily within their own idiomatic system. Occidentals usually experience some disorientation when they visit countries such as Morocco or Japan, whose communication symbols are incomprehensible to them; without training, their brains cannot handle the incoming stream of auditory and visual sensory inputs. Learning of a language opens the door to participation in a given culture. During the decisive years of childhood, most of the information that is shaping the individual brain is chosen by educators with a deliberate purpose, usually following traditional lines for the preservation of established values within the system.

Going one step further, we may analyze the neurophysiological correlates of learning a language. The first word spoken is often "Mama." The mother repeats this word again and again, perhaps while holding her baby and saying other affectionate phrases. A spoken word causes a pattern of vibrations in the air, which reach the baby's timpanic membrane, producing oscillations transmitted mechanically to the inner ear, where a series of waves is produced in the endolymph liquid. Consequently, specialized acoustic sensory organs are stimulated, transforming the sound waves into chemical responses and patterns of electrical discharges which circulate through the acoustic pathways, establishing very complex and poorly understood stimulation of a multiplicity of neuronal nets. At the same time, the visual input of the image of the mother determines another series of electrical discharges circulating through optic pathways. Simultaneity of determined optic and acoustic phenomena may induce a functional association between the two patterns of evoked electrical discharges in such a way that the presence of one facilitates—or even induces—activation of traces of the other.

Learning the meaning of a word is very complicated and requires, among others, the following processes: (1) acoustic coding of the word as a temporal succession of air vibrations; (2) induction of mechanical vibrations in the timpanic membrane; (3) mechanical transmission of the vibrations to the inner ear; (4) transduction of their mechanical waves into chemical and electrical phenomena at the sensory neurons; (5) transmission and circulation of electrical impulses through the brain with a new coding of the received information; (6) intracerebral evaluation and interpretation of the coded signals with respect to the frame of reference of past signals. For this purpose, a cross correlation is necessary between present information and past experience accumulated in memory storage of the neurons. This fact is very important because *without a frame of reference, evaluation of reality is not possible.* Moreover, the frame of reference must be based on past experience, related to previous reception of information through sensory inputs. *The genes do not provide this frame of reference.* The empty brain of the newborn does not have the necessary information to interpret the environment. *Reception of sensory inputs and learning are absolutely necessary for the construction of a personal frame of reference.* This is one of the reasons why early experiences are so decisive for individual destiny. Acquisition of the frame of reference is the most essential aspect in the integration of personal identity. Because the informational building blocks for this frame do not originate in the brain, the source of your thinking and behaving is not inside you but in the outside world, and it must be made available to "you," and penetrate through your senses before it is used to construct the "yourself." (7) Conscious understanding of meaning is a process we have all experienced, but very little is known about its physiological mechanisms. Somehow the circulating coded signals are decoded into a "mean-

70

ing" which reaches our awareness. (8) Functional association between determined acoustic and optic sets of coded signals, circulating in the brain, will be established after a repeated number of temporal correlations. Although information about this process is scarce, memory storage is obviously involved; the temporal sequence of two signals must leave a trace which facilitates their future association.

Even if cerebral mechanisms were ready at birth to receive and elaborate information, in the absence of messages the brain would remain unused and nonfunctional. The cables and equipment of an excellent telephonic network are inoperative if no one talks. The best highway system is wasted without traffic. The adult brain contains areas analagous to parking lots (memory storage), where many cars await a summons to circulate. Each of these cars (bits of information and experience) originated in the environment. A baby learning to talk assimilates and uses an established system—English, for example—but does not invent it. While people may have a larger or more limited vocabulary and may vary in their tastes, associations, creativity, and general skill in the use of language, they handle it according to rules composed by culture. Even the most original writer is merely borrowing an established language: His originality consists of giving a new sequence to his chosen symbols.

Certain languages are unsuitable for the communication of certain types of information. A primitive tongue will not contain the terminology required for a discussion of electronics or music. While language is made by man to serve his special interests, it also makes man, since the possibilities and limitations of expression inherent in a given language will be transferred to the person using it. Intrinsic characteristics of the information received will influence the reactivity, expression, and functions of the mind which is being shaped by this information. If your native tongue is Spanish, you will think and dream in Spanish, and express joys and pains in Spanish. You will understand the ideas of other men when they are explained in Spanish and participate in certain shadings of emotionality uniquely expressed in that language.

We may conclude that personal identity and mental functions do not exist at birth, do not appear suddenly, and cannot develop merely by physical growth of the brain; they are related exclusively to genetic endowment and sensory inputs. This statement emphasizes the causality of these two elements and rejects the idea that any other factors are involved in structuring personal identity. It also denies the preexistence of a mythical "you" upon which genes and environment could act. The self, the ego, and "you" cannot exist in the absence of a genetically determined brain, or in the absence of a materially and functionally enriched brain determined by sensory stimuli. Personal identity is the very complex product of a functioning mind which is structured by the intracerebral elaboration (involving genetically determined biases) of extracerebral information (involving inputs originating in the environment).

SUMMARY

Evaluation of recent developments in the neurophysiological understanding of brain functions leads to the following conclusions: (1) Complex symbolic thought, a species-specific human quality, depends on transitory organization in the depth of the brain of elements borrowed from the environment. (2) These elements are the only building blocks for construction of personal identity. (3) There is no mythical "self" pre-existing or present at birth; there is only a very immature—and mentally empty—brain with the potential to construct a human personality by reacting to and organizing information received from the outside. (4) The purpose of education is not to "unveil the true personality of the baby," because such a thing does not exist, but rather to *construct* the personality by providing suitable experience. (5) In a vacuum of sensory stimuli, the brain cannot function, and the mind will not evolve. Anything that we do or do not do in relation with the baby will influence the structuring of his mind. The only choices are who is going to provide the mind-forming information, what the purpose of education will be, and what kind of human being we would like to shape. Parents' withdrawal from intervention is still a choice and affects the child decisively. Blind chance will leave its mark if parents abdicate, reluctant to favor certain patterns of development in the child. (6) If personal identity is the product of genes plus received information, if both are given to the child, and if he has no initial possibility to select or defend himself from any element in his surroundings, we may ask whether human beings are automats without responsibility or freedom. This is precisely the case at birth and also during the early months of life. Babies are so totally dependent on parental care that they cannot survive by themselves. At this time, babies lack the attributes usually considered essential in humanness. (7) We should not fall into the error of potentiality, assuming the present existence of a future state which requires a series of circumstances not available at the considered moment. A worm is *not* a butterfly, nor has it wings, nor can it fly, although the metamorphosis is possible, provided that food and time are available. A seed is not a tree, nor does it possess leaves, nor can it give nice shade in summer. A newborn baby does not speak or understand. He is not responsible for his behavior; he has no freedom, and his clumsy movements are essentially automatic. (8) The birth of personal identity and behavioral reactivity is a slow process contingent on the progressive accumulation of sensory inputs which leave material traces within the brain cells. The highest quality of man is not inherited but acquired: It is the possibility to escape from automatic behavior by using his experience, for with knowledge and planning he may gain the freedom and responsibility to direct his destiny intelligently.

Delgado, José M. R.   Physical Control of the Mind: toward a Psychocivilized Society. Vol. XLI, World Perspectives Series, R. N. Anshen (Ed.), New York: Harper & Row, 280 pp., 1969a.

Delgado, José M. R.   Radio Stimulation of the Brain in Primates and in Man. *Anesth. Analg.,* 48:529–543, 1969b.

Delgado, José M. R., Johnston, Victor S., Wallace, Jan D., and Bradley, Ronald J.   Operant Conditioning of Amygdala Spindling in the Free Chimpanzee. *Brain Research,* 22:347–362, 1970.

Eccles, J. C. (Ed.)   Brain and Conscious Experience. New York: Springer-Verlag, 591 pp., 1966.

Scher, J. M., (Ed.)   Theories of the Mind. New York: The Free Press of Glencoe, 748 pp., 1962.

Sheer, D. E. (Ed.)   Electrical Stimulation of the Brain. Austin, Texas: Univ. Texas Press, 641 pp., 1961.

Skinner, B. F.   Waldon Two. New York: Macmillan, 1948.

Skinner, B. F.   The Design of Cultures. *Daedalus,* pp. 534–546, Summer, 1961.

Father Daniel Egan

Father Daniel Egan, S.A., a Graymoor Franciscan at the Graymoor Friars' house in New York's Greenwich Village, presented the Jennings Scholar Lecture on February 20, 1971 in the John C. Baker Center, Ohio University.

Father Egan is reverently known to millions as "The Junkie Priest." For the past 20 years his parish has been the streets, prisons, jails, criminal courts, emergency wards, and the morgue. His experiences in the deep subculture of crime and drug addiction are the subject of the best-selling book by John D. Harris, *The Junkie Priest,* now in its tenth printing. Father Egan's articles on drug addiction have appeared in many professional periodicals.

Frequently called to testify at federal, state and city drug addiction hearings, Father Egan was once the only priest in the country subpoenaed to testify before the U.S. Senate Committee on Juvenile Crime. He has appeared on National TV in both the United States and Canada. A major movie about Father Egan's life is now in the making. Probably he has lectured to more people on drug abuse than any other speaker in the country. He is most at home at high school assemblies, where he talks in a style that students really "dig." In the past few months he has lectured to thousands of men in the armed services.

He is the founder of The Village Haven in New York City, the first live-in therapeutic community for female addicts. He insists that kindness, patience, and honest confrontation have succeeded in obtaining protracted abstinence and even cures from addiction, where years of prison and psychiatric treatment had failed.

Father Egan has his A.B. and M.A. degrees from the Catholic University of America.

DRUG ADDICTION: A SYMPTOM OF
A PROBLEM

My dear people, Patricia and I basically believe that drug abuse is a "people-problem" and so we address you as "people." We fundamentally believe that drug abuse is a human problem, not a socio-economic one, not a pharmacological one, and certainly not a criminological one. We believe it is a sad indictment on what's happening that human beings must look for chemical or scientific solutions to problems that are basically human. What a human being should do when he hurts has always been a human problem. Ever since the dawn of civilization, man has been frustrated when he was unable to find within his humanity the answers to human pain. For once we box man in and say man is above the ape, that man is beneath the angels, or that man is more than a stone or more than a diamond; once we box him in and say he is human then, of necessity, he has human limitations. This is why man experiences frustrations when he feels the human feelings of loneliness and boredom and rejection. What does a man do when he hurts? Socrates, Plato, all the ancient philosophers struggled with man's limitations. But they accepted the reality that man does have limits beyond which he cannot go. At such times man always looked within himself for answers. Not finding them, he sought help outside himself.

Today our young people are experiencing nothing new in human feelings. Some kids actually believe this is the first time in the history of mankind that people feel bored. "Man, I'm bored," or "I'm alienated, man" or "I'm bugged" or "I'm frustrated" or "I'm misunderstood" or "I feel different." These are age-old human feelings. If you listen to some of the troops in Vietnam, you get the feeling that this is the first time in history of mankind that we have known battle fear. Actually, it's been around a long, long time but it's different today because young people don't know what to do with this feeling. Happiness doesn't mean the absence of fear. Neither does it mean the absence of pressure or pain. It does mean knowing how to cope with these feelings instead of copping out. Kids today are becoming a race of cop-out artists. They don't know how to cope; so they cop—cop out.

In other ages, in other generations, in your day and my day, when we were bugged or frustrated, we got out of ourselves, and, without feeling any shame or guilt, said, "God help me!" We humanly turned to God as we understood Him. Limited by our humanity, we prayed, "God, help me to remember what I studied, help me keep my girl friend good, help me not to punch my father." It was always, "God help me," when we couldn't do it alone and had reached the end of human endurance. But today too many kids are becoming the victims of what we have told them about the new heresy of secularism. Today we don't take time to deny God. We keep Him

77

up in Heaven where He belongs. "When we need you, Man, we'll let you know, but in the meantime don't crowd us. On earth we're going to solve earth problems with science and chemistry. But stick around, God. We may need you to blame an earthquake on, to blame a war on, to blame sickness on. But outside of that, don't crowd us!" Kids are saying this. Let's not pass judgment on it, but let's understand it. Youth are turning now to science and chemistry for answers. But can chemistry solve the problem of loneliness? Can science help a kid when he feels different or can't relate? Can science help when he doesn't know how to love because he never has been loved or doesn't even know what the word means? To what does he turn? To whom does he turn?

There was a day, not too long ago, when we could withdraw within ourselves to certain Absolutes that didn't depend on conditions or feelings or the weather or a system of politics. They were always absolutely true. But if you want a very frightening experience today, take a few sophomores, seat them in a circle, and ask each one to come up with three Absolutes—values, realities, ideals—they are absolutely sure about. What are they sure about? "I'm here, man, and I didn't ask to be born either. I'm here and someday I'm going to die." But between here and there you'd almost think they've been reading Sartre for years. So to what do they turn? These kids are part of a shook-up generation. They see values tumbling down. Those that are left are being jeered at and ridiculed. So what Absolutes do they have?

We come face to face with the causes beneath drug addiction. No good doctor treats a symptom unless the symptom gets out of control. A doctor doesn't deal with a fever unless the fever gets out of control. He asks, "What's the cause of the fever?" A doctor doesn't treat a rash unless the rash gets out of control. He deals with the cause of the rash. Drug addiction, to me, is a rash on the body of society. Underneath that symptom there are causes.

We could spend all the time during this lecture speaking about what is dramatic, observable, visual—the symptoms: the overdoses, the dropouts from school, the kids who come in nodding, the marks going down, the lack of initiative, the alienation. These we can see. But what's underneath?

It takes two things to make a drug addict. Since teachers always take notes, it's worth writing down that addiction comes from two Latin words, "ad" and "dicere." It basically means "to give up," "to go over to." The wealth of our country, our country's greatest natural resource, is in a disaster area. Our youth are becoming bankrupt by turning over to, giving up on drugs. Two things make a drug addict, a drug and the person. What kind of drug? With all the things you are getting mimeographed and printed from the Department of Education, you know more about the pharmacology of drugs than I do. But what kind of person, what kind of kid, goes from popping a pill to liking the pill for what it blocks out? What kind of kid, halfway through a joint of marijuana, will like it enough to need it and go on from need to dependence and abuse? I believe he is the kid who, by conditioning, by home or national environment, doesn't know how to suffer. He doesn't know how to hurt. He is the kid who has fallen victim to the greatest internal threat to our country, the heresy of hedonism. Hedonism is a philosophy which makes pleasure an end in itself, the end-all of everything. Ninety-nine per cent of all the advertisements on television sell pleasure. Pleasure isn't wrong as long as it serves as a means to an end. But when pleasure becomes an end in itself then kids get caught in a trap of no return. What is the result of kids' constantly looking at TV advertisements and billboard displays that sell only one thing—pleasure, pleasure, pleasure? In talking to some of the young kids today, you get the impression, that hurt and struggle and endurance and stick-to-it-tiveness are evils and that everything must come easy. There must be quick, easy solutions to everything. We seem to be reverting to the old primitive idea of the tribal magician. With a magic poof he could bring rain or dispel clouds. Today we have the idea that there must be an easy way to get up, an easy way to go to sleep, an easy way to be educated, an easy way to relate, an easy way to overcome shyness, an easy way to date, an easy way to do everything. But there is no easy way to be truly human! There is no easy way to grow up. There is no easy way to go from 13 to 18. One must be 14 and 15 and 16 and 17 before he gets to be 18. We wish we could skip 15, but we can't. We wish there could be no sophomores, but there must be sophomores. We wish there were no 13-year olds, mean and defiant. But they're 13 and they have to be 13 and they can't skip it. We wish every kid could remain 14 the rest of his life.

Years ago, when I used to hear confessions of high school students hour by hour, I'd often say to a girl who sounded as mean as hell, "Are you 15 yet?"

She'd say, "Yes. How did you know I'm 15?"

"Well, relax. You won't always be 15."

"I won't?"

"No, there's hope."

You wish they could escape those years, 13 or 15—I don't know which —when they're meanest. As Shakespeare once said, "I would wish there were no years between something and something, but there are." Kids believe today, because they are conditioned to believe—that they can be human and real without hurting. If there is anything we must teach our students (rather, educate our students, because education is more than teaching facts, data, statistics—education means the formulation of attitudes, a philosophy of life, an outlook on life) it is the attitude of mind that suffering is a necessary condition of human existence. We have to keep telling youth: "Kids, if you're going to be real, you've got to suffer. If you're going to be human and stay in the human condition, you must feel all human conditions. You've got to *feel* them, not block them out, not run from them, not drug them. You can't know the feeling of joy without knowing the feeling of sorrow."

Once in my life, I looked at a thalidomide baby, physically deformed through no fault of its own. Then I thought of all the students across the country, who because of softness and moral flabbiness in home life are emotionally deformed through parental fault. Kids who get things too easily without working for them or earning them or deserving them. These kids who come to our schools morally and ethically flabby, so soft. They don't know how to hurt. When hurts *do* come, they don't know what to do with them. They don't turn to God; they don't turn to their elders. They turn to what is available: drugs. Drugs are more and more available, even in your schools and in your rural community. In this drug-oriented society, kids are turning to drugs to make something easy. Drugs make it easy to date, easy to rap, easy to get to school, easy to deal with sex, easy to get up, easy to get down.

More and more classes today, we have to put on the blackboard real life situations, not ancient Egyptian history. We have to put on that blackboard real life situations that the kids can deal with. We have to show them. We have to say, "Do you know why that lady in the TV commerical can't sleep?" Can't you see why she needs that chemical to sleep, sleep, sleep? You know why—because she's not tired! Do you wonder why she's not tired? It's because she hasn't done a day's work in months. The only way to sleep is to get tired; that's *the human thing.* We must explode the myth that there must be an easy way to get out of bed. There's no easy way! There's no quick way to education and learning a la Leary, a la acid. For years Dr. Leary, like the Pied Piper, told our college students to "tune in, turn on, and drop out." today the greatest argument against acid and speed is Dr. Leary. Today when he lectures, he walks off the stage befuddled. If you want to stop the methedrine problem in this university, invite Dr. Leary to come and give a lecture. The audience will walk out in the middle of it. Today, he can't finish a sentence. Dr. Leary is the argument against any quick way to contemplation or to learning. There is no quick way to learning except hard study. Four years of high school—that's the way to learn, that's the way to be educated. Not on speed, not on acid.

Today our kids are in a crisis of identity. They have reached a point where they really and truly don't know "Where are you coming off from, man?" "What wall are you coming off?" "Where are you coming from, out of what bag?"—in their own terminology. Throw this out in your class sometime. Who's real and who's phony? Students are challenging you because you're over 50, over 40, over 30. You're not with it, you're not real. Why not have an in-depth discussion on the meaning of being real? What does it mean to be phony?" Now no kid likes to be phony. A phony is a kid who can't run from first base to second without taking "speed." That's phony, and they can see it. Then bring it up to eighth graders and first or second year high school where the highest level of drug-experimentation begins. Confront them with the whole meaning of real vs. phony.

The problems on a university campus are not the seniors but the young kids just coming in. They are contaminating our universities. That's probably what's happening at all the various armed force bases throughout the country. Some say that the Army is contaminating our youth with drugs. But, rather, they come into the Army, the Navy, the Marines with the attitudes they had in high school. They experimented with marijuana and pills before they came. The Army isn't going to change it. The Army can't exist in a vacuum. Neither can any university.

How real, how human are the kids you're dealing with? Say to them, "If the only way you can put your arms around your girl is on marijuana, you're a phony. Your girl should challenge your identity and say, 'Whose arms are these? Joe's arms or marijuana arms? And if they are marijuana arms, then, nuts, you're a little phony.' " And this girl who is talking so glibly, with her eyelashes blowing in the wind, is this Mary talking or is it speed?

Are we doing things humanly or chemically? I am more human when I'm more real and I'm more real when I'm more human. The meaning behind the words of de Chardin is that a person can never grow to full human potential unless he has known the meaning of suffering and pain. And until we have endured and felt suffering, there is a whole area of our human development that is untouched, untapped. We remain stagnant. We go through life limping because we have not *felt* loneliness. We have *drugged* it! We have not *felt* rejection. We have *drugged* it! We have not *felt* the difficulty of talking to our parents or talking to a guidance teacher. We have *drugged* it!

Too many kids can't get to school without taking ups. Too many kids can't get through a weekend without taking drugs. Too many kids can't deal with anything unless they're dehumanized a bit through chemicals. If there is anything you have to hold up to your pupils, it is basically this: Drugs dehumanize.

Thanks be to God, maybe less than 10 per cent of the kids who experiment with marijuana across the country will ever go to anything higher. But if even 8 per cent went to drugs higher than marijuana, can you imagine the epidemic that is breeding itself? You're in the same situation now that New York was 10 years ago. We did nothing about it. What will you do? It is not a problem that will be solved by itself. It cannot, like a raging forest fire, burn itself out.

Some national disasters, once identified, can be prepared for. But the human person is quite different and quite difficult to deal with. Every addict breeds ten addicts before he dies. The pushers you're speaking about are not the Mafia pushers. The pushers you're speaking about are the Patricias. The girls who go through high school selling two pills to get one free. So be careful when you get on the bandwagon to "kill all the pushers." Don't be that naive and don't be that stupid. The pushers you should be concerned about are the nonaddict pushers. I grant the fact that in your school you have the obligation to care for the common good of the student body rather than the right of any individual student to sell drugs. But what about the student addict? What is he like? Why do some kids go from experimentation to use?

I've struggled with this question for 20 years. I came up with this basic answer: Underneath it all, our young people are not oriented to deal with problems. They want quick, easy solutions! But there are no quick, easy solutions to life's problems. By definition a problem is a problem because it

81

does not have an easy answer. If it had an easy answer, it wouldn't be a problem. Our kids are not oriented to deal with problems. They look for quick answers. They want easy answers in this age of quick solutions. But there's no instant way to be 15; there's no instant way to deal with financial problems or sex problems or dating problems or how to talk to a parent. To suffer is part of the human condition. To be human one must feel hurt. We must endure it and know that this is humanizing, maturing, purifying. It makes me a better, more rounded, more whole person. Pat didn't believe this at one time in her life. Her schooling and her parents almost conditioned her to be a drug addict. I'll let Pat tell her own story. I feel sure it will lead to some productive discussion.

(Pat's story)

I started using drugs when I was in the eighth grade. At that time I wanted to be accepted. It was more like peer pressure; my friends were using drugs, so I wanted to use them. I started smoking pot. The problem began when I started to *like* it. I liked the feeling it gave me. I didn't like to go to school, so I went to school stoned on pot. It blocked out the feeling that I did not like about school. After smoking pot for a year, I wanted something better. I was bored with pot, and it wasn't giving me the same feeling that it used to when I first started smoking it. Sometimes this happens with a lot of people who end up becoming addicts. So long as there is a possibility, I don't see why anyone should have to take the chance of losing his life maybe three or four years later, like I almost did. So I went to pills, and after taking pills for a couple of months, I had to have something better. It wasn't so much that I liked drugs by now; I *had* to have drugs! I would be in school, maybe in my chemistry class, stoned on pills. I couldn't even stand up! The teacher never bothered to ask me what was the matter. I went in to take my chemistry mid-term and just signed my name at the top of the paper. He never bothered to ask me why I never finished filling it out.

The teachers, I think, at that time didn't feel that drugs was their problem. I wasn't their child, but I was in school with them more than I was with my own parents. I feel this is a problem for everybody. This is going across the country. It's everybody's problem! It's your kids that are going to be involved in this if nothing is done about it. My parents basically made drug addiction easy for me. They never made me earn anything. If I wanted money to go to the movie or money to buy clothes, they just gave me the money. If I wanted the keys to the car, they just gave me the keys to the car and off I went. If they told me to be in at 12, I'd come in at one or two. I thought that I was responsible. But I couldn't even make my own bed—that's how responsible I was. Then I went to heroin. When I was on heroin, I kept getting arrested. The last time I was arrested, my parents didn't come running down to jail to bail me out. I had to stay there. I got hepatitis for the third time and almost lost my life. I kept getting relapses. So from there I went to the hospital. Then I felt there should be something better than the way I was living, because it was nothing. Needing to make money, I had to get up in the morning to steal. I had to go to bed at night with drugs. I had to leave school four months before I was supposed to graduate. At this point I became fed up. Besides, it was either go into a program to be rehabilitated or go to jail. So I decided I was going into a program. I've been with Father Egan for eight months, and now I'm in re-entering society, learning how to accept the problems of society, learning how to accept the Vietnam War and Nixon and Agnew.

I like to read our New Hope Manor philosophy. We read this every morning at our house. It's something that I believe in. It helps me get by each day. I think each and every girl there does believe in it. "Today I am freely living at New Hope Manor because I now see that I was rapidly losing my most precious possession—my life. For too long a time I wasn't a free or happy person. Drugs had imprisoned me far more than prison itself. I had no hope without drugs and so, wishing to live yet drowning in a lonely sea of despair, I cried out for help. Somehow I knew that I couldn't help myself. Neither could my parents, children, husband or friends help me. So New Hope Manor is now my lifeline. I must not, I dare not let go of it. God give me the grace to cling to it, a day at a time. Here at the Manor with people who care and understand, I humanly feel the life pains of struggle and growth. Here amidst people who love and understand me in the truer sense, I humanly feel the slow birth-pains of a new life. When the pains are most severe, I will trust that these pains are doing me more good than the pains of drugs. When I hurt most I will trust my sisters more than I ever trusted drugs. For I now know that this suffering, shared and understood by others, is the price that I must and will freely pay for the life I came here to save. There is hope without drugs."
(End of Patricia's speech)

Father Egan's concluding remarks

I would like to make some general statements which may provoke discussion later on. The surest way for you as a teacher to notice the beginnings of experimentation or use of drugs is to know your pupil well enough. Not just on paper. I mean humanly, almost by identification. This is the best kind of education. Fortunate the pupil who can identify something with his teacher because he sometimes talks about the first stupid thing he did when he was 13. Or he talks about getting up in the morning when he doesn't feel like getting up. This is important because today kids are so subjective. Everything is feelings. If you are able to identify with your students on a human level and know them humanly, then you are able to notice dramatic changes in behavior patterns. Every word there is important—*dramatic changes in behavior patterns*. For example, if one of your students is leaving the room more often now than he ever did before, this is a change in behavior. You stack that up with some other noticeable signs. I don't think drug abuse in a school can really get out of control with any pupil if you are very scrupulous about taking attendance, scrupulous about being on time for every class, and scrupulous about checking how long a student is out of the room to the washroom and back? As in Patricia's case, thousands of girls and boys can be out for 20 minutes, 30 minutes, yet no one pays any attention. They can come into class every day 10 minutes late for a whole year, and there is no big deal about it.

So notice any dramatic change in behavior. If the girl was always on time, and now she's coming in late, that's a change. If she's frequently leaving the room, but never did it before—that's a change. If marks were consistently 80, and now they go way down, there must be some reason for this. Just don't say it's spring or she's in love again. That may be too superficial. If your student was never known to be too, too tired and now he is sleeping a lot in class, is that human tiredness or is that a chemical tiredness?

When I was giving a drug seminar some months ago at Hartford University in Connecticut, a teacher from Brooklyn came many miles to share with the eighth-grade teachers a tragedy she had had the month before. She had watched this boy in her class nodding every morning. She cast it aside saying, "Well, he's looking at the late show." He continued nodding. "Maybe he's looking at the late, late show." But he continued nodding. She was then in a situation too many teachers find themselves in today or allow themselves to be in. "I don't want to look at the problem, because if I look at it, I might have to do something about it. I don't want to open the washroom door; I don't want to look in there because I might see something that I might have to get involved with and I don't want to. It isn't my problem. It's a parental problem." This teacher did nothing about it. A week later, they found the boy dead in the boys' room right across from the classroom. Dead of an overdose of pills.

If you notice that a boy is eating too much, chewing all the time when he never used to, ask why. Sometimes one of the surest signs of marijuana smoking is a revenous appetite. Now don't go home and wake your kid up and say, "You're a pot head." Sometimes you go the other extreme. You stack this up with lots of other things. If the kid was never known to chew ice, but now he does, ask why. That's a change in behavior! If his eyes are more red than usual, what's the reason? Suppose his appetite goes down suddenly. It may be the same reason your diet pill takes away your appetite. There is an amphetamine in every diet pill. Some kids may be losing appetite, losing weight, because they're taking downs—seconal. I don't mean that you be medical people, that you should be the school nurse, that you should be the policeman or the psychiatrist. But you can notice changes in behavior maybe more easily than a parent can. Maybe.

Secondly, if you are ever in doubt about how to interpret this change in behavior in a pupil, I would rather you take a risk and find out that you're wrong rather than not take the risk and find out too late that you were right in your suspicions. Today, at times, teachers have to put their reputations, their jobs, on the line and run the risk of parental anger or run the risk of getting into a battle with the principal. Take risks. I have to every day. I was sent out of the country for two years for doing "unpriestly" things. Now suddenly working with addicts is the highest kind of social ecumenism. Ten years ago, it was stupid. Now it's the highest kind of priestly commitment. But ten years ago I had to make some ripples. I had to take risks. As a good teacher you must, at times, take risks, hoping you're going to be wrong. But if the principal won't do anything about it. take the risk and put your job on the line. Even call the parents and say, "Look, I'm a parent myself, or someday I hope to be one. If I were in this situation, I would hope that someone would call me. Now I hope I'm wrong, but here's what I'm worried about. Let's the three of us work it out together—you, I, and the student." In Pat's case, it would have been far easier for one of the teachers to reach out and show some concern. Sometimes the marijuana comes between yourself and the student. In a strictly humanistic approach, if you're a real human being and not just a professional teacher; if you're a human being who happens to be not just a teacher but a good, rounded human person; if you can relate to a pupil on a one-to-one basis because you care, then that pupil will tell you things he cannot tell a parent or cannot tell the principal. Maybe you are the only link between that pupil and a happy, productive life. But if you do nothing about it, no one else will. Take the risk.

Be that kind of dedicated teacher. True, there is no fair "pay" for that kind of service. That's why there has to be a Heaven. And, maybe that's why you hold in your hand the key to the whole problem of drug prevention. Don't throw the key away. Use it.

Dr. Orlando Taylor

Dr. Orlando Taylor, Director of Urban Language Education, presented the Jennings Scholar Lecture on March 20, 1970, in the John C. Baker Center at Ohio University.

Dr. Taylor is one of the nation's outstanding linguists. He has spanned the gamut of activities in the fields of speech, audiology, and linguistics. His three degrees—a B.S. from Hampton Institute, an M.A. from Indiana University, and a Ph.D. from the University of Michigan—are in speech pathology.

His professional experiences echo the broad scope of his educational background. His early career involved clinical speech therapy. His post doctoral activities began at Indiana University, where he was an assistant professor of speech. He then became an associate director of the Center for Applied Linguistics in Washington, D.C.

Dr. Taylor serves as president of the Black Caucus of the American Speech and Hearing Association; chairman of the Committee on Communication Behaviors and Problems in Urban Populations, American Speech and Hearing Association; a member of the Board of Editors, Journal of Black Studies; and an associate editor, Journal of Speech and Hearing Disorders.

Dr. Taylor is a valued consultant. His honors include recognition in the 1967 listing of Outstanding Young Men in America; Who's Who in the Mid-West and Who's Who in the South, 1970 editions. Indiana University also honored him with their annual award, "The Leather Medal," given to a faculty member for outstanding ambassadorship for the university.

BLACK LANGUAGE IN URBAN EDUCATION

In preparing remarks for this occasion, I faced the somewhat difficult prospect of addressing a group of some 200 to 250 teachers from southeastern Ohio with a background largely unrelated, at least professionally, to the types of schools and types of children most of you see and teach daily. I specified "professionally" because I grew up in an area which could be considered the southern extension of southeastern Ohio—the state of Tennessee. As most of you know, there are numerous phonological (sound) and syntactic (grammatical) similarities between the speech patterns of Eastern Kentucky and Eastern Tennessee and those heard in this area. Despite my personal kinship with you, I have had no professional experiences in the region. (However, I did teach at Indiana University, which is located in southern Indiana.)

My recent professional experiences have been focused primarily on the urban scene—a scene which is primarily black and Spanish-speaking and, as near as I can tell, quite different from the settings in which you work. I believe, however, that the kinds of things we are learning about language and its variation in urban settings is applicable to your setting inasmuch as both contain a large number of speakers of so-called Nonstandard English dialects. Thus, I have decided to present some general linguistic and sociolinguistic concepts and discuss their implications for classroom teaching.

I suppose that it comes as no great shock to you when I say that by the usual measures of educational achievement, millions of American children could be placed in a category called "nonachievers." These are children who by standard educational achievement tests demonstrate that they are not acquiring information at rates comparable to those of children of similar chronological and mental ages. Ironically, we can define these children according to some very specific parameters, and it turns out that they are related to the social classes, ethnic groups, and geographical groups which have long been ignored by the American educational establishment and, on a larger scale, by the American people. In short, we are talking about Black, Chicanos, Puerto Ricans, Indians, and people who live in such areas as Appalachia.

Many educators have used a "pathology" model for viewing the black child and his culture. In essence, that model states that the reason the black child fails to achieve in the classroom is because of some deficit in him (e.g., cognitive, linguistic, genetic, etc.) or because he is from a disadvantaged culture.

Recently, some educators have been raising questions as to whether American education, as we now know it, is organized in such a way that it takes into account the legitimate (and notice I said legitimate) behaviors, languages, cultures, etc., of the nation's pluralistic population. In other words, they are trying to determine whether the educational problems of nonachieving children is in the children or whether they are related to the ways educators approach them, their communities, their parents, etc.

By profession, I am a psycho-sociolinguist. I am interested in the study of language. However, I do not limit myself to dealing with the structure of language as do most of my linguistic colleagues. Instead, I attempt to look at the psychological, sociological, anthropological, and neurological underpinnings for language. When I talk about the urban black child and his language, it is important to begin with a historical review of the study of the topic.

Prior to about 1920 or 1925, virtually all the research that had been reported on the language of black people, which obviously includes black children, by noted historians, sociologists, historians, etc., always talked about it from the perspective of pathology. Typically, the language was described as being somewhat "savage-like." Indeed, from these readings one would get the impression that when blacks got off the boats in places like Charleston and Savannah, their greatest level of linguistic maturity was something akin to that of the brothers in the Tarzan movies. If you will recall these movies from the 1930's and 40's, you will remember that the blacks always spoke some sort of mumbo-jumbo. From these and other views, one gets a negative view of the language and culture of Africans and forgets that they were faced with the arduous task of trying to acquire a civilized language and culture when they came in contact with whites in the New World. This view is really a traditional view, and how it has been institutionalized into the fabric of the early history of this country can be shown. For instance, it is seen in the way black people were treated in the early Constitution as property—not people—and then, later, as compromise people (three-fifths of a person). It is seen later in Ku Klux Klan folklore and in early movies like "Birth of a Nation." From these and other examples, one gets a general picture of black people being something less than completely human. In a sense, language represents the highest form of human behavior. Therefore, it is not a great transformation to understand why the language of black people was cast in a savage, cannibal, inhuman way when black people, as a group, were viewed in this manner.

In the 1920's, some important things happened. During this period, linguists got involved in the study of various regional dialects of English and many of the American Indian languages. Though minimal formal data were reported on the language of black people, it was widely held that blacks spoke a version of Southern white English, and whatever differences existed were related to segregated institutions, not cultural, physical, or psychological deficits. While this view of black language failed to reveal recognition of African influences on black speech, it at least implied that the language of blacks was legitimate, and that whatever problems existed were not related to the speakers or their culture.

Now the problem with this view is that people reveal language in the contemporary sense in the context of their linguistic and social histories. Thus, it is not an accident of hills or sunshine that makes people in southeastern Ohio sound different from people in northern New England, for example. This fact is related to the linguistic history of the people of this region, where they came from in Europe, the type of interactions they have had, both in Europe and in the New World, their migration patterns, their social contacts, etc. We know, for instance, that people from this region originally came from Virginia and North Carolina, as opposed to the more Yankee type of migration that moved into Northern Ohio. Indeed, you get differences in speech between northern and southern Ohio. Of course, you know all of this and know that the points relate to history. If linguists made the claim that peoples' contemporary language usages are related to their history, it becomes somewhat difficult to claim that black people have no African origins in their language—unless, of course, the claim is made that blacks had no language in Africa.

In the late 1930's, Lorenzo Turner, a linguist on the faculty of Fisk University, described the speech of blacks living on islands off the coasts of South Carolina and Georgia. Scholars refer to these residents as Gullah people, though they are known colloquially as Geetchies. Because the people had been largely isolated from the mainland for nearly 150 years and had relatively minimal contact with white southerners, Turner thought they provided a good population for assessing the extensions of African speech in the New World. In his book, *Africanisms in the Gullah Dialect,* Turner reported the presence of numerous Africanisms in the phonological (sound), vocabulary, and grammatical systems of the Gullah dialect. Based on his data, Turner concluded that it is inaccurate to claim that the language of American blacks is only an extension of white southern linguistic behavior but, instead, has to be viewed in the context of its African underpinnings.

In the early 1940's, Melville Herskovits, an anthropologist from Northwestern University, wrote a book called *The Myth of the Negro Past.* Using substantial pieces of Turner's work, plus the work of numerous scholars on such topics as art, literature, family structure, religion, etc., Herskovits exploded the myths that black people had no culture in Africa and that Africanisms did not survive in the New World. In short, he asserted that Africans had a rich culture; it was brought to the Americas; and valid views of contemporary black Americans have to be couched in an African model.

In the 1940's it was considered racist to suggest that blacks came from an African culture, since it implied that they were *different* from whites. After all, racial differences had always been used to justify racial segregation in the United States. Of course, racial and cultural differences are not inherently problematic. Problems arise from how differences are viewed and dealt with. Thus, differences can be recognized as being legitimate and positive, or they can be used to alienate or polarize people so as to cause all kinds of social problems. Unfortunately, the latter option has been traditionally selected by white Americans for viewing the cultural and linguistic differences of blacks.

In the 1950's another view emerged in the study of black language. Basically, that view stated, "Let's deny black-white language differences." After all, this was the beginning of the integration era, which claimed that "we are all alike." In fact, many people would "compliment" blacks by telling them such things as, "I can't tell you are a black person," "you are just like me," "I don't really think about color," etc. Notice, of course, that these "compliments" always implicitly asserted that blacks are as good as whites, and not that whites are as good as blacks.

In the 1960's, some very important events occurred which affected how the language of blacks was viewed and handled educationally. They began during the presidential primary in West Virginia when Mr. Kennedy focused heavily on the theme of poverty and its various impacts. Indeed, after he was elected his famous "17 million Americans go to bed hungry every night" line was used to launch a program in the Congress called the "War on Poverty." These developments led eventually to the establishment of the Office of Economic Opportunity (OEO) which resulted in the availability of millions of dollars to study the effects of poverty, including the effects on language, and what could be done to change the poverty cycle, especially as it influences the educational prospects of children from so-called "disadvantaged" or "deprived" cultural settings. These developments were extremely important because, for the first time, a payoff was provided for raising serious questions about how to educate prople who can more appropriately be called the "havenots." I emphasize the payoff point because I want everyone here to recognize that everybody who got involved in these new programs was not necessarily more interested in the poor than he had been before. It was simply economically rewarding to use such words in proposal writing as "poor," "black," "Puerto Rican," "disadvantaged," "deprived," etc. Indeed, some people built their careers, their programs, and their pocketbooks from strictly dishonest motivations.

During this same period, some other important events were occurring. They evolved around the emergence of the Civil Rights era that began with sit-ins in Greensboro, and moved through Freedom Rides, bus boycotts, demonstrations, civil disobedience, etc. These events resulted in the passage of major pieces of Civil Rights legislation in the areas of housing and employment, not only on the national level, but also in the various states. As a result of these laws, and for the first time in the nation's history, everybody had the legal right to expect decent jobs and housing without regard to race, creed, or color. This fact suddenly meant that black Americans, who had been systematically discriminated against, suddenly had the legal tools for seeking employment and homes in areas previously denied them. Almost expectedly, employers and real estate people proclaimed that blacks were not "ready" to enjoy these new freedoms and, as a result, decided to focus on new criteria for maintaining segregation, mainly in the areas of language acceptability and level of education. What happened, in short, was that attitudes against blacks' use of language hardened, or at least surfaced.

The third important development of the 1960's was that white Americans gave up the city. For instance, Washington, D.C., was a mecca of white charm in 1954 when it was 65 percent white and had a student population in schools which was 60 percent white. Fifteen years later, however, the city was 75 percent black and the schools were 96 percent black. This pattern was duplicated to some extent in virtually every American city. Indeed, by 1980 most major cities will have a population of more than 50 percent "have-not" people. As a result of the racial and cultural shifts in urban school populations, and because the systems were historically white and middle-class oriented, a crisis in urban education emerged. Reading scores fell. Math scores fell. Percentile ranks on the College Boards fell. Naturally, the question What is happening in the nation's urban schools? was raised. All too often, the simplistic answer was given that "blacks and other have-nots made up the bulk of the school population and you can't expect any better." In other words, the answers always implied that black people are intellectually inferior to white people, or that poor or culturally different people can't learn. Rarely was the answer given that the schools need to be redefined to meet the needs of the changing population.

The fourth development of the 60's was the internal political pressures within the city by the have-nots, who demanded that the institutions, of the city including the educational institutions, become responsive and sensitive to their needs and aspirations. In short, people demanded "community power." (I use that term because I find that people can deal with it a little easier than they can with the term "black power.") All groups want community power. They may not label it in ethnic terms, though some have, like the Irish in Boston or the Poles in Chicago. In any case, black community people saw that their children were being mis-educated in the schools and often destroyed psychologically. Thus, they demanded change, and school authorities scrambled for new alternatives which could begin to make education meaningful, relevant, and of high quality for the new inhabitants of the city.

Enough for history. What does all of this mean for the development of quality education for black and other "have-not" children? Linguists believe that they have something to say on the subject. Why? Linguists claim that language permeates education. Children need linguistic skills in order to read the books in schools, write compositions, express themselves in ways that teachers will accept, etc. In short, language is a critical skill for acquiring any kind of information in the school setting. It is a vehicle, one might say. You can't really learn history, even black history, if you can't read or understand a teacher. You can't really perform in a college, even in a special program, unless there is an agreed upon language system. Now, I want to make something very clear, and that is I am not giving a hard line which says that there is only one way to talk, and all children have to conform to it. I am simply saying that an agreed upon system must be present. In the past, the language of education rarely considered the language of "have-not" students.

Another reason why language is important in education is that educators are interested in measuring or evaluating the effectiveness of instruction. Typically, the evaluation is done through the medium of some kind of test, and irrespective of the subject area of the test, information is requested in an oral or written language, and subjects are required to respond in a language. The language of virtually all intelligence and educational achievement tests is standard, middle-class, white American English. Obviously, children who utilize language patterns different from those used on the tests are placed in a disadvantaged position. In other words, the test systematically discriminate against those who use other dialect patterns inasmuch as there is high probablity that their skills and potential will be underestimated. Many modern linguists are demanding that educators reevaluate their tests so that they can alter those which are salvagable and discard those which are not. By the way, I think you should be thinking about your children here in southeastern Ohio at this point and start asking the same questions about their performance on the standard I.Q. and achievement tests. Although I haven't seen the results of their tests, I am willing to wager that the scores are not in the upper percentiles. Is that a true assertion? If so, what does it mean? I doubt that it means that teachers can't teach or are disinterested, or that the children are dumb. It probably means that the tests you are using systematically discriminate against your children, or that your teaching materials do not take the cultural and linguistic backgrounds of your students into sufficient account. If you can buy the notion that language is important to education and that differences in languages can cause educational problems, you can begin to see the bases of my claim about the mis-education of urban black children.

Presently, there are two groups of people looking at the language of urban populations with special reference to the black child. Many have developed programs, philosophies, and programs for educating children of this group. One set of experts can be dubbed the deficit theoreticians. In essence, they claim that black children fail to use Standard English because of some sort of cultural or social deficit. This notion is used to account for behavioral differences black children demonstrate in relation to white children of similar chronological ages. Among the reasons usually cited for these differences are disintegration or lack of family structure, poor motivation, inability to delay gratification, and underdeveloped language and cognitive abilities.

Many educators have accepted the deprivation view of black child language. Frequently, this acceptance has resulted in attempts to eradicate black linguistic forms and to replace them with a more "proper" form. It has prompted many teachers to refer thousands of black children to speech therapists to "improve their language." It has also stimulated many scholars to compare black English with white linguistic norms. While it would be interesting to understand black English in relation to other dialects of English, it is an ill-afforded luxury at a time when hundreds of thousands of black children are being destroyed in the nation's schools. Thus the time is inappropriate to focus on "pure" theoretical work, except as related to specific applied purpose. More importantly, attention must be placed on new educational philosophies and practices to meet the needs of black students.

The second group of scholars can be called difference theoreticians. These individuals assert that there is no such thing as an inadequate culture or an inadequate language. They claim that it is inappropriate to make judgments about the quality of a culture or the quality of a language. They state that if you approach the educational mission trying to eradicate something in a child, you are implicitly telling him something very negative about himself, namely that he is inferior. Even if you are successful in eradicating the old and teaching him a new culture and language, he is given an argument for rejecting the culture of his home and local community. Difference theoreticians say, "Let's not try to eradicate language differences but, instead, let's try to understand them and their historical origins." In fact, they propose that educators should try to utilize some of these language and cultural behaviors in the classroom. On this latter point, the difference group divides. One group says that language differences should be used as a vehicle for teaching the standard language as a second language. The other group questions the notion that everybody should use the standard language, except maybe to read and write.

For years, educators have claimed that education should begin where the child is. Unfortunately, we often don't have valid views of where the child is. More than likely, teachers ignore where the child is and approach the child in terms of where he should be. Difference theoreticians believe that we should really practice what we preach by beginning where the child is, and then proceed to bring the child through the educational process by teaching him other forms of language and culture. Ultimately, the child may begin to become bicultural, bilingual or bidialectic. In so doing, he is taught to recognize that difference does not equal inferiority. Linguists are largely difference theoreticians. They study the structure of language, not people, teachers, or educational philosophies. At the moment, many linguists are simply trying to develop a theory of all natural languages. Presently, they claim that all languages appear to have some things in common. In fact, they talk about universals of language.

Teachers should not wait for linguists to provide educational panaceas. Linguists are not teachers. All they can do is say enough about the nature of language to enable teachers to improve their philosophies and procedures. For instance, they can help teachers improve teaching in such areas as reading, composition, and the language arts. Thus, teachers must begin to learn basic linguistic premises so that *they* can adapt that information to meet their own needs.

All linguists are not the same. One group is more interested in the psychology of language. In fact, they are called psycholinguists. Psycholinguists are interested in language *behavior*. Their interests are not in language structure but, instead, in such topics as language production, language comprehension, language acquisition, and memory for language. All are relevant to the topic of education.

The topic of language acquisition is extremely interesting, since all children in the world seem to be able to acquire language with no formal training or Head-Start programs or lectures from linguists. Simply by having a human brain, being in an environment that produces language, and having the desire and motivation to acquire language, all but about one percent of all children become adult speakers in the first eight to twelve years of life. It's not a difficult feat to acquire the language of one's environment. Indeed, some psychologists think that language acquisition has very strong biological components and that it may not be all learned. In short, it may be partially "wired-in," in the same way that birds are "wired" to fly or fish to swim. Why are these biological arguments advanced? First, all people have language. There is no variation within species. Second, all languages show a good deal of overlap. There was never a national or international meeting among the nations of the world at which people agreed that all languages would conform to certain rules. If they did, agreement would probaby never be reached. Finally, the pattern of language acquisition appears to be about the same all over the world.

Another group of linguists is interested in the interaction between language and culture. They are called sociolinguists. They operate under a basic set of assumptions (many of which have already been discussed or implied) which can be useful to teachers. I will now present you with some of these assumptions.

First, most sociolinguistic scholars agree that all cultures have concepts, and all cultures have linguistic systems to represent these concepts. They also assert that all human languages are adequate for expressing the concepts of the cultures in which they exist. While there are phonological, semantic, and syntactic differences among languages of various cultures, there are also numerous similarities. On the basis of these similarities, linguists have developed the concept of "linguistic universals,"

Another basic sociolinguistic assumption is that linguistic differences typically exist within a given culture. These differences are usually based on cultural, social, and historical facts. Variations occurring within a language are called "dialects." Dialects within a language usually have a high degree of mutual intelligibility. Many dialects of American English have been recognized and discussed in the literature.

In most cultures—especially in highly competitive cultures with a codified linguistic system, i.e., a writing system—the concept of a "standard" language exists. A situation of this type exists in the United States in the form of collection of dialects called "Standard English."

In discussing the concept of Standard English, it is important to note that it appears to be as much a statement about "standard" people as it is about a set of linguistic systems. In other words, there is nothing innately good about the standard dialects of American English. They are simply spoken by the socially prestigious portions of the American population, i.e., the white, educated, and middle-class segments. To the extent that these groups are perceived by a substantial portion of the population as being "norm makers," their speech is used as a standard for judging everybody else—an obvious ethnocentric absurdity. Obviously the idea of Standard English is broad enough, by necessity, to include a number of "standards." In general, Standard English is more of a notion about grammatical matters than about phonological and vocabulary features of language. It suggests that white, middle-class, educated speakers utilize a standard set of syntactic rules for sentence production, though they may vary in other aspects of the language.

Now what do all of these theoretical notions have to do with teaching? I have implied several already, but now let me be explicit.

First, teachers would develop positive attitudes toward their students' culture and their language. They must recognize that virtually all students come from legitimate cultural and linguistic backgrounds and that they are capable of learning.

Second, teachers should learn to utilize the student's language and culture in everyday teaching situations. This language can be used for the whole gamut of education missions, including the teaching of reading, composition, and content areas. If one of the standard dialects of English is to be taught as a tool language or for reading purposes, teachers should not only utilize the child's first dialect but be certain that the teaching does not imply to the student that his language is inferior and should be eradicated.

Third, teachers must be extremely cautious in interpreting test results. They must remember that tests are valid only insofar as they test populations for which they are intended. Most school achievement and intelligence instruments have assumed the normalcy of white, middle-class children and process to assess all other children from these norms. Cultures differ and people differ. Thus, culture-fair tests (which generally do not exist) are the only instruments which are valid for evaluating potential and achievement for students in America's pluralistic schools.

Fourth, linguistic, psycholinguistic, and sociolinguistic principles can be quite useful for developing effective, educational programs, especially in the areas of composition, reading, and the language arts generally. Such topics as the structure of language, language acquisition, and language and culture can be helpful for developing innovative and effective philosophies, classroom procedures, and materials.

These are just some of the implications of what I have been saying. I am certain there are more. If you have further questions or desire more information, you can write me in care of Federal City College in Washington, D.C.

The main thing I hope all of you remember is that this country can no longer afford to mis-educate and undereducate the have-nots. The job appears massive. Language changes alone won't solve the problem, but the elimination of antiquated ideas about language, culture, and language behavior might help.

Dr. Ethel J. Alpenfels

Dr. Ethel J. Alpenfels, Professor of Educational Anthropology at New York University, presented the Jennings Scholar Lecture on April 17, 1971, in the John C. Baker Center, Ohio University.

She has been acclaimed "Woman of the Year," "Teacher of the Year," and New York University's "Great Teacher for 1970," and was elected an honorary member of the International Teaching Fraternity.

Dr. Alpenfels was the first person to receive the Alpha Delta Mankind Award in recognition of outstanding contributions to anthropology-sociology, education and the humanities. Among other awards and honors accorded her are the Alpenfels Award for excellence in educational anthropology presented annually at Montclair State College, New Jersey, to a graduating senior who has demonstrated outstanding promise in relating anthropoligical concepts to professional education; an award for teaching excellence from the Albert Einstein Medical Center, Philadelphia, Pennsylvania; the Judy Award for teaching; the Dorothy Hutchison

Award; the Colorado Silver Dollar Award; and the Distinquished Service to Humanity Award. She has numerous honorary degrees at universities throughout the country and abroad.

A native of Denver, Colorado, Dr. Alpenfels received her bachelor's degree from the University of Washington in Seattle, where she was elected to Phi Beta Kappa. She attended the University of Chicago for graduate work and was one of six students selected nationally to be trained in field work among the Modoc Indians under the direction of Dr. Leslie Spier of Yale University.

Before becoming a professor of anthropology at New York University, where she currently conducts four courses and counsels students, Dr. Alpenfels taught at every level of the school system in the United States. She has taught in the Virgin Islands, Mexico, Peru, the Scandinavian countries, Austria, and Japan.

Dr. Alpenfels shares her thoughts with a public that reaches beyond the confines of her discipline and the walls of the university. Her intimate knowledge of foreign countries enabled her to become known as an outstanding tour leader of trips throughout Central America, the Orient, and around the World.

She has published widely in both periodicals and books. Two of her best-known works are an article; "The Anthropology of the Human Hand," and a book, *Sense and Nonsense About Race*. She served as a fellow of the Encyclopaedia Britannica, editing the one-million word section on Anthropology. More recently, she wrote articles on Anthropology for the Junior Britannica.

Currently in progress is a series of tapes and film strips, *Man On the Move*. These explore the origin of man and his spread across the globe; the Sub-Sahara, its culture and its people; and the American Indian. The areas already completed are "Prejudices" and "Japan: A Study in depth."

Dr. Alpenfels has served as a consultant to the United States Army, The President's Commission on the Status of Women, and the United States Department of Health, Education and Welfare, where she directed a study on Cancer and Anthropology.

CHANGING VALUES AND THE AMERICAN FAMILY PATTERN

The best definition of anthropology I ever heard was at the University of Chicago, where we had the famous Bronisav Malinowski. Asked by one of his students to define anthropology, he answered, "Anthropology is the study of man, parenthesis, including women, end of parentheses." In fact, I often thought he should have said "embracing women," end of parentheses.

I came into anthropology by the way I have since learned is the best of all possible ways, that of a public school teacher, first of the third grade and then of physical education in Denver, Colorado. I had taught in Denver about four years, when one day my principal suggested that I go to summer school to get some more education. I took the hint. I went out to the University of California. I had a delightful summer and when I came back, I thought I had more education.

I had taught four more years when again the principal gallantly and gently suggested that I had better go to summer school. Well, after eight years I realized that the Denver school system meant business about me, so this time I took a full year off and went to the University of Washington. As students always do, I began looking around for a snap course. Everybody said, "Take anthropology." I took anthropology.

I spent the next 10 or 12 years in study and in teaching, and then one spring I received an invitation from the Denver Teachers' Association to speak at their fall Teachers' Institute. I went back home to give a talk about my new science and what I might have taught had I known more anthropology when I was there. I returned to New York City, and my brothers, who still live in Denver, saw to it that I received the clipping that appeared in the Denver Post after my talk. It was headed "Ethel Alpenfels Shows Need of Eduction." That is a true story, and as every one of you knows, it is the fate of us who make it our life work to teach.

I am going to talk as an anthropologist. We are concerned with everything that every other discipline has left over. Those of you who are social studies teachers know that the historian is concerned only with people who have written language. We in anthropology push time back to before man wrote. The psychologist, the guidance people, want to get us into the laboratories under controlled conditions. We who study man in his natural habitat found out a long time ago that man is not always going to stand still long enough to get him into a laboratory. This is why the anthropologist has been forced to make the world his laboratory. As I think of all the leftovers in the American culture today, I think one of the major ones is this whole business of the American family, of the changing values of the American society and the family patterns that stay the same. Constantly as the family looks at education, it blames the educator, it blames the teacher for the problems that begin in the home.

So I chose to talk about the family patterns, some of the American culture values. For in every society, anthropologists tell you that the key institution is the family. We say that the American family is not in as much trouble as many of its scholars and critics say it is. For any society to remain healthy it must have a healthy family. And a healthy family, like any other institution, be it the institution of religion or economics, must change with the changing times. So we allow freedom of change and economics in our system. We allow freedom of change even in our religion. But anthropology will tell you that the two institutions that will not allow change are American public education and the American family. For we continue to talk about the farm family. And I who came from Colorado talk to you from Ohio, where farms are so important and have been so important. You and I know today that less than five percent of our country lives on the farm. We spend billions of dollars in the United States to help the farms, and all we do is make them more mechanized and less family oriented farms. But we saved the American farm family and we hold our present family against it. We talk about the Victorian family but I suggest to you that if we had the honesty and courage to pull back the curtains on those Victorian homes, we wouldn't like what we'd see. I remember my own first field work among the Amazon Indians in South America. They had a word for adult which, when translated into English, is "he who walks around remembering." Remember when the American family was stronger? Remember when spring came earlier in Ohio? Remember when students in public schools and colleges were more respectful of their faculties?

We remember public education and the American family. I think that what we have to do is look with honesty at the American family and ask the values of the family. What are the values we anthropologists are talking about? I think it is important to distinguish between two kinds of values. There are the moral values that the religions and the theologians tell us are the absolute. Anthropologists do not talk of absolute values—they talk of universal values. And this is almost the same. There is no society, no family in the world, that does not teach its babies and its children and its youth that it is wrong to lessen the dignity of another human being. All people in the world, even the head-hunting tribes, teach this. But each society has some scapegoats which it is all right to persecute. In every society parents teach their children it is wrong to kill another man. But each society has certain men it permits its society to kill. So all societies teach respect, and one of the things bothering Americans today is the lack of respect among our young.

The Japanese teach that it is a sign of respect to take off your shoes when you enter the house. We teach our young men it is a sign of respect to take off your hat. So in one society you bare your head, and in another society you bare your feet. There have been wars as to which end of your anatomy is the important end to bare to show respect.

But all societies have these universal values. So we talk of loyalty and

102

respect and the rest of these. You will find them universal. This is one kind of value. The values about which we can do something are the values of anthropology called cultural values. I don't have to define culture to a group of teachers like yourselves. At the University of Innsbruck, I had 500 young men and women who had come from every part of the world. Being an American, I am ethnocentric. When I arrived, I asked my young interpreter, "Are there any students from the United States?"

He said, "I think there are a handful."

I said, "Would you find out how many?"

The next morning in that very rigid school room that is European higher education, he showed up to escort me to the classroom, where all the students stood at attention until I got there. I asked him again, "How many of my students came from the United States?"

He smiled and said, "Quite a number."

I said, "How many?"

He said, "I can't tell you yet, but I'll tell you after lunch."

So just before dessert, he took me up to a tiny balcony that encircled the vast dining room. As I stood looking down, I suddenly realized that he had arranged with all the waitresses to place slices of pie with the point either toward the front or to the side. As I stood looking down, I saw all the young men and women who came from Europe, Africa, Asia, and from the Islands of the South Pacific eat those slices of pie exactly the way the waitress had placed them. But all of those who came from the United States turned the point toward them. That is *culture*. I spent the rest of the summer trying to convince the young man that our way was the only correct and intelligent way to eat a slice of pie.

I remember a young man from India who said that Americans are dirty. When you're abroad you resent this. What did he mean? Americans are the the cleanest people in the world! He simply broke a twig off their sacred tree, the banyan tree, dipped it in water, and thoroughly, almost endlessly, brushed his teeth. Then he tossed the twig aside and said, "In your country you use the bristles of a dead animal, and you use the same dirty tooth brush morning after morning after morning."

Patterns of cleanliness, patterns of morals, right and wrong. When I used to teach the third grade, I taught about the American Indian. I must confess I didn't know very much about him, and I taught an awful lot of untruths. Then I went to live with the famous American Plains Indians. There the father taught his sons that the highest honor a man could claim was to steal an enemy horse. In battles, far better than to kill a man, you rode up, pushed him off his horse, stole his horse, and rode away. Then we of the East coast moved West, and you know very well what we thought of horse thieves. There are about 12 new Westerns this season on TV, and they tell us what to do with horse thieves. We hang the horse thief from the highest tree. So in one society fathers were busy teaching their sons it's better to steal a horse than to kill a man. In our society we worry about violence. Look around a little. Our mass media are busy teaching our children and our youth it's better to kill a man than to steal a horse. Each society says it has the only right value.

Go with me today 102 miles from Mexico City, where this morning a little child is born. It will not be the doctor or the nurse who brings the spark of life. It will be the mother, who must dip each newborn baby into a barrel of ice-cold water. Or go to Arizona or New Mexico, among the famous Hopi or the Zuni Indians. A baby is born this morning, and it won't be the doctor or the father that brings that spark. It is the mother-in-law the most sacred person, who must shake the baby towards the East, because it's the East that's sacred. And only from a sacred spot could the life soul come.

However, it is with the crisis of your birth and mine that we met our American culture. And never so long as we live, no matter how long we live or how far we go, will we ever escape that culture. So it seems to me that the key to education today is to turn and look at that American culture, to try to understand these values that are not acts themselves. We in anthropology call these cultural values "the silent language"—the "non-verbal language" "the unspoken language" of your behavior and mine that speaks far louder than any words we could use. So we know the silent language between the nations, and you are teaching it.

When I was teaching at the University of Chicago, we had 200 American soldiers who were going to be sent to Japan to stand between General McArthur and the Japanese people. These 200 young men spoke Japanese; they learned the Japanese culture. But if we in anthropology helped them at all, we helped to listen to and to hear the silent language of the Japanese. We had 150 different things. The one I always remember saying to them is "Never call a Japanese man as you call an American man—Hey you come here.' That's the way a Japanese calls his pig or his dog, and he'll turn and run away from you. So when you leave a large city like Kyoto or Tokyo and you want to call a Japanese man, you just bend your fingers toward him." So we are learning the silent languages today among our many ethnic groups. You have them here in Ohio. On the East coast for the first time we're getting the Puerto Ricans in large numbers. A Puerto Rican boy is taught by his father that a respectful son never looks his father in the eye when he speaks to him. He must always talk to his father with his eyes on the floor. Try it sometime. But he comes into my classroom and what do I say? "Now look me straight in the eye." You and I know that in 1971, looking people in the eye has nothing at all to do with honesty. It has a lot to do with etiquette, but most important it is the silent language we are teaching our youngsters. When we talk to someone, it's a sign of respect to look him in the eye. But that Puerto Rican boy has to remember, and remember well, that when you're home you keep your eyes on the floor. When you're in the classroom you look the teacher in the eye.

There is a silent language that is disturbing the adults of our country! What is male behavior and what is female? How do you tell a young man from a young woman in Greenwich Village where I live? As you walk down the street, it's a little like out here on the Ohio campus. How do you tell them apart? The same black pants, the tight shirts the long hair, the untaken bath. How do you tell them apart? Watch how they carry their bundles. Men always carry bundles with arms straight down. Look at their fingernails. All the men in this room will turn their nails like this. The women, particularly if we've just had a manicure, will begin flying our fingers in the air.

Their is also a silent language in your attitude toward pain. If you have an Italian boy in your classroom, two or three generations removed from Italy, he will express pain quite differently than a boy whose father is of Jewish faith from East Europe, and both of these quite differently than a Polish boy. If your're lucky enough to have a Polish boy, get his father in for an interview sometime. Let his father tell you, as he's dying to do, for five minutes, how sick he is. Then for the only time in your life, you'll have undivided attention while someone let's you tell him how sick you are. Then you can both get down to business.

There is a cultural behavior in alcoholism. In this country, there's a great deal of difference between the alcoholism of the Irish, of the Italians, and of various national and ethnic groups. There is an emerging pattern in the differences in the drug addiction of youngsters that come from different backgrounds. Even in mental illness there are differences. In the mother-dominated Irish homes of the United States, Irish schizophrenics behave quite differently than do Italian schizophrenics in the father-dominated Italian homes. Two ten-year studies in greater Manhattan showed that the Irish schizophrenic tends to withdraw, but the Italian schizophrenic becomes aggressive.

But of all the cultures that it is necessary to understand, the one that brings real problems into the school is the culture values, the silent language, of our poor. The anthropologist calls it, unappropriately I think, the culture of poverty. As in all the other cultures, money is there, but money is not the most important factor. It doesn't matter how much money we pour into our inner cities. The key for teachers is the understanding of the way they see their world, the way they relate to the policeman, the way they relate to the teacher, and, above all else, the different patterns in family living.

As I talk about family patterns, I talk about middle America, about you and me who teach young people and expect to find within their families patterns the same as ours. But they are completely different. Whereas we teach our boys to be obedient, in the inner city boys are taught not to be obedient, but to be aggressive.

What are the values then? Simply ways and clues, I think, to understanding the way they relate to you, to the teacher, and I would like to look quickly at the values of the American family and to try to illustrate how the family still continues to teach in its home certain values and divide its world into two cultures: the ideal culture, toward which it wants its youth to act and to behave and to become, and the real culture, which all of us live. A mother punishes her daughter for lying. Yet, when the telephone rings, the mother says to her daughter, "Pick up the phone and tell whoever's on the other end of the line that mother isn't home." The ideal and the real. We had a young man on our faculty whose son had just been picked up for speeding. He was frantic. How do boys in this country learn to speed? He had never taught him to speed. It took me two weeks before I was able to tell the father who had really taught the son. He lives in Connecticut, where I do, and every Friday for the last ten years we've gone bumper to bumper up the West Side Drive, up from work to that playful weekend in the country. There's one thing to be sure of when you come to Connecticut and New Jersey: Those signs about the policemen really mean what they say. Our licenses are going to be taken away, and we know it so we watch. I drive like a good honest American, because someone told me I could get by with five miles over the speed limit, I usually go four, with one eye on the rearview mirror. For ten years, just as we hit the Connecticut line, he would go by me ten miles faster than I was going, and in the back window of that car was a little boy who grew older every year, watching what I was watching for in my rearview mirror, the dreaded Connecticut police. So the boy was picked up for speeding and the father said, "Where did he learn to speed?" He learned to speed in his father's car. So the ideal and the real.

One of the values of the American family today is that marriage is and must be the life pattern of everyone, that if you're not married you're not quite normal. So when I went into the field of teaching, my mother was a little disturbed. Why had I chose the profession of teaching. Why not the profession my mother and grandmother had chosen as wife and mother? My mother said that all women have always gotten married. Then a sociological study of some 20 years ago showed that not all American women got married. Not more than 150 years ago, no more than 61 percent of the women in this country got married. I wondered how my mother could have been so wrong; she was no longer here, and I couldn't tell her. Then I bought a house in Connecticut and got the answer. Just off my kitchen is a little room where they put queer Aunt Ethel, who never got a husband, and thankfully forgot about her. Earlier than that when they had the salt box they put her upstairs and closed the trap door and forgot about her. But there's one place where they couldn't forget about her—in the cemeteries of New England. The best history books in the United States are the cemeteries of New England. For at the end of all those stones are the names of the spinster daughters. By 1960 that 61 percent had risen to 92, by 1970 it had risen to 93 and there's one report that it may be 94 percent of us who can confidently look forward to getting married once before we're 65. I had greater hopes of 85. And if you invite me here, no man in this room is safe, for I believe around the corner is my future, and around the corner may be the law of diminishing returns, too. So we have taught that all men and all women shall be married. I just noticed that we now have TV dinners for couples. This is a couples society. And we pressure our youth. We pressure, not our boys, but only our girls. Ruth Benedict says that every one of us in every society of the world learns certain behaviors, certain ways of thinking and acting, that we'll never have to unlearn as long as we live.

Each of us also learns certain ways of thinking and acting that we'd better unlearn sooner or later in order to remain emotionally healthy. The continuity that none of us in Middle America has to unlearn is that we're going to get three square meals a day. So deeply do we believe it and with such dispatch do we teach it, that by the time our babies are two years old they are already eating on the adult feeding schedule. You say this is not unusual; I say it happens nowhere else in the world. If you go to Burma, a little two-year-old boy would appear before his village and his family and demonstrate that he could smoke a cigar with skill and with grace. He's not on the adult feeding schedule until he's five. A two-year-old boy in Bali must play a musical instrument. And I have heard it played beautifully, too. Little girls in Java are perfectly at home in the water. At two, they swim beautifully. By the time these children are three or four, they're not eating three square meals; they're eating six. For the coffee break, morning and afternoon, is a national institution, and the bedtime snack at night makes six.

By the time our little girls are in kindergarten they know the purpose of their lives. It is to get their man. There isn't a kindergarten girl in the laboratory school here that doesn't know how it's done! The way to a man's heart is through his stomach. I close this one with just one last point—we are the only people in the world who sentence a man to death and give a man as his last choice in life—his choice of his last square meal. If the newspapers tell you nothing else, they will report whether he chose southern fried chicken or a Minnesota t-bone steak smothered with onions. This is the continuity. You only have to look at the food we sent to Biafra and the food we sent to the poor of Mexico to know that food is the answer for everything.

Our boys today do not have the continuities that girls have. We teach our little boys to be obedient to everyone. If they pick on a boy littler than they are, we call them bullies. If they pick on their sisters, we sisters know how to handle brothers. I had five, and they gave me extra practice. But I never could get into any trouble. Every time I parked on Look-out Point, a brother was in the car next to me. In other words, there was no chance. There was an older brother who always tattled about it, so I took care of him. Just as my father's footsteps were heard coming up our front porch steps, I would kick my brother in the shins, take off for the only room in the American household with a quick lock on the door, and my father never failed me. I think the neighborhood heard him. He would say, "Now, Theodore, don't you dare touch her! Remember, she's just a little girl." This nasty little girl took care of her brothers. For years the only place a boy had any authority was over his little dog. But you will remember a boy who lived in the White House a couple of years ago who picked up his two dogs by the ears, and not only the United States, but the entire world discovered that over his little dog a boy has no authority at all.

To boys we say, "While you are young you must be obedient, and suddenly you become adults and get married, you must be an authority." When do we teach that authority? When do we come to understand the difference from the lower class of poor in this nation, in which authority rests with the boys from the beginning? Then they storm into our schools, completely unaware of this change, unaware of the different family patterns that enter Middle America. So marriage then is the life pattern.

Second, you must stay married only so long as you are happy. The moment you are no longer happy, you now can get a divorce. On such shifting sands we place the most important institution—the marriage and the family. I think you have to look at the law of limited possibilities to see what we're teaching in our homes. For there are only a limited number of ways in which we can react. There are only four ways in which you can get married. You can have group marriage; you can have polyandry—one woman and several men; polygamy—one man and several women; or you can have monogamy. There are only three ways in which we can orient our children. Based upon a fact of life known as sex, which has led to the institution of marriage and the family, we can honor marriage. Or based upon another fact of life, childbirth, which has led to parenthood, we can honor parenthood. We can honor either marriage or parenthood. There is a third possibility—both. But no society does that. Most of the world honors parenthood. Many of the children you teach, if they come of Chinese background, Spanish-oriented background, or Jewish background, tend to honor marriage. But most of us in Middle America do not honor parenthood. We honor marriage. I suggest that in our homes a little boy growing up is taught by his father, not how to be a good father to his future children, but how to be a good husband to his future wife. And little girls imitate their mothers. In the old days it was up-lift brassieres—now it's no brassieres at all—high-heeled shoes, and false eyelashes. Is this motherhood? I doubt it. Therefore I think Mother's Day has now become a day of atonement in the United States, when we atone for all the things we should have done for Mother all the rest of the year.

Well, you say, honoring marriage is right. For our girls are marrying earlier. I'm sure you know the statistics of last year: 40 percent of all the women who married in this country were between the ages of 15 and 19. Of the women who walked to the altar, from 15 to 50 to 78, one-third were pregnant. Let's take that little girl of 15 who's pregnant. That child will be born in less than nine months. By the time she's 19 or 20 the child will already know more than she does because she's had no education. In other words, we're marrying earlier. But you will say that we've always married earlier. That is one of the great myths of American society. Less than 10 percent of this nation, up until modern times, married earlier. We've got the widespread myth of the farm girl who marries earlier. The statistical answer is "no." Not only do we marry earlier but we have our children earlier. The latest average figure for a woman in this country to have her last child—even her fourth child—is twenty-six and a half. She'll only be in her early 30's when her child will be in your classroom. As we marry early and have our children earlier, something else is happening to America. We're becoming grandparents earlier. I cannot tell a grandparent in my class. They look like some of my undergraduates. So we are grandparents at 37, at 40, at 42. You are going to be a father and a mother for 20 or maybe 25 years at the most. You're going to be a husband and a wife maybe for 30 to 40 years. In fact, the figure for children in elementary school today has just been given; 58 years of married life. Perhaps if we begin to teach not for good parenthood but for good marriage, we might produce better fathers and mothers in the next generation.

And so the third value. The adolescent years are the best of all possible years and the years the most to be desired. I think today many of us are kind of jealous of those young people. We think the years they are in are the best years, and we constantly remember what we did or what we failed to do. Because we think they should know enough to use those years, we constantly watch them, no matter what they do.

I took a group to Europe. These young students from NYU talked with men in Germany, France, England, and Ireland. It didn't matter how they asked the question; it didn't matter how the answer came; these men, when they thought of their lives asked, "Is it a success?" For example, they never looked down to their children; they always looked back to their fathers. If they had a job as good as their fathers had, these men in Europe would say, "Yes, my life is a success." But if you asked the parents of your children, "Is your life a success?", I wonder how many of them would look back to their fathers. They would instead look down to their children. Their boys and girls get a better education, their boys and girls strain to be professional, and no one knows what we're going to do with all the professional people in nursery schools of America. But most important for Americans, they're on the happiness kick, too. If their children are happier than they have been, they will say, "Yes my life is a success." I think it is not unfair to say that youth is the time of all play and all learning, middle age is the time of all hard work, and old age is the time of all regrets. So we send our in-laws and our grandparents, and they indeed asked to be sent, to retirement towns in Florida and in California, where they write their pathetic articles about how much they love their retirement towns.

There is a truth that we have got to begin to teach in our schools—we who are afraid of death, we who are afraid of older years. We have got to begin from the nursery schools, since the parents are not doing it, to open the picture of growing old, for growing old all of us must do. And we must bring back people. You may not agree with me but I think the senior citizens are one of the most awful things in America. We have a culture of adolescents and a culture of senior citizens, who are put away, many times at their own wish, saying, "I will not interfere with my children." We have to begin to have the reality of teaching our children about the whole of life. One of the major values here is that children should be shielded from adult woes and spared the tribulations of adults, so we shield our little children from all of life's realities. Above all else we shield children from death. So when suddenly death comes to them at 25 or 35, it is a complete shock. I think there are ways the school must find, the creative teacher must find, of looking at this with honesty, for our culture does not want to grow old. Our culture does not want to face death, and we must somehow find the way.

The next value I think important in American families is that there be a division between men and women in the family—that men do the work outside the home and the women the work in the home. You see the women's lib movement today and you look at young couples today and see something completely different happening, even though we constantly hold up the value of the family, of the man doing all the outside work. I think it is important to look at the changing role of men. When I was here three years ago, I spoke to this group of the study I was then in, of why our professional men are dying—our doctors, our lawyers, our teachers, our managers. Dying so very young. Seven universities studied this for ten years, and I went around asking the question, Why are men dying so young? The men over this country answered, "Because we work so hard." If they lived outside Chicago or Los Angeles, they said, "Commuting." And having commuted a little in the summer, I know precisely what they are talking about. But the anthropologist always points out that if you have an unmarried woman working with you, the chances are that she carries as heavy a financial load as many married men. For we've got a good old Protestant ethic in the United States—that the unmarried daughter helps support her family. She had no chance to choose. You would be surprised at the number of women who cannot finish their Ph.D.'s. I have one who's just finished hers from North Carolina. She had to drop out nine years ago to raise the children of her brother, whose wife had died. And these women don't have ulcers, they do not suffer from hypertension, and they do not die from heart attacks, as our men do. The question is why.

The answer this study gave is simply this: the failure to allow our men to show their emotions. I don't know how men are going to show their emotions. They're certainly not going to start crying because women can cry. Because you've let us cry, we're living longer than you are. I often say that the only place men really show anger is in the car in the morning on their way from home. They're mad at their wives, so they take it out on the woman driver next to them, and at night they're mad at their boss so they swear. The answer was that top management, the doctors, the lawyers, get their emotional expressions on the golf course. I won't give you statistics, but I'll give you a personal story. I used to play national tennis and I got beaten. I would look in the eye of the young lady who beat me, smile, and shake her hand, because all Americans are good sports when the camera's on them. I would say to her smilingly, "You played a good game." Well, she hadn't played a good game. Either I was off my game, my mother hadn't let me wear the pair of tennis shoes with my toe sticking through, or someone had miscalled a point. But I pushed it all down inside, and that is what is happening on the golf courses of America. If you want to really see it, watch those golf games every Sunday and all those tournaments around the country.

Then they said the next level is in the bowling alleys of America. I spent six months in alleys of northern New Jersey and the worse words I ever heard were "gosh" and "darn." In a seminar, one of my young men said, "You've been in the wrong bowling alleys in New Jersey." But the answer is that I think the family and educators must recognize that there is a whole new masculinity. There are no more forests for our men to cut down. There is no longer need of large muscles. Our men today get their masculinity from their status and from the titles that they hold. In the educational profession in this nation today, more than three-fourths of the high school and junior high school teachers are men. I don't know how many of you have elementary school principals who are women, but I told the superintendents last night that the elementary school woman principal is as dead as a dead dodo. Nine young men who are superintendents in northern New Jersey have been in my class. I once asked them, "What are you going to do about your women principals?" The superintendents can't wait until those women die or retire, and they've got the young men all ready for the jobs. What we need desperately today is young men teaching in our public schools. We need them in the lower grades, we need them at every level. But our new masculinity forces the men out of teaching. They must become the supervisors, they must become the superintendents, they must become the elementary principals.

So we have eliminated for women a chance for any way to rise, any need for status; and, what is more important, we have taken out of the classroom what youngsters really need—the man. And we have taken out from administration what all really need—an occasional woman as an administrator. For the division of labor is necessary if we're going to have a balanced society. The long men with the long hair are not growing feminine. Our men are getting what they have always got, what they want. American men want participation in their families and participation in their community. So the answer is, I think that our long-haired young men are living in the communes, and doing all the rest that makes for little work. The research job I'm doing in one of the communities in the eastern part of Greenwich Village shows that in these groups the young men have more to look forward to than their fathers or grandfathers ever had. I give you a story that illustrates far better than all the statistics I could quote. My own father, born in Germany, was an engineer, who, like all German fathers, was very strict with his sons. In fact, he used to lay down the laws of what they should do. He was very gentle, as Germans are, to his daughters. But my brothers never talked back as they might have today, had they lived in this age. They never even opened their mouths. They made a beeline for mother. And down through the years, my mother's gentle voice was always the same, "Now, sons, now boys, settle down. Wait till your father goes, and we'll take care of the matter. In my family we always took care of the matter the way my mother decided. I say to you, and my brothers agree with me, that not once in my father's life did she ever doubt that my father was the head of the household.

I give you just one example from the last question in a series answered by a group of 200 soldiers between the ages of 18 and 25 in New York City. How many of you were ever put to bed by your fathers? Only seven had ever been put to bed by their fathers, and they cut across every socio-economic group. How many had put their children to bed? Only one said he had not, and when we broke him down, he was the only unmarried man in the entire group.

There is a new masculinity abroad, and in the schools I think there is a job for us to do, because the family is not doing it. They are teaching one thing and the youngsters are practicing another. Oh the fear today of older people toward these long-haired young people! You have them right here on this campus, and in New York, of course, they are even more extreme. It is the truth that they are fighting out, I think, against the rigidity of what has been the role of men.

The last value is the heart of American society—that it will be individual values that count, not the family values. What do you as an individual want? This is precisely what we've taught. We've put our little babies in a room, we've closed off the light, we've firmly shut the door, and we've let them develop their little old individualism in this room all by themselves. That room has become a symbol of the American family. It's the place where you send the child when he misbehaves. It's the place where the teenager rushes when he can't stand the sight of his parents, and he slams the door louder and louder each time. So we say to young people, "Stand on your own feet, be an individual, think for yourselves, be independent." In the last four years you and I have seen the first generation of young people who are doing precisely what their parents taught them to do—standing on their own feet, thinking for themselves. As I teach them at the university level I must confess to you that I don't like what I think some of them are thinking when they look at me. But individualism is the key of American industrial technological society. For one day your son will bundle up your daughter-in-law and grandchildren and take off for Cairo or Tokyo. He'll give not one single backward glance at you. For we are training them to be alone, and ours is the loneliest society in the world. I ask you to think sometime in the next few weeks about how long and how lonely a trip each one of us has taken to be sitting here in this room this morning in this individualistic society.

We put a baby in its own bassinet and from there it moves to its own playpen, and in some homes there are walls around those playpens. They're growing higher every year that passes, because in those homes the wall-to-wall carpeting and furniture are sometimes more important than children. From our playpens we move to our own highchairs, where we eat alone and correctly. When I was in college, every Friday night my father picked me up and drove me home; every Sunday night he drove me back. Every Sunday night all those years my mother always said to me, "Now, Ethel, please this week don't forget your table manners. It won't be you they blame, it will be your mother." So I stuffed sandwiches down my throat in a drug store in New York and said, "It doesn't matter. It will be my mother they blame."

So this individual moves from playpen to a highchair to a bed. And there is a dream that the parents that you work with have brought into reality, a dream they share with every parent who lives in the United States particularly. If they live in one of the 14 of our largest cities, they're going to get out of Cincinnati, they're going to get out of Columbus, Ohio, they're going to move down here. They're going to have enough land, they're going to have a house big enough so that each of their children will have that symbolic room of his own. In that room we teach the child not only individualism but loneliness, separateness, and, above all else, apartness. Apartness from whom? Apart from the adults, of course. Because at the same time we teach individualism, we're teaching conformity. I used to stand before my poor little third grade-class and say, "Mary, why can't you ever keep your desk as neat and clean as Jane does?" In their attitudes and their skills I still compare my students.

Your daughter comes home one night and says to you, "Mother, may I stay out until one o'clock?"

It is Saturday night, but mother says, "No, you cannot stay out until one o'clock on Saturday night."

Your daughter gives the answer you have taught her from the moment she was born. "But Jane gets to stay out until one o'clock. Everybody in my class at school stays out until one o'clock."

You, sometimes for the first time in your life, say, "But I don't care what Jane can do. Your father says you must be in at 12 o'clock."

At this mystical moment that grows younger with each year that passes, we toss the learnings of a lifetime out the window and bring in new values, the ones that should have been there all along. You and I as teachers know the developmental pattern of each one of our children—the values of individual homes. You ask, "What does the young college student really want today?" as you watch what is going on. You and I know that in all our colleges we're seeing a new aliveness. So today I am doing the most exciting teaching I have ever done since I first began after World War II and had the young men and women back from World War II. When I started lecturing on some place out in the South Pacific, a hand would go up and a man would say, "I was in the Solomon Islands and I didn't see anything you've been talking about." So I had to go to the Solomon Islands. But today I cannot go to the islands of these youths, for everyone up to the age of 25 has no concern with change. Only those of us over 25 are concerned, for the only world they've ever known is a world of constant change.

So today we look at the individual in our society. Can we begin in the classroom to teach sone of the responsibilities that go with this individualism? It's heart of the matter. For, as I said, there are two cultures, the real and the ideal. The family in American society in reality is changing. It's lost many of its beauties and many of its functions, but I suggest to you that the family is still the place where love must be taught. For you and I cannot truly love someone else unless we have the good fortune to be born into a family where there is love. All over this country you see worry about sex education in the public schools. Many of the towns are divided right and left. Some even think that those who would teach sex education are communists who are trying to destroy our nation. Do you know what authorities in this field say? That there is no sex education taught after the age of five. By the time I was five, my attitudes toward men were already set by what had happened in my home, by the fact of how my father acted toward me. So you ask an authority "Well, then, what's all this business of sex education?" And the answer is, of course, that the only thing the public education can teach is anatomy. Maybe they can teach a few techniques, but we know anatomy. And after that what is the purpose? To produce better parents for the next generation. How a mother and a father respond to each other will set the pattern of our lifetime in our whole field of love.

The second thing that the family has and always has had is that the home is a place where respect is taught. I will not respect any of you and none of you will respect me unless we have the good fortune to be raised in a home where we were taught to respect ourselves.

The third value of the home that I think remains unchanged in most societies is that the family is the place where standards are set up. This is not a good word today. It's a little corny. But American parents and American adults must begin to recognize that there are only four ways in which children learn in all the world. They learn through imitation, above all else. They learn through the guiding hands of parents as they help them to walk or to play a musical instrument or to dance. They learn as we do our teaching, through precepts, by telling. We do too much. We just tell them what's going to happen; we don't let them experience. And lastly they learn through involvement. So parents who get a little sneaky on the income tax, or drive as I do, four to five miles above the limit, have to face the fact that it's what we do as adults that is the key.

For education the key is what we do in our classrooms. For automation, as all of you know, is here. In a certain little community, they're going to teach for 11 months. They're going to have six weeks of school, two weeks off, then six weeks of school; they're going to have a chance to go to the Caribbean at Christmas time instead of in the heat of the summer. These things are changing. The school will not stay as it is. We have to have the courage to change some of the structure if we would keep what is good within society. We know there is no skill you can teach a child in kindergarten or in college, unless it be the skill of thinking, that will not be obsolete in 10 to 15 years. Every machine we teach youngsters to run, even a typewriter, is going to be in a museum in another five to ten years. What can we do? I think the only thing we can do is to link up the facts with principles, with concepts, and above all else, teach our youngsters attitudes. How can we keep alive some of the attitudes we pride? We've got to begin in the home, and the home has got to begin teaching and not leave it entirely for the teachers. I urged you the last time I was here to keep alive the attitude of curiosity that is so rich in the early elementary school. As youth goes through junior high and senior high school it disappears, and by the time they finish, at least at NYU, it's almost gone.

I had one undergraduate class of 420. Walking in late and forgetting it was afternoon, I said, "Good morning." Not a single student answered me. They were all busy writing "Good morning" down. It might come on the exam. How to keep alive the attitude of honest doubt so good in science and therefore good in family life as well. How to keep alive the involvement. Will we lose these young people as we lost you between the ages of 25 and 35, when you and I were creating a job or a home or a community? I think we're going to lose these youth just as we've lost every generation before; but, most important, I think the heart of the matter for education and the one thing we can do is to begin to teach responsibility. There is no amnesty in life; there is a responsibility. I don't care how much youth today wants to clean up the environment, it had better clean up the environment where it is, in our own halls at NYU. They're out marching to clean up environment, but in the environment they create we have to hire extra help to clean up after they're gone. How do we begin to teach responsibility? And so Lillian Smith sums it up. She says, "This is the sin of you and me and all of us, to have more power than love, more knowledge than understanding, more information about this earth than of the people who live upon it, more skill to fly to far-off places than to stop a moment and look at the secret spots of our own hearts; for freedom is a dreadful word unless it goes hand in hand with responsibility, and democracy is going to disappear from the face of the earth unless the hearts and the minds and the souls of men grow mature."

THE MARTHA HOLDEN JENNINGS

SCHOLAR LECTURES

at

BOWLING GREEN STATE UNIVERSITY

1970—1971

Dr. Marcus Bach

Dr. Marcus Bach, Director of the Foundation for Spiritual Understanding, Palos Verdes, California, presented the Jennings Scholar Lecture, on December 12, 1970, in the John C. Baker Center, Ohio University.

Author and specialist in inter-cultural and inter-religious relations, Dr. Bach was for fourteen years on the staff of the School of Religion at the State University of Iowa, where he received his Ph.D. degree in 1942. Four other schools—Bradley University, Hillsdale, Carthage, and Elmhurst Colleges—awarded him honorary degrees. He has been the recipient of numerous citations in the field of writing and research.

Unlike most professors, Dr. Bach has had the opportunity of alternating his teaching program between a year on campus and a year in travel. "An excellent arrangement," he contends, "if you can work it." His research has taken him into many areas of the world, where he has lived among various religious and ethnic groups in an effort to "empathetically interpret their ways of life and subjectively enter into their experiences."

His work has brought him into as-sociation with many outstanding leaders, including the late Dr. Albert Schweitzer in Lambarene, Africa; Vinoba Bhave in India; and Buddhist leaders in southeast Asia. Two State Department assignments under the auspices of the Educational Division of Cultural Affairs took him to Pakistan, Cambodia, and the sub-continent.

Recently Dr. Bach helped establish the Foundation for Spiritual Understanding, which is designed to explore new approaches to the total circumference of concepts which unite humanity on deep feeling levels of response. He takes a new, bold look at the convictions men live by and interprets them against the discoveries of his years of intimate and unbiased research.

Dr. Bach is the author of numerous interpretive books including *The Will to Believe, Had You Been Born in Another Faith, God and the Soviets, Spiritual Breakthroughs for Our Time,* and *The Power of Perception.* His inspirational book, *The Wonderful Magic of Living,* brought out by Doubleday in January, 1968, was Dr. Bach's fifteenth publication.

119

THE COMING OF THE NEW MAN

While the Jennings Lecture Series is not directed primarily to the field of formalized education but rather to a broad spectrum of the total overview of life, in the talk this morning I would like to emphasize a directive which applies to all of us interested in the educational process: Education should be looked upon as a creative experience, and this experience should in no way be hampered by didactic and academic studies.

In a day when force is met with force, war with war, violence with violence, and terror with power, we should not lose sight of the fact that a creative breakthrough is still possible to turn the tide and solve, to some degree at least, the impasse and the dilemma in which we often feel we are inextricably caught and out of which there seems to be no apparent escape. It is creative thought in all fields that has contributed to the progress and refinement of life.

Now, this creative breakthrough is the assignment of a new breed of individuals, the coming of a "new man" who will bring a new approach and a new way of thinking without destroying that which was helpful and constructive in the past. The old concept used to be that we belonged strictly to the genus Homo sapiens. A favorite expression has always been, "Let's by all means be *human* about it!" Or, "Let's by all means be *smart* about things!" Homo sapiens, the man of intellect.

Now, however, it seems as though we have reached a point of challenge in life when just being human or being smart is no longer enough. Circumstances challenge us to be superhuman or, if we are not afraid of the term, we are asked to be "divine" or at least emphasize a certain divinity in life. This, in itself, suggests an insight into what our contemporary consideration of the educational process should be, though heaven knows I am not thinking in terms of an institutionalized religious emphasis! I am referring to the coming of the new man, who in many instances has actually defected from organized religious movements.

Some of my favorite lines relating to the assignment confronting modern man go something like this, "When God made the earth, he could have finished it but he didn't. He left it as raw material to invite us to be copartners with him in building a better world, and it may be that in this very fact lies life's greatest meaning. God gave us an unfinished world so that we might share with him in the joy and satisfaction of finished perfect things." This, it seems to me, is where the idea of the new man comes in, and to better understand let's go back a bit and take a reflective look at Homo sapiens.

Homo sapiens was an individual who, until a few short years ago, was bound in a four-dimensional or even a three-dimension world, and he thought within this frame of reference. He was also restricted to his five sensory aptitudes. As I remember, and let me say I have a good deal of respect for him and for the kind of world he tried to make, his basic policy seems to have been self-perpetuation self-aggrandizement to a point of rugged individualism, self-propagation, and a policy of "making good" in life.

By "making good" in the western sense he meant security and success, linear thinking, the fulfillment of his ambitions and goals. Again, not forgetting all the admirable accomplishments of Homo sapiens and without doing discredit to the world and the "Establishment" with which he became identified, let us consider some of his basic beliefs.

Feeling that he had come to grips with the life of his time, he concluded that his soul had been born with his body. He was of the opinion that heaven and hell and purgatory were locations, almost geographic. His prayer was communication with an anthropomorphic God made in the image of man as man had been made in the image of God. This Deity was usually quite remote from man. He was, in a way, a vague and hazy shadow God.

This man of old looked upon breakthroughs in the parapsychological field as unrelated to religion. Hypnotism was for a long time regarded as fraudulent; psychism and its attendant phenomena were construed as fakery or some satanic hokus-pokus. He grew up in this kind of consciousness.

He was more interested in things that exist than he was in existence. The archetypal world, if the phrase occurred to him in a Platonic sense, was less real than the phenomenal world, the world round about him, the world of things and beings. Outer space was beyond his premises. Inner man had been theologically defined by way of an institutionalized faith with various sectarian inferences. All of which is recounted with no intention of belittling or writing off either the greatness of Homo sapiens or the world which had become so very much a part of him.

It is mentioned primarily so that we can understand the change that has taken place. With a suddenness we can hardly sublimate or absorb, a whole new conceptual world has burst upon us. All at once a revolt has been instituted against many concepts once held sacred by the Homo sapiens world, the Establishment so-called, a revolt very real to us who are intimately engaged in work with the onward-coming generation. Actually, isn't it part of our responsibility to bridge the gap between the counter-revolution movement and the Establishment?

I have a feeling that this concept of a new man may be able to effect a creative breakthrough in this field, for this is an ideal that exists in the minds of all generations. The potential of this person may already exist within someone in your classroom or in your own family or in you yourself. Is it possible for him to arise, and if so what kind of a being will he be?

It is difficult to make any generalizations about the hip-culture group. There are so many contradictions. I saw a cartoon recently that showed a long-haired-type fellow standing on the highway holding a placard saying,

"Ban the automobile," and he was hitch-hiking. I remember another cartoon equally poignant. It showed a messianic-appearing hippie carrying a placard that said, "Peace." He was being stalked by an armed squad of police, and they knew they were going to get him because he was heading straight into a lake. However, when he got to the water he kept right on walking.

This new man reveals himself at least in a fringe way to the needs and dilemmas of our time. For example, he realizes he is living in an unfinished world. He knows that whatever cosmic force created planet earth, imposed a responsibility upon man to maintain and preserve the balance of nature. He realizes that he is no longer circumscribed by a three- or a four-dimensional world. He is already exploring new dimensions. He is no longer bound by his five sensory aptitudes. He now deals familiarly with extrasensory perception. He has been awakened and alerted to a whole new range of parapsychological insights and phenomena in what he calls the psi field, phases of which have escaped the church and the academic world.

This new man no longer thinks in terms of the soul as a distinct entity created with the body, but speculates that the soul force has conceivably been around before. In fact, for the first time in the history of western thought, the concept of reincarnation is being taken seriously by the traditional churches and is one of the favorite subjects in the "rap sessions" of the youth generation. Both reincarnation and karma are now looked upon as hypotheses worthy of consideration.

Cybernetics, psycho-cybernetics, synthesis, psychosynthesis, synergetics, the concept of simulsense, in short, the reach of technology is now the reach of the mind, and the reach of the mind is the reach of the soul. Depth meditation is part of the program. Did you know that transcendental meditation brought to America by a bearded maharishi changed the lives of thousands of students on west coast campuses, for a time, at least, and still. constitutes a serious spiritual discipline engaged in by young people and adults alike?

But even this is moving on into new fields of exploration. Now we are beginning to hear about electronic meditation and electronic yoga! While we seek to perpetuate traditional methods of education and while the church endeavors to maintain its ancient forms and practices, a new generation is experimenting in such things as bio-training feedback, an attempt to induce and sustain the alpha consciousness, a state of tranquility, a new approach to modern mysticism, a quest for the kind of world in which the new man may feel at home. He has taken the whole bit of esoteric thought into his field, from the Tibetan *Book of the Dead* to the apocalypticism of the Christian scriptures. He claims he is finding what Christianity has continually been emphasizing, the "I Am presence." He has a saying that "The search for meaning is the search for Self." In short, we are dealing with a new type of mind in a new-dimensional world.

Is it any wonder that education must be looked upon as a creative process in which self-discovery plays an increasingly more significant role? Isn't it understandable that we must think in terms of the coming a new man? Even at the risk of over stressing the current phenomenon, let me suggest a descriptive term for this innovative individual. He is no longer merely Homo sapiens. He is Homo sapiens subliminalus, a type of being living in an extrasensory world in which he realizes that ideas and concepts that get into life above or below the limits of consciousness are those which most directly shape and influence life. The real communication is non-verbal. The deepest communication is always non-verbal no matter how evocative words may be. The real communication is subliminal.

We live in a world in which vibrations and sensitivity have been so heightened that we need speak less because we feel more. We have never lived at a time when we were so conscious of the unconscious as we are today. There is a feeling of immanence today, a sense of the "fullness of time," a time of advent of the new man, a leader, an avatar of synthesis, so to say, and this new man need not necessarily be one individual but a group representing and personifying new dimensions of the age. People more interested in existence than in things that exist. People to whom heaven and hell are no longer locations, but states of consciousness. People who believe in a new sense of values, to whom war is obsolete, to whom war is an illusion built upon the misconception that the logic of force is stronger than the logic of love.

Occasionally in chapel talks in colleges, I ask young students if they would care to read a scripture passage to open the meeting. They say, "What do you want me to read?"

"Something out of the Psalms," I suggest, "or something out of the Sermon on the Mount."

They shake their heads about reading something from the Sermon on the Mount. They say, "It doesn't make sense to read words that our generation has rejected. What are the sayings and precepts of Jesus? Merely symbolical? Who lives up to them? Who among us turns the other cheek? Who walks the second mile? Who loves his enemies? Where do you find examples of these sayings demonstrated in life?" Alfred North Whitehead once said, "If anyone takes the sayings of the gospels literally in a world like ours it will mean sudden death."

Yet the new man says he would like to accept the challenge. He feels that a new breed of individual is rising out of the turmoil and violence, out of the matrix of terror, rising to represent a new approach to life. Whether this is true or false—and I think it is true—if you and I can catch the vision and begin to enter into what is the mystique of a new life-style and a new approach to things, we can become that bridge that is so desperately needed. The new man needs our help, and he knows it. He needs the benefit of our maturity and experience. All he wants is an assurance that we also need him.

Let's take a look at the triad of life and see how our new man is seeking to relate the body, mind and spirit and how we who are involved with him in education, religion and consultation may have missed the boat by not taking cognizance of the world in which he lives.

For one thing, this new emerging man takes a different view of physicality than the Establishment used to take. The body is the vehicle employed by the spirit of God to express itself, to particularize itself. I am speaking idealistically now and not in generalities because there are surely evidences galore that many among the hip culture hardly persuade us that they hold to the maxim of "Cleanliness is next to Godliness."

But if you have ever attended any of the big yoga camps or modern youth camps that are springing up across the country, you know what I mean. I was at a yoga retreat where some 600 young people came to develop and respect their physical bodies and to harmonize them with mind and spirit. Their day started at five in the morning with yoga exercises and chants. For three months groups came and went, learning how to walk, learning how to breathe, learning how and what to eat, learning to look upon the body as the temple of God.

Perhaps I am overly enthusiastic and, as I have said, idealistic about all this, because I know what this kind of training did for me and I know what it did for my Christian meditative practices and all that. I know that the more I learned about yoga disciplines, the more I understood Christian disciplines. The more I learned about Krishna, the more I respected the Christ, and the more I respected the Christ the more I respected Krishna, too. And when I was with the Zen Buddhists in Japan, the more I learned about the Buddha the greater he became; and the greater he became, the greater the Christ became; and this is the way it will be with the new man.

I went to a meeting with high school and college students where a medical doctor was talking about the birth of a baby. He explained that life begins with an egg, a quarter the size of the point of a pin, and it is impregnated by a sperm 50,000 times smaller than that. He made clear that in the process of growth there is the beating of a heart before there is a heart, there is a pulsation before there is a pulse; the power of something beyond human mind has begun its work.

He stated that after 30 days all of the major organs of the body have begun to form, that the color of the eyes are determined at the time of fertilization, and I sat there as enthralled as those young people were. When we walked out of that classroom, I am sure we all felt as if the body were a holy place and that it is the manifestation of some profound spiritual force. We *are* fearfully and wonderfully made, and if we could somehow communicate about such basic convictions with this new man who is struggling to be born, struggling to grow, hoping as we are for some kind of breakthrough in the next rung in the ladder of human evolvement, then we would be better equipped for the kind of world in which we find ourself.

Secondly, Homo sapiens subliminalus looks upon the mind differently than we used to. He looks upon the mind as unlimited, or limited only by its sense of limitation. When I went to school, teachers said, "Don't clutter your mind with things that are unimportant." I always had the feeling that the mind could contain only so much and that if I crowded too much into it there would be a minor explosion. Young people these days know differently. They know that the mind is like a sponge. It is, to quote, "like lungs with air pockets."

It will take everything you give it, and the more you give it the more it wants. It is not only the greatest memory bank and computer in the world, it also has subsidiary banks and computers tucked away in the unconscious. The brain of man, neatly set in our funny-shaped skulls, wonderfully protected, marvelously made, is infinitely greater than any instrument man has ever devised.

Talk seriously with 16- and 17-year-olds these days and, while many may seem to be adrift, more have already "made up their minds" which directions their lives are to take, the careers they plan to go into. They are ahead of me when I was in their age bracket. I wish someone had persuaded me during my teenage years that education is a creative process and that the mind is unlimited. I wish someone had told me that the search for meaning is the search for self.

I was telling George Keith during our drive over here that my ambition had once been to become a violinist. My dad thought that anyone with a name like Bach had an advantage in this field, and he put a violin under my chin. I was studious and tried very hard to gain virtuosity, but I never made it. For one thing, I never learned the relationship of the mind to the reactive or unconscious mind. I did not think in those terms. I was always playing consciously. Homo sapiens subliminalus thinks in subconscious and superconscious terms as a matter of course.

If you saw *Woodstock* or if you ever attended any of the great rock festivals, you know there are moments when the young performers demonstrate the ecstatic truth that the instrument and the player become one and indivisible. There is a time when you cannot say that this is the guitar and this is the hand or the person; they are unified.

I remember seeing the same phenomenon during a performance of the famous Spanish riding team in Vienna. What makes these riders the greatest in the world? Because there is a moment when, through an empathic force, the horse and the rider blend and become one. You no longer think in terms of fragmentation; horse and rider have been perfectly blended into a creative experience.

This is it, and this is part of the mental adaptation of the new generation. I am not making a case for the fact that it is exemplary. I am merely saying it is unique and on a new wave length. But so are we. The new world, the nondimensional world, has been opened to us. The extrasensory world is all around us. We will never be the same again. We dare not be the same again. Life is much greater, God is much nearer, all of these things are more real because we feel within *ourselves* the coming of the new man.

One reason for the rise of interest in psychedelic drugs was that some of these young people were sincerely involved in the exploration of mind. Some of them were serious and honestly seeking. Many went into this for kicks, in protest, in revolt, and so on. I am not trying to make a case for the practice. I am simply saying that the new world that we as Christians used to glibly talk about, the unseen world, the world of spirit, is what many young people were actually seeking—through chemistry.

I was in San Diego as a resource person during a Young Christian Fellowship meeting sponsored by the San Diego Council of Churches. I sat with some 20 young people who were discussing, of all things, the "nature of God." Each one presented what he felt was basic in the nature of God, and then a boy got up, about 17 years old, and he said, "You can talk about God if you want, but you don't know what God is until you've taken LSD." Then he gave a testimony about what he had seen on his trips, how commonplace things throbbed with life, how time stood still, how his world expanded. The young people who listened to him had little defense against what he felt he had experienced.

I took a walk with him afterwards. He said he had been on 17 trips and wanted to go on just one more. I suggested that he had been lucky, though perhaps unwise, to have taken the chances he had, that he could make it an adventure by beginning to explore the inner man through deep meditative practices.

I had a copy of one of my books and I gave it to him with an inscription, "To Jim, a fellow spirit." The next day his mother came to see me and said she wanted to share something with me.

"Jim came home," she said, "with your book under his arm. He threw himself into my arms and began to cry. He said, 'Oh, Mom, I've found a man who understands what I've been talking about.' "

I mention this only to suggest that the things I've been talking about, the mystique of life, the point of contact that we must establish, the creative contact in which our communication is of the spirit, in which it is not enough any longer to just be human about things, are challenges we must consider if our teaching and our counseling is to effective.

If the new man has a different approach to the body and to the mind, he also has some advanced ideas about the soul. As he believes that there is a non-atomical substance in the brain called the mind, so he suggests that there is a non-anatomical soul in the physical being which never dies. The soul and the mind are connected by the spirit, as many occultists have always suggested and as many of the great teachers have speculated. The new man, of course, accepts the total circumference of spiritual experience as his rightful domain. His faith, if it is liberal, is syncretic; if it is conservative or fundamentalistic it is, nonetheless, psychically involved.

He takes psychism seriously because of the spiritual nature of life. In short, it helps him in his understanding of the triad—body, mind, soul. In thinking of the body, the new man feels that what was once considered rational is no longer sufficient. There must be an "irrationality" which becomes rational because of an over-belief. As an example, it used to be irrational to believe that a person can live as long as he wills to live, but now there is a growing belief that we die only when we will to die.

In his approach to the mind the new man says it is no longer enough simply to relate to intellection. We must begin to relate to intuition, to paranormal experience, to a conviction that what we feel intuitively is as valid as that which we figure out intellectually, that in fact, intuition is the basis of intellection.

And according to his belief, the soul is truly immortal. It no longer embarks on a final journey to a geographical heaven or hell. It is eternal, God living in us, living in man, each one of us being a particularization of God for a specific purpose with an inner knowing of what that purpose is and the inner conviction that death does not end the story.

In his search for meaning which is the search for self, the new man says something like this: "When God made the earth, he could have finished it but he didn't. He left it as raw materials to tantalize us and challenge us and start us creating and thinking, and therein lies life's greatest meaning. God gave us an unfinished world so that we might share with him in the joy and satisfaction of finished, perfect things.

"He left the electricity in the clouds, the aluminum in the clay, the oil in the rock. He left the rivers to be bridged and the mountains to be trailed. He left the forests to be felled and the cities to be built. He left the minerals to be mined and the diamonds to be cut. Perhaps he left poverty in the world so that we would know what it is like to share affluence with people. Maybe he left sickness so that we could better appreciate well-being."

The new man says that God left most of nature's beauty to be discovered and most of nature's mysteries to be solved so that we might be partners with him in the progress of ideas. The challenge of the educational process and religion is to keep life creative and to serve as a bridge between generations, between worlds of varying ideologies, and between historic periods in the great transitional hours of time.

However it may be, a new man is arising faster than we have been aware of, and we are all nearer to him than we realized or dreamed.

Dr. George Z. F. Bereday

Dr. George Z. F. Bereday, professor of comparative education at Teachers College, Columbia University, presented the Jennings Scholar Lecture on November 7, 1970, at Bowling Green State University. He has been on the faculty at Columbia since 1955.

His professional experiences also include: associate of the Russian Institute, member of the Faculty of the School of International Affairs, exchange professor at Moscow University, Fulbright professor at Tokyo University, visiting professor at the University of Hawaii, and director of the Japanese-American Teacher Program.

Dr. Bereday has been a member of cultural missions to the U.S.S.R., Finland, and Japan and was chief of the STAG Mission to Western Europe in 1970. All of these missions were sponsored by the Department of State.

Dr. Bereday has degrees from the University of London and from Oxford and Harvard Universities. He has. language proficiency in Polish, his native tongue, English, French, German, Russian, Italian, Spanish, and Japanese.

Among the books he has edited are *The Making of Citizens, Essays on World Education,* and *Studies from the Center of Education in Industrial Nations.* His articles are published in several professional periodicals.

TOWARDS INDIVIDUALIZATION
OF INSTRUCTION

Dr. George Bereday

Dr. Bereday presented this lecture in the series at Ohio University. Please refer to page 21 of this volume.

Dr. John B. Calhoun

Dr. John B. Calhoun gave the Jennings Scholar Lecture at Bowling Green State University on January 23, 1971.

Dr. Calhoun is a member of the Unit for Research on Behavioral Systems of the National Institute of Mental Health, Bethesda, Maryland. He is working on the behavioral aspects of high density populations and the influence of space on animals, including man.

He holds M.S. and PhD degrees from Northwestern University. In 1943–44 he taught biology at Emory University and from 1944–49, zoology at Johns Hopkins University. From 1946–49, he was a research associate in parasitology at Johns Hopkins University.

Although Dr. Calhoun's basic training is in ecology, since 1949 he has been closely associated with psychologists, psychiatrists, and sociologists, orienting his studies to provide insights relevant to concepts and problems in these disciplines. Concentrating on the ecology of behavior, Dr. Calhoun has been with the National Institutes of Health and has served as a consultant or special fellow to other institutions. He has published numerous articles in the fields of ecology, social behavior, zoogeography, and genetics.

THE STRATEGY OF LIFE

I really feel very much at home here this morning. I feel, in many ways, that I am coming home. My wife's home was in Bellevue at the time we married. My grandmother was born in Clyde, which is also very close. There is a town nearby called Fremont; a cousin of mine, Kit, journeyed around the West with a man that city was named after.

And, I hope in some way, that I may be a guide this morning to new frontiers, frontiers that require new maps. But it's hard for some people to read a map even if they have one. In illustration of people not reading the map: In our Washington suburbs, early winter is a time of preparation for junior high science fairs. Every year we are deluged by calls from mothers and scientists who think they have a connection through to us. Students rarely call, which is very disappointing. The last request we had was made in this way: "My son is doing a science fair project. He wants to do a study on population with mice. It's got to be completed in three weeks." In mice, the gestation period is three weeks!

This is a very logical trap. A friend of mine who has been doing bio-chemical research spends on the average of about three weeks for each publication. During the past 15 years he has published 300 papers. He just received a Nobel Prize for this. (He's also contributing to some studies I'll remark on this morning.) This is one avenue of research in which we have been able to focus on smaller and smaller segments of our total life spheres and make very significant contributions. That is one trend.

We have to go back in time to see another trend. If you can, think back a little over a century ago, to the publication of the *Origin of Species* by Darwin. He spent 30 years on this particular study. Now we're down to where we can spend three weeks and accomplish something that is worth a Nobel Prize. But that has been just one trend in science and understanding: We have reduced by one five-hundredth the amount of time to accomplish a significant insight!

The other trend has been just in the opposite direction, probably by fewer people. This relates to the magnitude of the problem. The time required to accomplish its final understanding has increased five hundred fold rather than decreased. That is, we are involved in problems now initiated which will take, instead of three weeks to finish, 1500 years.

The problem with the junior high school student is that he was confusing these two trends. A task that takes 1500 years to complete he was trying to do in three weeks. This is a very common misconception on the large part of our society. It's probably at the root in a great many of the total academic settings which, I understand, came into focus in this part of Ohio last year, also. It's not the only reason, but it's one thing.

We're getting the time scale which is increasingly shortening, increasingly devoted to simplistic problems, mixed up with the time scale which is very long and very complex. You can't get instantaneous solutions for the latter. They are two quite different problems. And it is with regard to the very complex and the very long range that we will be talking about this morning. Darwin was concerned with understanding evolution. We now are also concerned with the design of evolution—the design of our future. Here is where road maps can help.

You may have great difficulty reading my abstract. Mr. Waple asked me to prepare a short abstract. I felt in the mood to write a poem, and I did. It may not at first make much sense, but I hope, it will make more sense as a road map when I get through. (The poem is printed after the lecture.)

We can put one letter, R, on the front of evolution, and we have the word "revolution," which was the termination of the President's speech last night. His emphasis was on revolution. We could put one mark on this word, and we would then have discovered a pass through the "mountains." That is, revolution is a kind of barrier, a kind of mountain. We react against this word, although our forefathers didn't. We could put one slash mark through R to form R_x. You've all seen this in drugstores; it means prescription.

To the early Roman pharmacists, this was derived from R for recipe. They combined this with the symbol ♃ for Jupiter to form R_x, which forms the symbol for prescription. It was a prayer to the god of destiny, as they understood it, to look favorably on this compound which they had designed. So that $R_x$evolution now becomes the design of evolution if it is written this way. The sign of $R_x$evolution is a kind of pass through the mountains to develop a new kind of understanding and a new kind of awareness. That is all evolution is about, all life is about, the development of awareness.

Now I would like to go back briefly to my legitimate life, and I try to be legitimate, which has to do with the day-to-day research which helps me to be a guide searching through the maze of the future. We're going to talk about mice for a few minutes.

We designed a Utopia. What do you do to design a Utopia? Taking care of physical needs is one of the things, so we built a large environment. It's 16 apartment units around a big court. There is a fence around this; the mice can't get out of this total complex. It is a very large space. All the food, all the water, all the living spaces were provided so that somewhere between three and five thousand mice could live there happily.

We introduced four pairs of mice into this Utopia. It's like a new continent being invaded, being colonized. There was trouble at first as the individuals tried to learn the environment and each other, since they were strangers to each other. Then the population began to grow. It began increasing very fast. In fact, it doubled every 55 days, since these animals have a very high reproduction rate. It grew until the population was a little over 600 mice. This rate of doubling every 55 days started with the first group of young, which numbered about 20, and it went 20, 40, 80, 160 . . . very rapidly until there were over 600 mice.

All of a sudden, the population growth rate decreased; instead of taking 55–60 days to double, it took 250–300 days to double. Still, many more individuals were born until there were 2200 mice.

At that point, another shift occurred, like a change in physics—a phase shift. The population became stationary. This is where the ZPG movement is going—zero population growth. This became really zero. It became zero when many of the mice were still quite young. There were no deaths for a while, but no more young were produced either. We have studied several of these populations but have continued our observation only on the one which reached a peak of 2200 mice. For a year's time since this peak, the equivalent to 35 years in the human span, very few young were conceived and none reared. Now there are none conceived.

So what would the world of man be like if we were to look back and observe that there had been no young born for 35 years? You can see, at this time, in our mice that menopause in both males and females is being approached. Our population is dying off. It has dropped from 2200 to 1700 by natural aging processes. By the time the population drops to 1000, all individuals will have reached menopause. We anticipate that the population will go to zero.

That is just part of the story. Now why did these rapid phase shifts occur? There were never more than 150 mice in our Utopia. I have been calling them mice, but they weren't. There were never more than 150 mice in this total universe. We call them universes. The mice—to be a mouse—have to engage in activities necessary for survival. They have to be members of social groups, to get involved in their total society. In this physical space, the mice would tolerate only 14 social groups, each of about ten or a dozen mice of both sexes. The first 150 mice, including some of the initial colonizers, filled up this social space.

They produced a lot of young by the time of the first change in the rate of population growth, so that there were three times the number of living mouse bodies around as there were socially organized adults, and when they matured, there was no place to go socially, no place to get involved. They tried, but they were rejected. These individuals then withdrew psychologically and socially and became extremely violent in their attacks on each other. They were ignored by the socially dominant mice. They were just so many sticks and stones to the organized members who were real mice.

But for these individuals who had become non-mice, though they were once mice, the least change in the surrounding stimuli might trigger one mouse to attack an associate in some irrelevant type of unmeaningful, extremely intense aggression. And the mouse being attacked wouldn't flee. Everything was disoriented. These were very inactive, very withdrawn mice except for eating and drinking and flurries of intense violence. That's the first phase shift. This is when something says to us that there is something wrong about this system. But this is minimally very good. Getting violent is at least some kind of involvement.

Then some very strange things began happening while the last several hundred were born. As the young matured they never engaged in courtship behavior. They didn't conceive. They didn't fight. Animals that still were territorial or members of social groups paid no attention to them. These roughly 1500 mice, ten times the organized ones, grew up being non-mice from the beginning. They gave you the impression of being like autistic children and of still being juveniles even as they entered physical adulthood. Those animals who were blocked from the very beginning and rejected by their mothers had no opportunity for social involvement. So, as youth just developing, they emerged and tried to enter as juveniles into society. Every time they tried, they were interrupted by some associates.

Some of you are familiar with the early stages of child development and the theories of René Spitz and his theory of interruption of action cycle. There are so many individuals meeting each other, young individuals who never carry out anything complex without another mouse bumping into them. This is part of the problem, but we really get non-mice.

These individuals are unstressed. That's why we call them the beautiful ones. Their only activities are eating, drinking, and grooming themselves, so they keep physically fine. And my colleague, Dr. Axelrod, whom I mentioned just a few minutes ago, did win the Nobel Prize in medicine this year. He examined some of these animals and confirmed our suspicions that these beautiful ones, physiologically were unstressed. They have never been stressed. They don't know anything that is going on. These are images of the result of a kind of Utopia. These are real experiences on which we have to base judgment.

I may wander a little bit here, but most of you are concerned with education in some way. One of the reasons that I have thought about education is because of the present world situation. Many people think we are in a crisis that is so critical that we have no opportunity to gain real experience. There's no longer sufficient time. But how do you build into the educative process, with our own experiences, the ways of understanding the sorts of problems we may get into—one from which we can never return? This kind of study with mice is one that may help us look at such problems.

We'll look at man the same way we look at mice. We're now taking this very long time perspective to see where we are now and where man is. So, let's go back more than 100 million years ago and follow the lineage from which man himself stems. Piecing it together the best we can, let's look only at numbers and the size of animals. If we go back to this time, approximately 100 million years ago, there were probably one million individuals in the human lineage inhabiting a relatively small area, probably some place in Africa, possibly in Asia. There had been some migrations. But that's irrelevant for the present time. Over the next 100 million years, the size of the animal increased and the total world population of our ancestors increased to about four and one-half million. At the end of this long evolution, those individuals looked just like us. So this 100-million-year span showed a rather slow increase in which one thing was constant, and this was biomass. Probably the total amount of protoplasm, the total amount of flesh of our lineage, per square mile, through this whole 100-million-year span, varied somewhere between six and seven kilograms or somewhere around 15 pounds of flesh per square mile.

About 43,000 years ago, a sudden change took place. As we watch the numbers from that point of time on, there is a phase shift. The population increased rapidly, and we can describe it in this way: Most things in life are very simple. Now this is a basic philosophy. Life is very simple. The problem is trying to find out the simplicities. So let's take population and change in numbers. The equation which describes this can be stated in words: The population doubles over time. What was four and one-half million approaches four and one-half billion in less than 50,000 years. Each doubling of population required half the time of the previous doubling. That's the process. This pattern of population increase defines man, simply and totally. Everything else is dependent upon that. You start with the first doubling of four and one-half million to nine million; this took about 20,000 years. The next doubling took about 10,000, the next, 5,000, the next 2,500, and so on. We're in the tenth doubling now, requiring about 40 years for a doubling of world population. The next doubling will take only 20 years.

This ever shortening of the time required for the world population to double, in essence, describes man. Continuation of this process leads to an instantaneous doubling. This is impossible. Yet, this impossibility means that that which has been man for the last 50,000 years, culturally, (not biologically, because biologically man has been around for a long time) is about to end. So, that which enabled the breakthrough from being simply biological man to being human, which started 50,000 years ago, is coming to an end. And you can calculate when. It should end at about the end of the first quarter of the next century if what happened in the last 50,000 years continues. Man is over with. Period. This may or may not be so.

Let's look at it this way. We've got some abstractions here. One may mention biomass, an idea derived from wild life management and ecology. We take the number of animals, let's say rabbits, per square mile. Take the number of times the average weight of the rabbit and get a product of these. When W equals the average weight of a rabbit and N equals the number of rabbits per square mile, NW equals B where B is biomass. So there would be so many pounds of rabbits per square mile. That is the idea of biomass.

Over the time that man has been human, that is, over the past 50 thousand years, his body mass, his weight, has increased very little. And yet man has increased greatly in size, in his capacity or potentiality for creating and utilizing ideas. So the population problem is not just one of numbers only. It must take into account this other kind of increase in the magnitude of the individual, his potentiality for understanding and his potentiality for executing the ideas he has generated.

Let us use the symbol d'' to represent this new diameter of man, his potentiality for creating and utilizing ideas. Like weight, potentiality is a measure of the size of man. Again, if we let N represent the total number of men living at any one time, and if we let d'' represent the potentiality of the average individual at that time, then the product, Nd'', represents the total worth of all mankind. This total worth of all mankind may be said to be ideomass, I. $Nd'' = I$, or ideomass, just as $NW = B$, biomass. Through theoretical studies conducted in my laboratory, we have come to the conclusion that up to now every time the world population has gone through two doublings, the potentiality of the average individual doubles. Thus in the time that there has been a thousandfold increase in population, the potentiality of the individual has increased some thirtyfold. That is to say, the total worth of mankind has continued to increase as a result of increases in his numbers and in his potentiality.

These are rather simple relationships. Part of the insight says that about AD 2025, the further increasing of the total worth of mankind will come to an end. There is a limit here, just as there is a limit for so many rabbits in the fields per square mile. There is a limit to the total worth of mankind which will be reached. At this near date in the future, the total worth of mankind will become constant! And this worth is made up of just these two variables: the number of individuals and the worth of the individuals. It leaves us with three choices. I hope you can begin to see that. If this is so, simple mathematics reveals this relationship of $Nd'' = I$. The number of individuals times the average worth of the individual is the total worth of mankind. That total worth is becoming a constant.

We may continue increasing the human population to a point that determines the upper optimum population, which is about nine billion at most, with about three and one-half billion adults. This point will come early in the next century. If we let the population keep increasing, more and more and more people, the worth of the average individual, his potentiality or d'', will continually decline. He will be less aware of less and less. This is a judgment based on my examination of human evolution.

We can also take as our choice the zero population growth model developed by ecologists. However, I think this ZPG movement and this philosophy is an extremely insidious misapplication of a basic wild life management principle. It says: Beyond this point of attaining a world population with 3.5 billion adults, the numbers of people will forever remain constant. Now, if the worth of mankind is becoming constant, then the worth of the average individual will become constant also. So every social role, every expressive capacity, will be refilled with another individual just like the one whom death removes from the scene. This ZPG model will lead us into a rich and sensuous life, unchanging here afterwards. And there are models of this having happened. Take the lungfish, which are close to the stem of the beginning of land vertebrates. Lungfish live in Lake Manyara in Tanzania. This lake often dries up; you can drive trucks across it. Underneath are these fish, which have made a capsule, hiding from changes in the environment. They live there for a year or so until the rains come and their mud capsule softens. Then they come back up into the water. By this tactic they avoid all change. They have avoided all crises and opportunities for further adaptation.

And this is what we can become if we make the ZPG choice. Maybe that's the way to live. It's up to us. That is a value. We're concerned with the value of our future. Our other choice: We can say our value is in the individual. If this is so, we have to begin a slowly declining population after we have finally gotten worldwide in a total communication network, which is like Teilard de Chardin's concept of the noösphere, the total mind of man. We can do that by gradually declining the world population. We have the opportunity of further increasing the worth of the average individual.

So these are the kinds of things that we can look forward to in the future. Our studies of mice give us some insight if we take the first choice. It also probably tells us something if we take the second route.

There are three periods to the extent of evolution with which we are here concerned. The first lasted from the formation of the first social, primitive, group-living kind of mammals in our lineage some 100,000,000 years ago to a culmination some 50,000 years ago at the beginning of cultural man. The second is this little flash period of 40 to 50,000 years in which man is human. This next period that is coming, whatever it is, is beyond human, an extension of humanity into somewhat different form. It can't be a very long time to this third period. Which route of these three I mentioned earlier we will then follow will probably be irrevocably decided within 50 years. And once we're on this course, we won't be able to turn back.

It's the understanding of complex systems that provide us a warning. Once they get on a course, beyond a certain point, the probability of returning to some other state gets very difficult. So the point of no return for that system which is man and what he may become, is 50 to 75 years away, at most. But, where we are going depends on which of the three major paths we choose to follow.

The path is being decided right now, and the next 15 years are probably the most important in the decision process. I hope that is what President Nixon meant when he was talking about Revolution last night. I hope he was talking about $R_x$evolution. I think he was, in part, in the sense that he meant the designing of evolution. That's why now is so critical.

Someone asked me yesterday, in a discussion with some of the students, "Why don't we focus on the children under ten because creativity tends to get pretty well set by then?" Those individuals who are now under ten are important for our long-range future. But it is those people who have already reached ten who are already fixed, who will decide the total future. Because it is these people who will get into the decision process in the next 15 years. I think that's why the situation is so critical now. It is different

141

from anything that has happened in the past and anything that will happen in the future. It's just that we happen to be here now. Well, I could tell you more about mice—that's one way to get side-tracked from issues—and they do tell us a great deal.

But, that's the essential message. After a while you get evangelistic. I may be wrong and some of my colleagues who are thinking like this may also be wrong. But if we are right and these messages and insights are not examined, we could step beyond the point of no return. It's this kind of issue, getting a new perspective on life, which is very critical now. It raises many questions regarding education. We wonder whether the whole structure of primary and secondary education and life in academic worlds as here today, are appropriate to these sorts of problems. I wonder whether education is misfocused toward shorter and shorter decision times and simpler problems rather than toward the long-term problems which last hundreds of thousands of years and take more than any one individual's lifetime to solve. Unless the universities and the schools are being set up to approach the long-term problems, we certainly won't survive.

THE GREEN R_XEVOLUTION

Vistas opened by expanding walls
Reached with crutches electronic
Along paths buffered by compassion
As human neurones hand to hand
Bind the earth in noospheric net.

These things mice and shrews and rats
Provide us signposts, if we look
To involvements wished but wanting
Past autistic cozy blandishments
Into the twelve of us and others.

Suffering servants, deviants too
Creative templates offered free
Build ever new establishments
Encasing growing capabilities
Despite an N that ever dwindles.

This may but not assuredly will
Be the prospect of an earth
Now bounded, yet unbounded
As human and all other life
At a threshold finds a crisis.

Fifteen years are ours to say
What lies beyond the veil
Of one nine and eighty four
Senescence, stagnation, even death
Or awareness to be met.

John B. Calhoun
11 January 1971

W. W. "Woody" Hayes

Wayne W. "Woody" Hayes, the head football coach at Ohio State University, presented the Jennings Scholar Lecture, on February 27, 1971, at Bowling Green State University.

Under Coach Hayes' leadership the past 19 years, Ohio State football has achieved a degree of excellence never before attained in the school's history. His teams have won three national and five Big Ten championships and the three Rose Bowl games in which they have played.

Coach Hayes is best known for his strong running attacks. His philosophy of football incorporates many of the principles of military strategy. A tireless worker who has his players' best interests at heart, he is respected by his staff and his players for his honest, workmanlike approach to football.

At Denison University, Coach Hayes majored in English and history. He has an M.A. degree in education administration from Ohio State University.

SPORTS IN A CHANGING SOCIETY

A year ago when I was contacted about appearing here, the letter read something like this: "We are inviting outstanding educators." That played on my pride to the extent that I decided to come. I don't know if I would have if I had known I was going to be down in San Antonio, Texas, the day before and was going to lose my suitcase on my way here, and a few little things like that; but, actually, I am happy to be here. And because you have come here to a meeting on Saturday morning and are giving of your time, I'll try to see that it is not wasted.

I would like to explain to you what football means to me from an educational standpoint. If we can't see our profession in a broader sense than just blocking and tackling, or maybe teaching phonies, then I think we've missed the boat completely.

We talked about Professor Bode this morning, and some of the progressive educators at the Ohio State University who are really strong on student-centered schools. If you want to go back another 50 years, my dad started teaching with an eighth grade education. The type of school you taught in was usually a one-room school where you learned at your own speed and you learned by getting along with people outside your own peer group, in other words, older students. It's quite a learning process—one that we so largely ignore nowadays because we get in our own little peer group. A great tyranny exists, whether it's a meeting of Rotarians at the age of 50 or teenagers at the age of 15.

There is tremendous tyranny and, it takes a very strong person to break out of that tyranny. The thing we like best about football is that it is a personal game. It's an individual game first. We studied about the individual back in progressive education. That is exactly how I coach. Coaching is not of a team at all; it is a personal responsibility because we're going to make that off-tackle play of ours. We're very well known for that one. Actually it's not quite as simple as people would think because we reverse it. We don't just run it to the right. Sometimes we run it to the left.

Strosnider said not too long ago, "Coach, how long has that been the center of your offense?"

I said, "About 17 years."

He asked, "How come you've stuck to it that long?"

I said, "Because we're going to run that darn play until we get it right!" Sounds like a school teacher, doesn't it?

But actually on our plays it is all individual, because of that tackle whose prime job it is to handle the man over him, who is going to go through literally hundreds of maneuvers. If he is going to handle him, it first is done individually. If the fullback is going to make a goal, he will read the block of that tackle and know what is coming. It is not only personal for the tackle and the fullback, but it becomes a team element because, in that very simple play that the sportswriter likes to ridicule, we run it seven different ways. Yet when we study the films at the end of the season, in which we put each one of those plays one after the other, we find that never twice in the whole season did the day go the same way. So it becomes a very considered thing.

Now you get on into team play. And that tackle has to make a decision when he looks at that defense and sees who makes a call. He may say, "1) Get it, 2) rack it, 3) run it, 4) hit it," and for any one of these seven calls he needs a different blocking pattern.

Jim Otis, the fullback, used to complain in the huddle. He'd say, "Damn it, you're not yelling loud enough, I can't hear it because I'm one of them and I want to get there very quickly." He must use a cross-over step because it is the most direct action he can get to the point of attack. He's got to pull that defense out of position and wait until they get pulled out of position. He's got to use a leadstep and sort of curl into there. But he has to do what the tackle tells him to do after the quarterback has already told the play to run. Of course the quarterback may, as he did in the Rose Bowl one time, mistakenly call the automatic and call, "Hold one," "Hold one" means the same play to the other side. The tackle didn't get his call made quickly enough because 102,000 people were pretty loud. Fourth down and six inches to go, and he didn't get the right call made. So there is breakdown occasionally, but that is not what we anticipate.

We anticipate full-team play, so we start with the individual, who has to do his job, and then he has to tie it into the work of the other men. Now what formation you use depends on whether you can make some calls, because we try at the point of attack to establish a four to three blocking ratio, which means we have one extra blocker. But there are times when that halfback is not there. He's out there flinching to try to pull the defense out of position. The tackle has to do that because normally he can only make a call that is one-on-one at every position. How he may call, "Run it," which means just block the man over you, but more often he'll call a cross-it, which tends to pull one man out of position and let another fellow hit him in the stern seat while we trap the outside man.

You see it is a little bit technical. But it starts out individually. It's first what a man is going to do individually. The whole play breaks down if one man does not do his job. The Negro has made his greatest advancements in football because in this field a man is known for what he does. It's just that simple. If he can get the job done, he is going to play. If he can't, he'll sit on the bench with some other unfortunate individuals. He's not going to get in there because he's black, but he's not going to be kept out because he's black. If he can contribute to the team effort, he's going to be in there. That's why the Negro has gone farther in our sport than in any other area. True, he has been outstanding in other areas—music, stage, things like that—but he has gone farther in our sport because we judge him on what he does, and that's a pretty good way to judge people. If he cops out, or if the white man cops out, we won't use him again. We have no use for him. He can't play unless he's going to contribute to the immediate benefit of that team.

One other thing that we get from football: We have to live by the rules, and I know that connotes some things that are not popular in education or politics today. If we get a bad rule, we change it. But we have to live according to these rules. Along that line, as one of the professors said to me one day, "Tell me, coach, if the opposing team's halfback fields a punt of yours and breaks down the side line, comes right down past the bench, and goes all the way to score, except that as he passes the bench, he's just out of bounds just that far, is he really out of bounds?" Yes, he very obviously is out of bounds. We do have to live by rules, because without rules we have nothing.

Now that doesn't mean the situation can't change radically. I talked to a military man about the planes that sunk the Jap fleet. They went in and got four carriers in one day—three in the morning and one in the afternoon—and they had to get them. We sacrificed eight lives of great people to do it. It was all with team effort. When they went in there, they went in at 180 miles an hour. Now a plane would come in at 1,000 miles an hour. Now if we had a halfback who usually runs at 110 and then comes out some day and runs 102, our defenses would not hold up at all. The opponent obviously would beat us badly.

But we don't have great changes in physical ability. Now we do a much better job than we used to. One of the great things that has come into football in the last few years is our program against injuries. We've found that we can fix up knees almost as good as new with an operation, if the boy goes through the therapy work afterwards. If you do it after an operation, why not do it before, and avoid the injury altogether? We've done that. We've cut our injuries way down. We don't get really bad injuries on the field. If you were the mother of a football player, I would tell you one thing above all else: Make sure he has a good neck. Make sure because the neck is the basis of the worst injury one can ever get. Several years ago at the University of Minnesota, a father said to me, "You know, my three boys come in here every morning."

I said, "I know they do because I've seen all three of them."

He said, "How did you spot them?"

I said, "By their bull necks."

Coach Willman knows that a player must have a bull neck because it is the basis of the more serious injuries to the so-called brain stem and the brain itself. If you don't have men with bull necks, you better write notes to their mothers and tell them not to buy shirts for their sons until after they have come to school in the fall because we're going to build their necks up. So we have done a great job in reducing injuries. We worry much more about injuries when a youngster goes home for the week end than we do when he stays on the campus and plays football. Actually we've had more

149

injuries in basketball because of the hard floor. If a man has any trouble with the knee, it's going to show up in basketball because of coming down on the hard floor.

I'm not against basketball, because we love to have the kids play basketball. It does make them agile, and again it's a team game which they love. Kids love to bounce that ball, and they love to pass it off. All of our great quarterbacks have been great basketball players.

First it's the individual; then it's team play. We have the best laboratory course in team play of any class on the Ohio State campus. It's under emotional situations, it's the living now, the thing youngsters are always talking about; it's right now. The decision has to be made in about a twentieth or a tenth of a second, so many of these decisions are made by sight alone; they don't have time to do it by word of mouth. The player must, as we say, *read* what's happening up there. It is imperative that the quarterback always put the ball at the right place because the fullback pays no attention to the ball. He merely puts his arms there until he feels the ball. Then he takes the ball and goes in there because he must not look for the ball. He doesn't look *into* the hole, he looks *through* the hole, and by *through,* we're talking about peripheral vision. He has a very very short time to make decisions.

One of the great problems in society is that people will not make decisions. They are always searching for a life style in which they will not have to make decisions. But they find that these life styles do not exactly fit *them.* Then they go in search of another life style. We do not do well at making decisions. I think you have to make decisions by making decisions. You have to make decisions by practicing. I wrote a chapter in a book on decision making because the coach not only makes decisions, but he makes them for as many as 86,000 people. How do you make decisions? We won't go into the whole thing, but you always have to start at both ends of the line. Making a decision is a compromise. It must be a decision that is workable, or it is not much good. It must be a decision made in time to affect the situation, or it is no good. So many times people make darn good decisions for me on Monday!

I would like to talk now about some of the concomitants, in other words, some side effects of football. Among the concomitants this one of decisions is a great one. It does teach a youngster to make decisions in regard to other people and in regard to other factors. There is nothing that builds confidence like some decisions well made. Of course, nothing builds confidence better than success.

It's a learning situation on the football field. The friendships stick. Even 20 years later you can start talking as you did 20 years before. Now that's rather boring to your wives, of course, but your wives understand that sort of thing. So many times the friendships we make now, as Toppler points out in his *Future Shock,* are transient. You feel you're getting old, and you are getting old when you think of some good thing you should do and then immediately think of the reasons why you can't do it. You're getting old, whether it's at 23 or at 73. We need to say here, "You know you should do that. You're too darn lazy. For God's sake get on the ball." And then do it! Then you look around, and there are a lot of people behind you. I saved a man his job this fall. He was fired in the middle of the season and his team was to play the next week. An Athletic Board at a Big Ten University had been very cowardly, and they were going to back down and humiliate this person by firing him in the middle of the season. The man said he deserved to be fired, but that he deserved it at the end of the season, because he hadn't won enough. They're going to fire you if you're a coach and don't win, because people can unload their own quiet complexes and say, "See, he didn't win." But they are talking about their own lack of winning. And the coach that doesn't accept it had better get out of the profession. What was it Harry Truman said? "If you can't stand to eat, get out of the kitchen." But these men were totally wrong in humiliating him and knocking him out of the chance for another job by letting him go in the middle of the season. I knew his team would be steamed up because if they were the right kinds of kids, they weren't going to like any mistreatment of the coach. As I walked off the practice field on Friday, this pipsqueak kid, who had been writing for three months came up to me, and I said, "You're the guy that fired the coach here."

"Oh," he said, "I didn't do that."

I said, "You're a liar, and I'll tell you one other thing about your article. You know about as much about football as a hog does about Sunday." Because he didn't know what he was writing about. Then I turned my back on him and talked to the other writers. What do you call that? Positive reinforcement. You give credit for doing a good job and turn your back on the one who did a bad job. It worked, too. I told one man on my squad who was getting married one thing to never do. You should never beat your wife. And one worse thing: never ignore her. The one thing people cannot take is to be ignored. But I said this, "If I were fired for the same reason, I'd take it to court to see if there was cause to fire me in the middle of the season.

This writer had said that the players were down on their coach. But I was afraid I was going to find out the contrary and I did, because in their next game they played great ball. In other words, they followed their coach. After the game, the whole team walked right into the dressing room and voted unanimously that, if their coach didn't get to finish the season, they wouldn't play any more football. They took care of that situation in a hurry. The Athletic Board had to back down. They had been working on false information. At the end of the season, the coach was let go, and he should have been let go because he didn't win enough games. If you don't win enough games, you're going to be out of it—and that's all there is to our profession. It's a pressure profession. There's not any way to avoid it that I know of.

To get back to friendships on the field—these friendships are very lasting. That is one of the great problems in society today; the friendships.

These are not lasting, because not only do we have to make decisions fast, not only are the changes too accelerated, but our life styles force us to move from place to place so fast that we don't get to sink our feet. That's one of the big reasons we are becoming a pragmatic society. But the men who play football at times don't like the coach. At times, I prefer to be disliked because I find you take advantage of people you love. When a coach is pretty rough on a player, that player says, "I'll show that old so and so." Then he does exactly what I want him to do. I want to challenge him, but I want to challenge him for a definite reason, because I feel that any man that is not prepared for an ordeal will not do well. The occupation troops in Japan and Korea in the '50's did not do well for two reasons: They were not ready mentally or physically to do a good job. And of the men who were captured over there, 33 percent of them defected. That's the report that President Eisenhower withheld for four years. In those compounds, the man who squealed on his buddy to try to get an extra food allotment, who took the piece of carpet given to his buddy and pulled it over his head, died within 21 days. What do you call that? You call it withdrawal symptoms. When a man takes himself away from many people and tries to live alone, he dies. That'll happen to a baby. If no one pays any attention to that baby, other than to give it food, it'll die. The same thing happens to a man when he pulls the carpet over his head. He will die. Those are the withdrawal symptoms. Man cannot live alone.

A Cornell professor wrote a book which is a comparison between our grade-school education and Russian grade-school education. What he said, in effect, is that we do an excellent job of training the individual, whereas in Russian schools, if the youngster is tops in his school or in his town or in mathematics, this is a great honor for the schoolroom and for everybody in the class with him. For us, it is an individual honor. But right away you must translate it to the rest of the squad. Every All-American says, "I wouldn't be an All-American if it weren't for these men up front blocking me." Yesterday morning down in San Antonio, I called a youngster at 6:15 in the morning, and he said, "Coach, I'm going to come to Ohio State."

I told him, "Son, if you come to Ohio State you'll be a better back than you'd be any place else because you're going to play behind the greatest line any team ever had." And I honestly believe that. I believe it because we're getting some real quality kids. The one thing we have to have in their education is this great individual input. And then it comes out as a team output. It is so much of our education program and so much of our living. But we ignore that.

I don't believe anything worthwhile comes easily. Football shows a man what's inside him. The thing we find about every football player, is that a man is a better football player than he thinks he is. As a matter of fact, I've always said, and not entirely jokingly, that there is one man I'd never want to meet as a football coach, and that is Ralph Waldo Emerson. Here is a man who had a great ability to build a man up, who knew that the great strength is within the man and he must exploit it—he must use it. A fellow who can talk like that and get that across can build football teams that will come out on the field ten feet tall. Because a man is never worth a nickel unless he has great respect for himself. That's the thing football does. It shows a man what great power he has, particularly if he means to exert that power with other people. We had a coach on our staff who is the head coach out at William and Mary now. He used to use this expression so often: "A majority is one man with courage." Because courage is catching; leadership is catching. There are too many people today who cop out, who try to get along without their best effort. They talk about love, but love doesn't mean to them what it does to you and me. Love to me means only one thing: helping a person do something he is unable to do. If you do for him what he can do for himself, you'll destroy him. You're taking his initiative. I had two math teachers. One of them was great. He'd make me work hard. Good teaching is hard work. The other one would go to the board, work out the equation, and ask if we all got it. We'd all get it, and then we were ready to go again. That's the easy way. You don't learn anything, and if you do it's very little.

The thing you can do in football is teach a man what's inside him. So many of us manage to isolate ourselves. I don't need an automobile. I'd rather walk across campus than drive because I meet no one when I drive. And I get a little absent-minded, and I might get in trouble. But when I walk across campus I meet so many people who are not totally in my life style. That's how I learn. I don't learn by talking to people who nod their heads at everything I say or with whom I agree. I can't evaluate that way.

I'm also doing a little something about pollution, because pollution, you see, is me. The night before I left for San Antonio, I had a whole bag of cleaning out and my wife told me to go get it. When I got my shirts back, I had a whole basketful of junk: six straight pins, a piece of cardboard, some crepe paper, and cellophane. It looked pretty, but I don't need all that to wear. I had to get rid of it. Somebody has to get rid of all of it. And you know it takes seven times as much of that junk for us as it does for a Chinaman, so our problem is just seven times as much as his. You want to travel light, don't you? Well, that's not traveling light.

These problems are individual problems. I get so bitter when a group says, "We've got a problem here, so let's go to Washington and get a federal grant." That federal grant is coming right out of our pockets. I get so disgusted with people who say everything is wrong, but how many of them ever went down to the inner-city and tried to tutor some kid? That is hard work. But it pays off because now you are doing for a youngster something he cannot do for himself.

I said to a Lions' Group one time, "Our great mistake in Vietnam is that we didn't win. I've been over there four times and I want to go once more because I like the people I run into over there. They're great. You always hear about the My Lai incident. I've always been amazed there weren't more of them because recognition over there is darned difficult; you don't know who your enemy is. It was a fabulously great tragedy. I know one time I got into a barber's chair and got a hair cut, and the next year I went back to get a haircut and I asked, "What happened to that good barber that gave me such a good haircut?" The answer was that he didn't work there any more because he had turned out to be a V.C.

So recognition is a problem. We went over there to fight their war. They had problems, and we went over to fight for them. We weren't going to let them do it. Our machines were all too difficult for them to understand. That's where we made the mistake—not letting them do it. You can talk ethically or any way you want to about that; we were trying to give those folks their freedom. At least four Presidents thought that way, and I thought they were pretty smart men. Actually we didn't do such a good job over there. Are there any language teachers over there? It would never have happened if we had bothered to learn their language. The people who learn new languages do it to earn money. They learned our language so they could do business with us. We didn't bother to learn theirs. You cannot have any kind of understanding with a person unless you can talk on common ground. If they learn only your idioms, that's not good enough. We Americans have always been so lazy. We can pass out money. A man who married a German girl asked me the other day, "How did you get around Germany?"

I said, "It was easy. I ran into English whereever I went over there. Sure I had a little more money than they had. Every hotel had somebody who spoke English there; I had no trouble at all."

Now I did get down in a little Italian village on the side of a mountain one day. I was driving a German car with a German license on it, and the Italians thought there was a German in town. They couldn't speak to me, but we stood around the bar and we got along pretty well. You know what I thought of? They were great people. Not particularly lettered people, but you know I've always been amazed how well some unlettered people can think and evaluate.

That old fellow on the end of the broom in the gym—don't pass him by. He has watched a lot of people go by. He knows a lot more about what's going on than maybe somebody up in the staff meeting. So many of these unlettered people at least have had time to think and to evaluate. I'm always interested in those people. Who are the fellows I know best? Well, my garage man is one of them, and the barber is a pretty good friend, too. I stop by and talk to the bartender and almost never buy a drink, so I know he likes me. I learn from those people. They are the salt of the earth. So often we do not get to know people like that. Only look out for the people beneath you. If they are working for you, you may have some yes-men. They all agree with everything you say, and you learn nothing.

I find that when I talk to a youngster the greatest problem I have is listening. You know why? Because if he says something with which I don't agree, I start thinking of my rebutal, and I don't hear another word he says. That's no good. But if I can look at him, then look down at the floor, then look at the corners of his eyes, very often I can learn quite a bit. I may find out he knows more than he's talking about, or I may let him talk himself directly into a corner. Then even he knows that he is not thinking very straight.

Let's talk about the good teacher. What makes a good teacher? I know, and do you know why I know? I've talked to a lot of students. I never go into the Faculty Club but what I talk to the girl who serves me. These are great kids, great kids that are working their way through college. Education isn't coming easy for them. Are they going to make the most of it? You'd better believe they are. They have to work for it. And that's what we like about football. They work for it. We don't hand them the position; they work for it. I say to the girl, "Who is your best teacher?" The answer pops out almost automatically. I say, "Why?" Almost the first thing that comes out is that he makes the course work interesting. That work is always there: interesting. I had a niece, Mary, who was at Ohio State for several years, and she was a real good student. But it didn't look as if she was ever going to graduate because she just couldn't make up her mind which course she liked best. She liked everything they taught. There are students like that, and they have a real problem. So she got engaged to a boy, and I said, "I think you'd better graduate before you get married," and she graduated in a hurry. Motivation, you see, primary motivation.

Anyhow, Mary had a lady in a biology course. I asked, "How good is she."

Mary answered, "She's wonderful Uncle Woody, just wonderful."

Here's a lady nearing retirement. She wears her hair up in a bun, several years behind the times, she dresses drably, she is crippled a little in one leg, and she has a little trouble getting across campus. She isn't a pretty woman by the standards of what we might artifically call pretty. I said to Mary, "Why do you say she's good?"

Mary said, "In the first place, she knows her stuff. In the second place, she has a droll sense of humor and you have to keep listening or else you'll miss it. In the third place, she likes us."

So I made it a point the next time I was in the Faculty Club to sit down with this lady. The minute I talked about her students and biology, she lit up like a Christmas tree. I could see the very thing in her that Mary saw. Here is the great teacher.

One of the ladies down the block was telling about her son. Her husband was a doctor, and her son always wanted to be a doctor. In high school he started thinking, "I might want to major in English. I might want to be an English professor." Well, There had to be a reason. The reason was the teacher. So this lady went to the open house one evening and only then did she find that the English teacher was almost a total cripple in a wheelchair. Her son had never told her. Evidently he had never noticed it. But here was a great teacher who had captured his mind.

Whenever I talk to any teachers group, I say, "I would rather have a teacher steal money from my son's pocket than steal my son's enthusiasm."

How are students going to react to the teachers who are bent on getting out of the building at three in the afternoon, and the ones that say, "I'm teaching only because I'm here. I don't particularly like it." They're not going to like it at all. They're never going to like the course. Students are usually very charitable towards their teachers, but there is one thing they always do. Even if a teacher is too lazy to return the test paper or the theme or too lazy to grade the student, the student is never too lazy to grade the teacher. The student always grades the teacher. I know one student who is now a doctor. He made a C in history his first quarter as a freshman. I said to him, "How come you made a C in history? You're supposed to be a better student than that. Bad professor?"

He said, "No, Coach, great professor. I just goofed off and didn't study the right thing for the final, and all I deserved was a C."

I said, "Well, Carl, that might keep you out of medical college."

He said, "I hope it won't, but if it does, it's nobody's fault but mine."

I've had that experience a hundred times with kids. There is a fellow coming back to law school this fall. He'd been in the service four years; he was a captain back in 1965. He was in the Navy demolition movement off the west coast. He has a wife and two kids. I think he's nuts. But he asked to get into it. If there's a bomb scare, he leads his squad in there. They won't get a better lawyer, because here is a fearless leader, obviously. One day I said to him, "You were telling how good a professor a certain guy is. A couple of the other guys said he's no good at all."

Greg got mad. He said, "Those fellows don't know what they're talking about. If you believe that, then you come to class with me."

So I went to class with him. I knew he was right all the way; I just wanted to hear the professor. I wanted to see if he would stand up for what he believed. This man is retired now. I went to his last lecture. I should have been there long before that. This old fellow didn't like football, but he walked right over to the Faculty Club and practically cried when he said, "You know who came to my last lecture today? Woody Hayes, the football coach." He regarded it as a great compliment.

Last spring after we had had all that trouble on campus, I saw one man who I thought was just fabulous. He had hair a lot longer than my life style, sort of a boyish bob. I had heard him in faculty meetings. He was a lot more liberal than I was. He said, "I have taught and studied in many countries, but the freest place I have ever been is right here on the Ohio State campus. If we want to keep that freedom, we must keep this university open." And he had more to do with keeping this university open than anybody else. I went to his last class of the year in an auditorium about twice this size. People were sitting in the aisles. It was one of the most outstanding scenes of my college lifetime. He's a top-flight psychologist. Those kids stood up after the lecture and applauded for five minutes. He has that great ability to get to the kids.

I go to a basketball game, and it worries me when I hear my own stadium boo a player on the other team. This is not what sports is supposed to be about. I talked to a Greek lady who said she got in trouble in our stadium when she stood up and applauded. Someone said, "Sit down. That's the other team." She had a job on our campus with one of the physicians, so she was entitled to two tickets. She said it was amazing how many friends she got just before the tickets were given out. I've always been interested in our crowds, and I watch them very carefully. When a player on another team gets injured and is finally lifted to his feet because he is not badly hurt, I can always hear a sigh go through the stadium. "Thank God, he isn't hurt." Then they always applaud him. That's the way it should be.

If a team wants to win as a group, they have to become totally disciplined. There's one thing we have to learn above all else: that discipline starts with the individual. I picked a player off the field years ago because he wasn't playing good football. He kept saying "Come on me." What he was trying to do was rid himself of his guilt complex. He had no team spirit. If he had done his job, the team would have done its job. It's collective. And yet so many people miss that. The team is a great common denominator because the man who gets on that team is the one who can help us win. We overlook such superficialities as race, religion, ethnic background. We're in there to work for a common effort.

Now, I'm going to talk for a few minutes about the future. The acceleration of things is unbelievable. We're having great pains in this super technology, and it's going faster and faster. That's the whole problem. We can't always call this rapid growth an improvement. I was interested a couple of weeks ago when a man whom I knew quite well with great courage stopped the canal across Florida. Do you know who did it? The President. He stopped the canal because it was going to ruin the ecology of Florida. There might have been a lot of money made out of it. Don't underestimate that money, because you have to have money before you can have taxes. One thing that becomes very apparent today is that we're rapidly running out of money. We're going to have to compromise. You can't have schools if you don't have taxes. And you do not tax unless you have profits.

Dr. Nicholas Nyaradi

Dr. Nicholas Nyaradi, Director, School of International Studies at Bradley University, presented the Jennings Scholar Lecture on September 26, 1970, in the John C. Baker Center, Ohio University.

Born and educated in Hungary, Dr. Nyaradi came to the United States in 1949 and became an American citizen in 1955. He received two doctor's degrees from the Royal Hungarian University of Budapest—one in political sciences and one in jurisprudence. Dr. Nyaradi was an attorney for 13 years and the legal advisor and executive director of one of the largest banks in Hungary.

Having participated in the anti-Nazi underground movement in Hungary during World War II, he was asked to accept a position in Hungary's postwar coalition government. He was first the Under-Secretary of the Treasury and then the Minister of Finance of the Republic of Hungary until 1948, when, because of increasing Soviet pressure, he and his wife were forced to flee their native country.

Since coming to the United States, Dr. Nyaradi has written several articles for leading newspapers and magazines, among them the Saturday Evening Post, Fortune Magazine, and the Scripps-Howard newspapers. His book *My Ringside Seat in Moscow* was not only acclaimed one of the best books ever published on Russia but was also commended as an outstanding antisubversive document. Several of Dr. Nyaradi's articles and speeches have been inserted into the Congressional Record.

Dr. Nyaradi has a unique and profound knowledge of the Soviet Union. He spent seven months in Moscow negotiating a Russian reparation claim against Hungary. During these conferences he came to know personally many Soviet leaders. He is also well acquainted with many leading personalities in the United States, in Europe, and in the Middle East.

Besides this vast background of international experiences, Dr. Nyaradi has established himself as an educational and civic leader in the United States. For his work in connection with Hungarian relief activities, he received a diploma of appreciation from the American Red Cross signed

159

by its honorary chairman, President Eisenhower. Dr. Nyaradi is also a consultant for various government agencies and congressional committees.

His name is listed in *Who's Who in America, Who's Who in American Education,* and *International Who's Who.* The Freedoms Foundation at Valley Forge recently awarded him the George Washington Honorary Medal for his lectures throughout the country.

"THE ANATOMY OF DISSENT"

Last month I was invited to address a convocation at a small college in Indiana. I decided to drive, and suddenly my car developed engine trouble on the winding highways of the Hoosier state. It was late at night, the rain was pouring, and I was hopeless and helpless. Although I knew exactly what was wrong with my car, there wasn't a thing in the world I could do about it. The car manufacturers up there in Detroit are so very confident about their makes that they fail to include even a screwdriver in the equipment.

So I stood there on the edge of the road and on the edge of despair when suddenly one of those huge interstate trucks drove by, stopped, and the driver—one of those kind, always-smiling American truck drivers—readily climbed out of his cab to give me a helping hand in my trouble.

As the trucker was working on my engine, we started a conversation. I do not know how it happened, but he soon noticed the "Zsa Zsa Gabor" tyro delivery of my speech. And, really, I must admit, I wasn't talking to him in what you might call a strictly midwestern accent.

Suddenly the truck driver looked at me and said, "By the way, Buddy, what the hell are you doing here in the United States?"

I said, "Well, Buddy, this is a difficult question to answer."

Then I told him that originally I was the Secretary of the Treasury of the Republic of Hungary. But when the Russians took over my unfortunate native land, Stalin didn't like me, and I didn't like Stalin. They passed a death sentence over my head. I was offended and escaped Hungary.

Then I told him that due to the fact that I was fortunate enough to have two earned doctor's degrees—the one in jurisprudence and the other in political science—I was able to seek out for myself and my family a living in the United States. I became a writer, a lecturer, a radio and TV performer, and, then in 1965, I was asked to join the Foreign Policy Task Force of the Republican National Committee. In this capacity, I contributed the writing of the Foreign Policy Platform of the Republican Party, on the basis of which Mr. Nixon was then elected to the White House in 1968.

I also told him that in 1969, I was appointed as a consultant to the United States Department of State in the field of Eastern European and Soviet Affairs. I told him that, before and above all that, I am a university professor and a college administrator as the founder and director of the School of International Studies at Bradley University.

Listening to all of this, Buddy looked at me and said, "Wow, isn't this too bad? I thought you were at least a traveling salesman."

Well, my fellow teachers, the more I think about my conversation with Buddy, the more I feel that he was, after all, right. Because you might call me a traveling salesman, although the merchandise I am trying to sell you is very hard to sell indeed. Because it is cruel; because it is bitter; because it is hard; because it interferes with this easygoing, wonderful, American way of life of ours.

The name of my product is TRUTH . . . this horrible, ugly, cruel truth . . . as I saw it in my native land and in some 12 other countries, and among millions of people all over the world as it descended upon them in the form of a horrible, ruthless dictatorship. I am the traveling salesman of TRUTH because I see today the same horrible, dark shadow extending over our own country as it begins to engulf the heart, the mind, and the soul of our American people.

I see here, today, my fellow teachers, the fog . . . a fog of ignorance, of indifference, of complacency, of taking-for-granted attitude and of apathy descending upon our fellow Americans. And unless we are able to clear up this fog from the American mind, this fog inevitably will lead to blindness. And please remember the 3000-year-old Greek adage: "If the gods want to destroy someone, first they strike him with blindness."

Today, fog of confusion is descending upon our people in some of the most important aspects of our lives. On one side we hear outstanding, good-willing Americans telling us that we should completely forget about our commitments in the world. We must concentrate our efforts now on inner space instead of outer space. We have such tremendous problems ahead of us in our cities, in social welfare, in the problems of medical care for our people, that they have an absolute priority over everything else.

A distinguished senator, for instance, asked just recently that a new comprehensive medical program be introduced to all Americans, which would cost the astronomical figure of 58 billion dollars per year.

There isn't anybody in the world who sees more clearly the need of an adequate health insurance system than I do. Yet, at the same time, my fellow teachers, we have to maintain a measure of sober judgment, as we cannot allocate 25 percent of our total budget for this purpose alone. We also have to have other priorities, for we have to think about *all* the problems within our country, and we cannot neglect the problems which are towering on the international horizon of the United States.

My fellow teachers, I would like to ask you, if you would be so very kind, to drop a line either to the State Department or direct to the White House, and ask that President Nixon's *State of the World* message, which is a 180-page book, be sent to you. You will see there not only a full and honest explanation of the role our country plays in the world today, but also the somewhat subdued but increasing concern of the President about the tremendous expansion of Russian military might.

Ladies and gentlemen, during the time of the Cuban missile crisis, we had an eight to one superiority over the Soviet Union in the field of missiles and delivery vehicles, as a consequence of which we were able to call the bluff of Nikita Kruschev and could command him to withdraw his offensive missiles from the backyard of the United States, from the island of Cuba.

However, afterwards we adopted a very good-willing, a very honest, but somewhat naive philosophy. We believed that the reason why Russia

162

behaved like an international bull in the china shop, like in the adventure in Cuba, was because Russia had a tremendous inferiority complex because of our overwhelming military and industrial superiority. So the idea was that if we permitted Russia to catch up with us in nuclear armaments and completely stopped our own development in this field, then Russia would lose her aggressiveness and we would be buddy-buddy ever after.

In my opinion, however, this very honest and very good-willing philosophy made just about as much sense as if we had said that the best way to stop the crime wave in the United States was to permit the Mafia to arm themselves to the strength of the police. Because, if the Mafia achieved the same strength as the police, then it would lose its inferiority complex, and the crime wave would end at once and forever.

If you read the President's report you will see that Russia, unfortunately, was not satisfied with achieving parity with the United States, for today the Soviet Union is forging ahead relentlessly to achieve superiority over the United States. I don't want to go into the details of this report, which you should read, but let me tell you that, according to the estimate of the Secretary of Defense, Melvin Laird, if we are not able to reach some agreement on the limitation of armaments or if we do not increase our own defenses accordingly, then within the next five years the Soviet Union will have developed such a frightening first-strike capability that at the pressing of a button they will be able to destroy up to 140 million American lives without our having even the possibility of retaliating.

So as you see we have other priorities and obligations besides the very important problem of health insurance. No matter how overwhelming the issues of the environment, the fight against pollution, the ecology, the urban problems, the welfare problems, the medical problems are, yet there is also a problem which is simply not more and not less than the survival of the American people—the continued existence of the United States of America. During my seven-month-long ambassadorial mission in Moscow, I came to know personally more Russian government leaders than practically any other statesman or diplomat of the West. And to my great regret, I have to say that I came to know these men as understanding only one language . . . the language of iron determination. Everything else they mistake for weakness.

Now the best way for us to maneuver ourselves into the horrors of World War III is to create the false impression in the minds of the leaders of the Kremlin that we are afraid, that we are worried, and that we want peace at any price. Because, in this case, I can guarantee you that one day we shall be able to witness the explosion of enemy warheads over our American cities.

The only way for us to avoid World War III is to let those leaders know that we are ready, able, and willing to fight if and when they ever force us into it. Never before was the 2000-year-old Latin adage as true as it is today: "Si Vis Pacen Para Bellum"—"If you want peace, be prepared for war."

If after this you come to the conclusion that I am some kind of war hawk, please forget about it. In my frequent trips to Washington, I meet all sorts of birds. I have met the screaming hawks, I have come across the cooing, fluttering doves. And you have no idea how many chickens I saw there, too.

But let me also tell you that, if anyone knows, I know that war is hell. I still remember the horrors of World War I when I was a little boy as it swept over my native Austria-Hungary. How could I ever forget the terror of World War II when, as a member of the anti-Nazi underground movement, I stood up in the streets of Budapest to the henchmen of Adolph Hitler. I know that war is hell, and the last thing I want to see is that our two American-born children should one day experience one-tenth the suffering that their mother and I had to go through in our native Europe.

The second aspect of confusion, which even the President mentioned in his televised news conference three days ago, is the complete misunderstanding about our involvement in this tragic war in Vietnam. He pointed out that there are certain news commentators and TV personalities who simply don't want to understand that the action in Cambodia last spring and now the South Vietnamese action in Vietnam are the best ways to shorten the war.

Cambodia was used until five years ago by the North Vietnamese regular Communist army as a staging base against Saigon. When the American and South Vietnamese armies intervened in Cambodia last May, they destroyed these bases and, as a consequence of this, our fatalities have declined dramatically.

And when those commentators were crying—and so were certain politicians—that we had violated the neutrality of Cambodia and Laos, then we have to ask ourselves: *Who* violated *what?* Because, in spite of the fact that Cambodia and Laos were neutral by international agreements, for five years these countries served as the staging areas and transportation routes for the Communist army of North Vietnam. *Who* violated, therefore, the neutrality of these countries?

This reminds me of my favorite Hungarian joke, according to which when Johnny comes home from school, he is all messed up; his clothing is in shreds, and he sports a black ring around his right eye. Mother looks at him in horror and says, "Johnny, for goodness sake, were you again in a fight?"

Johnny admits, "Yes, Mother. Charlie beat me up."

And Mother says, "Well, Johnny, I told you a hundred million times never to get in a fight. Who started it?"

Johnny answers, howling, "Charlie started it. He was the first one to hit me back."

What the President is trying to do in Vietnam is very simple. He is trying to find a way in which we can honorably disengage ourselves from this tragic conflict without permitting South Vietnam to fall into the hands of its Communist aggressor.

There are a large number of people in this country who believe that we should set a "certain date" for American withdrawal. While I personally do not play poker, you might ask yourself the wisdom of or the strategy of the poker player who would show his hand to his opponent and let him know how long he has to hold out to win the game.

We hear about various distinguished senators who are introducing bills by which the President would not be permitted to commit troops. He cannot do this anyhow in connection with Cambodia and Laos, even in support of the South Vietnamese if they would decide to invade North Vietnam. While we are not supporting such a move, I am still asking you this question: When South Vietnam was the punching ball for North Vietnam's aggression for the last ten years, why would it be such an impossible thing to imagine if this unfortunate country were to repay in kind what it had suffered during all those ten years?

However, those of you who still remember the last years of World War II can imagine what would have been the American people's reactions if the United States Senate had adopted in 1944 a resolution by which it could have forbidden General Eisenhower to cross the River Rhine and to pursue the Nazis into their strongholds in Germany.

Or how would the American people have reacted 25 years ago to a Senate or House resolution in which General MacArthur would have been ordered to leave Okinawa and Hiroshima in Japanese hands, and in which he would not have been permitted to attack these Japanese bases in the Pacific Ocean?

Of course at that time we were fighting the Nazis and the Japanese militarists—two evil powers. But, may I ask you, when we are fighting today against Communist aggression, is this a different case?

The only thing I am objecting to is the application of double standards. There is a good old American slogan: "What is sauce for the goose is sauce for the gander."

At the same time, however, what our American people simply don't know—or do not want to recognize—is the fact that our stand in Vietnam was the result of the absolutely unanimous thinking and decision of three American Presidents: President Eisenhower, President Kennedy, and President Johnson. All three of them believed that it was overwhelmingly, absolutely important for the United States not to permit aggression to succeed in Southeast Asia. And now a fourth President, Mr. Nixon, joined the decision made by his predecessors when he declared that he is not going to permit peace to be turned into an American defeat, and he is not going to permit American withdrawal to be turned into an American humiliation.

Therefore, I am asking you what would have been the reason that four American Presidents, belonging to our two major political parties, made basically the same decision? Is it that these men were not wise enough to see what they were doing? Do you think that they were dishonest? Do you think that they were the captives of what is called the "industrial-military complex"? Of course you know very well that you cannot say such things about men of the stature of Eisenhower, Kennedy, Johnson, and Nixon! These men must have had a good reason for taking this stand, for not permitting aggression to prevail. What was the reason?

Red China, or as we call it officially The People's Republic of China is engaged today in an overwhelming attempt to reach nuclear superiority or at least parity with the countries which she regards as her two greatest rivals or perhaps even enemies: Russia and the United States.

Red China has already made considerable progress. She has a packable and deliverable atomic bomb. She was able to explode three or four nuclear devices with which she polluted the atmosphere to a greater extent than all the supersonic transport planes and all the automobile exhaust can do. (Interestingly enough, none of our ecologists ever mentioned what Red China did to the atmosphere when she exploded those "dirty" nuclear devices in the air.) Also, today, China is already orbiting a satellite around the globe.

Red China, whose government is both aggressive and irresponsible— please remember the basic thought in Mao-Tse-Tung's famous *Red Book:* "Political power grows out of the barrel of a gun"—has not yet reached an overwhelming nuclear capability. The only reason is that Red China has to use all her financial resources to buy food abroad for her teeming population of 750 million people. Today, Red China must import food; otherwise, her people would starve.

On the other side, the Rice Bowl of Southeast Asia is in the Mekong River Delta of South Vietnam. If the North Vietnamese Communists could extend their domination into South Vietnam, then this Rice Bowl would be at the disposal of The People's Republic of China; therefore, she could devote her full financial and economic strength to the expansion of her thermo-nuclear capability. In this case, our children and our grandchildren would be exposed 20 years sooner to the Chinese nuclear attack.

The real reason why 45,000 Americans have died in the defense of South Vietnam is to restrict the Chinese atomic gun from being pointed at the heads of our children and our grandchildren for years and decades to come.

There is, however, another aspect of this situation which shows you the confusion which is reigning supreme among our American people. In my position now I begin to see the clear evidence of the increased aggressiveness of both the Soviet Union and The People's Republic of China. We definitely want peace, but as the President has noted with considerable concern in his State of the World message, our prospects for peace as well as our negotiations and relationship with the Soviet Union do not show any improvement.

The reason for this is that the Soviet leaders came to the conclusion that the dissent, the explosion of bombs, the militancy which today had become commonplace in America indicates the beginning of the end of the United States as a world power. As I told you before, the leaders of the Kremlin respect only one thing, and that is iron determiniation.

You can read in your history books that when President Roosevelt had a discussion during World War II with Generalissimo Stalin, the President told Stalin what a great moral advantage it was for the Allies that the Vatican came in with a condemnation and denunciation of the cruelties committed by the Nazis. Then, ironically, Generalissimo Stalin asked, the President, "How many divisions does the Pope have?" The only thing *they* understand is strength.

When today the leaders of Russia and of Red China see what is going on here in the way of dissent, of opposition, of militancy, in the way of the exploding bombs, the shooting of the police, and all these demonstrations, then they come to the conclusion that the United States is weakening, that the United States is in its last stage of disintegration and decomposition, and this is the reason why they think that the time has come to increase the pressure upon the United States of America.

While I am presenting to you some of the unknown aspects of the anatomy of dissent, I am calling to your attention the disastrous effects of all this on our situation in the world, on our foreign policy. And, therefore, it will be worthwhile for us to explore the background, the reasons, and the causes behind this phenomenon which sometimes is called the "generation gap."

Let me tell you that in my position as both a university professor and a university administrator, I am not only interested but also involved in the affairs of our young people. So, therefore, I think I can tell you with full responsibility in this "Anatomy of Dissent" that it is my conviction that the overwhelming majority of our young people—at least 99 percent of them—are basically honest, goodwilling, straightforward young American men and women.

However, the tragedy is that this overwhelmingly honest group of our young people are suffering today from considerable weaknesses which make them the easy target for the troublemakers.

What are these weaknesses of the young generation today? The first is that they are so tremendously idealistic that their idealism borders upon naiveté. They walk down the road with their eyes fixed on Cloud Nine and do not see the rocks upon which they are tripping on the road. They do not really understand their position in the world. They do not understand their privileges in this country. They are dreamers in most cases. Why? Because so many of them have led a more or less sheltered life.

Only last week I had a conversation with my own son, John, who is a junior at Bradley University, and he is a cadet-captain in the Air Force ROTC. He has neatly trimmed hair, no moustache, no beard, no sideburns—and, amazingly enough, he wears clean shirts, too.

Johnny lives on campus, and around two o'clock in the morning he burst into our home; this is the time when we usually talk. This particular night he sat down on the side of my bed as I told him how pleased I am that he is enrolled in the Air Force ROTC program, because when he graduates, he will get his commission into the Air Force as a second lieutenant. With this he will get a $9500 a year job when some of his fellow classmates will be

167

walking the streets, still looking for positions or jobs.

And then Johnny looked at me with his big, dreamy brown eyes and said, "Oh, Dad, I don't think money is so important after all."

And I said, "Sure, Johnny, money is not important as long as you can drive up to the gasoline station and pay for the gasoline with Dad's credit card! And I am certain that money is not important as long as you can call your girlfriend in California, and I have the $7.50 toll charges on my telephone bill! But when it comes down to the hard realities of the world, the world is not as nice as you young dreamers imagine."

The second weakness of our young people I am sure will shock you because it is contrary to all you hear . . . that we have never before had such a well-informed, involved, tremendously well-educated, and highly intelligent young generation as we have today. Don't believe this. This is all baloney.

In many cases, unfortunately, our young people are abysmally ignorant. They do not know about their privilege of being born with the silver spoon of American citizenship in their mouths, and they do not know the conditions in this country and in the world. And let me tell you that each and every one of those kids—the best and the most honest ones—are firmly convinced that the American economic system which we call the free-enterprise economy, has outlived its usefulness, that it is dehumanizing the people, that American industry is polluting the atmosphere, that the American economy puts the almighty dollar on the throne and worships it. And therefore, according to them, it is inevitable that some kind of a socialism will replace the present American economy.

This was about the gist of the conversation which I had with the students of the college in Indiana after my presentation. I came to the conclusion that the students, no matter how honest they were, didn't know absolutely anything they were talking about. When I tried to find out from them what type of socialism they had in mind—whether it was a type of social democracy, the British type of Fabianist socialism, or the Russian and Cuban type of communist socialism, they didn't know.

So I asked them if they knew just what the situation was today in Cuba, and, of course, they didn't have an answer. Then I told them that they can study the results of a socialist economy just 90 miles to the south of the American boundary in Cuba, where it was established 12 years ago.

Cuba, until 1958, was the wealthiest among all the Latin American nations. While its government was a miserable, despicable, facist dictatorship, its economy was the strongest in Latin America. Cuba's main product was—as it is today—sugarcane. Its production in 1958 was about eight million metric tons per year. And today, 12 years and dozens of Castro speeches later, the production has fallen to about five million tons per year—40 per cent less than it was under the hated capitalistic system.

When I asked the students whether they knew what type of rationing system is in force today in Cuba, they, of course, didn't know. So I told them that today, at this very moment, each and every Cuban man and woman can buy for themselves per month four pounds of rice, two pounds of meat, a half pound of butter, and one bottle of beer. Accordingly, if a Cuban worker wants to buy his bottle of beer on the first day of the month, then for the rest of the month he is out of Schlitz and out of beer!

Then I asked the students, "Is this the type of economy, is this the type of economic system, is this the type of living standard that you want to have the American working man "enjoy"?

Yet, the most important shortcoming of our young people is really not their responsibility at all. It is the fault of their parents. The parents of our young generation today were young either during the depression years or during World War II. They went through very hard times, it is the desire of parents to always give their children something better than they had when they were their age. This is the reason that permissiveness has invaded the American family since World War II.

Those of you who are not only educators but also parents know that in order to bring up a child you have to keep him on a steady and very well-balanced diet. On one side, you have to give him love; and on the other side, you have to give him discipline. If you give him love only, you will raise wild jungle animals. And if you give him discipline only, your end product will be concentration-camp inmates. And you certainly do not want either of them.

However, the parents of these young people went overboard. They gave only love to their children also because they were influenced by the philosophies of certain baby doctors in Massachusetts who told them to let the little darlings run loose when they wanted to. The result: the bombs, the burnings of campuses, and the disorder on the streets.

After giving you the anatomy of dissent, I wouldn't be a good physician if I gave you only the diagnosis without giving you a prescription for the cure.

First of all, it is my conviction that permissiveness in the halls of Congress, permissiveness in the family, permissiveness in the courts, permissiveness among spineless school administrators who simply do not have the guts to enforce the rules in their schools has to come to an end.

I, in my own modest field, try to do something about it. Even with my present job in Washington, I still teach classes at Bradley University. I have in my classes only students who come from their own volition. Never in my 20-year career as a professor did I have a required class, as I don't want students to be held there by a rope. I have every semester between 250 and 300 senior and junior students enrolled in my classes.

When I begin to teach at the beginning of the school year, I always deliver a brief sermon to my students. This is what I tell them: "America was never a country of yes-men. This country became great, not because we all had the same ideas and because we agreed on everything, but because we always had different ideas, different viewpoints, different philosophies. Then we debated these issues, after which we reached either a compromise or a solution or both."

169

So I tell the students that as an American college professor, it is my duty to give them the facts, the best way I can, but I have also the privilege of telling them my conclusions, my opinions. Naturally, they will have to know the facts, and then, when the facts are asked for on the examination, there cannot be any difference between us.

However, when it comes to opinion, if they voice opinions which are 180 degrees different than my own, not only will I not punish them for thinking differently than I do, but I will give them a double "A."

Accordingly, in my classes I am not only going to permit, but I am going to encourage dissent, discussions, and oppositions, as long as they are presented in the spirit of American academic freedom, in the spirit of a gentleman-like attitude, mutual respect, and on the basis of intellectual honesty.

Then I continue, if some of you should have the mistaken idea one day of standing here in the door of this classroom and trying to prevent me from entering and fulfilling my contractural obligations of teaching, or if you should try to prevent your fellow students from receiving the education which they have paid for, then, so help me the Lord, I am going to call the police and have you all thrown into jail!''

Now, ladies and gentlemen, as a consequence of this, we do not have a "generation gap" in my classes. The process of education goes ahead smoothly, in the friendlist possible way. We constantly discuss, we constantly debate, but we love each other and we respect each other.

This is possibly the reason why last May, when I celebrated my birthday (I'm not going to relate to you which one it was) and when I entered the lecture hall, this is what I saw: Balloons were floating in the air, streamers were hanging from the fixtures, confetti was thrown at me, and on the blackboard there was a huge sign reading: "Happy Birthday, Nicky-Baby!"

At the same time, we all know that one ounce of prevention is worth more than a pound of cure. Therefore, we have to provide for a complete change in our curricula through a special emphasis in our primary and secondary education.

Today we are faced with a brand-new problem, and this is that the 18-year-olds have received the right to vote by an act of Congress which has now been confirmed by the Supreme Court.

Ladies and gentlemen, I have supported this legislation, because I felt that it was extremely important that we should remove this confrontation from the street corners and from the campuses and put it where it belongs-—in the ballot box.

Yet, at the same time, now that these young people have received the privilege of voting, I am wondering if they have the adequate knowledge and preparation to take care of living up to this great privilege, which is, at the same time, a serious duty.

My fellow teachers, the word "democracy"—the word of which we are so very proud, and rightly so—is a Greek word, composed of two words: "demos" meaning "the people" and "kratia" meaning "the rule . . ."

170

"Demos kratia"—the rule of the people. However, please remember, that the world "democracy" means not only the privilege to participate, democracy means not only the right to guide and to lead, but democracy means also the obligation to learn, democracy means also the duty to know.

How will these young people be able to make up their minds in casting their votes by which indirectly they will decide the most important problem which the world faces today? They do not have the background; they do not have the facts. They do not know the details.

Therefore, it is extremely important that in the earliest grades we should introduce certain aspects by which our students will receive an adequate background. By the time of their high school graduation, they should know three very important aspects: America's role in the world today, the working and the blessing of our American constitutional system of government, and the structure and advantages of the American economy.

Ladies and gentlemen, we can start this as early as the kindergarten. In one of the fine Jennings Scholar meetings in which we are participating, a young teacher asked me, "Well, Doctor, I have in my kindergarten class five-year-old toddlers. How can I explain this to them?"

I said, "Madam, I can remember when our kids were in kindergarten, and they had, around ten o-clock in the morning, a little "pause which refreshes." The kids were told to lie down on the carpets or to sit on their little stools, and the teacher served them milk and some crackers. How would it be if you asked the children, "Did you like the milk?" When 20 pairs of blue or brown eyes stared at you after hearing such a question, you could say, "Did you ever think about it, that of the approximately 1200 million children in the world, you are among the very few who have not only seen but also, tasted milk in their lives!"

We have to educate our kids to compare. What we have to educate them in is not hatred or negativism against different people, different colors, different races, different creeds, different religions. Our trouble is that there is too much negativism in our country today. On the one side you see the anti-blacks, then you see the anti-whites, the anti-Mexican-Americans, the anti-Catholics, the anti-Protestants, and anti-Jews, the anti-everything people.

Please remember that never in the course of history was a cause won by being merely "anti." If we want to survive, we have to become strongly and positively "pro" something, instead of being just "anti" something. This is the approach which you can inculcate into the minds of those little ones— even at the kindergarten age.

The reason why I am privileged to work with the Martha Holden Jennings Foundation is that we think that this is the most important instrument by which I can reach the most important people in this country—the teachers.

You and I, the teachers of America, are more important than the highest elected officials of our government, than the members of the Senate or the House of Representatives. We are more important than the captains of industry; we are more important than the bank president. Why? Because

171

you and I deal with the most important commodity, the greatest treasure which this country has: the young people of America.

Ladies and gentlemen, your work in the classrooms will determine the future shape of our country, the future shape of the world, in which you, our children, and our grandchildren will live for decades and decades to come.

Therefore my work with the Martha Holden Jennings Foundation results not just in meeting you here. We have also developed a program for you when you become the "alumni" and when we hold a regular workshop for you, discussing, more in detail, these particular aspects.

Now, ladies and gentlemen, I am asking, begging, and cajoling you and the Martha Holden Jennings Foundation, that, after this magnificent rapport we have developed with the teachers of Ohio, we should concentrate now, also, on the school administrators and on the members and presidents of the school boards.

I am asking, now, for a deliberate new effort of expanding the curricula of our public schools which in view of this new law of the 18-year-old vote will make it possible to give our young people an adequate, nonpartisan, non-ideological, completely factual presentation of those problems which they will be privileged to decide.

Now, my friends, you might think that what you have heard here is very hard, very cruel; some of you may even call it a controversial type of address. Yet, I have two very important reasons why I told you all this.

When my wife and I, together with millions and millions of people from all over the world, were forced to flee from tyranny and dictatorship, many of us still had a place to come—the United States of America.

But, in all humility, my fellow teachers, I am asking you, "Where will *you* go if such a terrible thing should happen *here?*" There is no place left in the world, so we've got to make this country as good as it can be, as safe as possible because this is our last hope. This is the last hope of decency; this is the last hope of democracy, of freedom, and of the God-fearing attitude in the world.

The second reason for my being so forceful is that 17 years ago, my wife and I stood in the Federal Courtroom of Peoria taking our oaths for American citizenship. At that time, inevitably, I had to ask myself a very pertinent question: How shall I ever be able to repay this country for the tremendous privileges which I am receiving here today? Freedom instead of slavery in my native Hungary. Opportunity instead of oppression in my native Hungary. Life instead of death in my native Hungary. How shall I ever be able to repay this country for all of this?

And then I came up with the answer. The only thing that I can give is knowledge, understanding, comparison, and before and above all, appreciation. And ever since I have only two overwhelming feelings left in my heart: The one is deep humility and the other is everlasting gratitude for being a citizen of this maligned country.

God bless you all and thank you all so much for listening.

Judge Philip B. Gilliam

One of the nation's leading authorities on the prevention of juvenile delinquency, Judge Philip B. Gilliam, gave the Jennings Scholar Lecture on April 17, 1971, at Bowling Green State University.

Judge Gilliam has heard more than 150,000 cases in the 34 years he has served as a judge in Denver, Colorado. In addition to his judicial duties, he has been an instructor in sociology and in domestic relations and family law at the University of Denver.

A graduate of the University of Denver Law School, he was admitted to the Colorado Bar in 1932.

In 1962 Judge Gilliam was appointed special advisor to President Kennedy's Committee on Delinquency and chairman of the Governor's Citizen's Committee on Delinquency. In 1968 the National Council of Juvenile Judges presented him with the Meritorious Service Award as the outstanding Juvenile Court Judge in the United States. He continues to serve as special advisor to various organizations and committees dealing with delinquency.

"CORRECTIVE TREATMENT vs. PUNITIVE JUSTICE"

I feel highly complimented that I should be asked to be with you and talk to you a little while about some things that might be of interest to you. I was so glad I accepted the invitation: First, because of my great admiration for the teaching profession and the Jennings Series. I think the idea will be copied in many states, and congratulations to you as scholars in the Jennings Lecture Series.

Another reason I am so glad to be here—I'll never see you in a courtroom. I deal with crime. I deal with delinquency. I deal with broken homes. I deal with broken people. I deal with the tears of the big city. I deal with the slag in the furnace, the results of poor planning and poor method. I deal with what's left over, and when I was asked to be here today I was thinking of the great contrast between the good and evil of my life.

I am glad to be here, for you have been so very friendly. I sometimes think it is a little difficult for a judge to be friendly. I have been a judge so long in the City of Denver it seems to me I have sent most of the people of Denver to jail. I never know if I should shake hands or duck!

It's been a good life, as I look back over the years. There's a tendency when we leave our home town to reminisce, and I realize now that I have been a judge for 35 years. It went by so very quickly. Life is a very fleeting thing; it seems like only yesterday when I was appointed in the criminal courts, and yet that was more than 30 years ago. And as I look back over those years I realize now that I have heard over 150,000 cases. You think of all the drunks and narcotics, thefts, gambling, stick-ups, robberies, murderers, drunk drivers; you think of all the dented fenders and all the girls who gave up babies for adoption. There were more than 30,000 girls who appeared in my court to relinquish babies; little kids who cried in a far western city. And then you think of all the wonderful people who adopted children. They were the nicest people I ever met. They loved those children so deeply. And then the very unfortunate children who were not adopted. And then you think of all the juvenile delinquents—38,000 kids in trouble. It was like a big stadium filled with law-breakers and I was the judge. Do you often wonder what makes a good person; what makes a bad person? You never exactly know, you only wish you had some magic way of solving the problems of people. Wouldn't it be wonderful to have a magic sulfa-drug for anti-social behavior? But you don't have that and you realize that you lose so many cases. You only wish you had a better solution, because these kids don't go to college; so many of them go to penitentiaries. You meet them later in the penitentiary and they all wave at you and say, "Hey Judge, remember when I was in your court? I was a kid, Judge."

And, you look at the man behind the bars and you wonder why you didn't do a better job. And then you think of all the family fights and the people who loved each other deeply and how they hated each other in the courtroom. And the battered, beat-up children, the little babies with the broken arms, the non-support cases, guardianships and the very young who married too soon. You realize you did run the House of Grief in a large city. I am sure many people would say, "Judge, you must become a cynic; you must become hard in dealing with the tragic side of life." And yet, I don't think you do.

It seems to me that the most unfair people in the world are hermits. The most intolerant people live in ivory towers. God was good to me. He gave me a very wonderful job, and I am glad that I was in the arena. The more I work with people the better I like them. There is something dignified about the individual. People are important. The lowliest man has the image of God, and God was so good to me to put me in that position. The only ones I worry about in my home town are the Chamber of Commerce. They are always going to clean up Larimer Street. Larimer Street is so tough that a cat with a tail is a tourist. And yet they're my customers. When I go down on "Tough Street" everybody knows me and everybody waves at me. I guess they're not so bad. I know when I was a kid I used to play cops and robbers. They do the same thing on "Tough Street," except they use real cops. I remember one time I went down on the street and I saw a little boy sitting on the curb drinking out of a bottle of beer and smoking a cigar, and I said, "Son, you shouldn't drink and you shouldn't smoke, and besides, why aren't you in school?" He said, "Damnit, Judge, I'm only four years old!"

I am so very happy that I was a Judge of Denver's Juvenile Court. The Denver Juvenile Court and the Chicago Court were the first juvenile courts of the world. I like the philosophy of these courts. I like the story of my predecessor, Ben B. Lindsey. He was a noisy, fiesty, one-man band. He was the Greatest Show on Earth.

It makes you feel good to be a judge. You wear a black robe, you walk into the courtroom, the bailiff raps the gavel, "Hear ye, hear ye, This Honorable Court now open and ready for the transaction of business." Everybody stands up and you sit down. It makes you feel very important. And we follow the law from the Common Law of England, the law that came down through time immemorial. The lawyers, the courts, the judges, live by precedent; what has gone before; things decided.

When you argue a case in law, you pick up a book and say, "If the Court please, this has been decided," and you are bound to follow, but sometimes the law gets into a rut. It's like the streets of Boston. They were started by a cow, and the cow walked along the path and the people followed. And then they built the buildings along the path, and there was a precedent. If you've ever been to Boston you can understand the winding streets. The law is like that sometimes. We get into a rut and we follow the winding path.

I presume that happened from the standpoint of children in the early days. We used to try a child the same way you try an adult. It was "The People of the State *against* John Jones." That's an awful lot of people to have against you at one time. Like the colored boy said, "Lord, what a majority!" I can actually see Ben Lindsey in the early days as he took the bench. He heard the rapping of the gavel, "Hear ye, hear ye, ----- This Honorable Court -----" and there stood Johnny. Johnny was only 10 years of age.

Lindsey was trained in the Common Law and knew that he had to go ahead as had been done hundreds of years before. So, he turned to the clerk and said, "Arraign the prisoner." The clerk, being very legalistic, said, "The District Attorney in and for the Second Judicial District does allege that you did break and enter a dwelling house of another with intent to commit a felony therein contrary to the statutes in such case made and provided and against the peace and dignity of the People of the State of Colorado—how sayest you plead?" Johnny looked up and said, "I beg your pardon." That ruined it!

Ben looked at the little boy and said, "Let us take a recess." He went into his chambers and said, "I would like to have a court that does something *for* people instead of *to* people. I would like the name of the action to be "The People of the State in the *Interest* of the Child. I would like to be able to find out what his teacher thought. I would like to find out about his father and his mother, and find out what kind of environment he came from. Then I would like to be able to do something *for* him."

The lawyers and judges said, "You can't do this, Ben. We have been doing it this way for hundreds of years and you're bound to follow." But, Ben was the greatest show on earth. He said, I am going to do it!"—and he did! He went all over the world and he talked about juvenile courts. Wherever I go in the world I am so glad when people ask, "Were you in the same court that Ben Lindsey started?" It makes me feel so good that I should follow such a wonderful person.

There are a lot of things that I didn't like about Ben Lindsey: He was very controversial, but he lived all of the time. He was an extraordinary person, and brought the juvenile courts to every civilized nation of the world. One of the greatest innovations in law since the Magna Carta. May his name live forever.

When I was asked to talk today, I was thinking in my own mind, "Well, what could I talk about?" So many times we're asked to make speeches, we read a book, we read a profound thought, we come to an audience and say, "This I believe." You didn't ask me to do that, you said, "Judge, you have been a judge for many years, you tell us how you feel about these things." One thing I know is that we become very impersonal. It is hard for you and I to know each other.

There is a new book out "Who Needs People?" I am afraid that we walk the lonely road. A woman is beat up on the street and everybody shuts their doors. The police officer is being attacked and no one helps. The world becomes more impersonal, but it was never impersonal with me. I run the House of Grief in a large city. I deal with the tears of the town and when I see what happens to people from the standpoint of crime and delinquency, from the standpoint of broken homes; no it was never impersonal.

I went around the world one time for the State Department. I lectured in many countries in the Far East. I debated with Communism. But, the thing that impressed me so very much is that when I looked out of my room at night in India I would see thousands of people lying in the streets. It was the only home they had ever had—a cobblestone for a pillow. The little guys and dolls would hang onto you and say, "I'm so hungry." When you come back to this country, you see the beautiful fields, wonderful cities, and the greatest standard of living that the world has ever known. And yet so many people seem to be unhappy. We choose up sides, there is a tiger in the streets. It is hard for you to understand this, and probably our lack of understanding is the fact that we never suffered too much adversity. I read a poem one time—

> "I walked a mile with pleasure,
> She chatted all the way—
> But left me none the wiser,
> For all she had to say.
> I walked a mile with sorrow,
> Ne'er a word said she—
> But oh, the things she taught me,
> When sorrow walked with me."

Well, I find happiness in connection with my work because I see so very much grief and so very much sorrow. As a result, the good looks so very, very good to me. I remember in the "Spoon River Anthology" it said:

> *"Choose your own good and call it good, for I never can make you see that no one knows what is good who knows not what was bad—and no ones knows what is true who knows not what was false."*

"Well, I have seen the false and I have seen the bad all my life, and as a result I have become very happy in connection with my work.

I realize that I came from a very fine family. My father was the greatest fellow you ever saw. He studied for the ministry in North Carolina, but he did not go on in that—he bought a gold mine in Colorado. There was only one problem with that mine. There wasn't any gold. It had a beautiful view. My father was a fun-loving, creative, intelligent, well-educated person, and the world was mine. I'm so glad he wasn't a bum. My mother came over from Scotland, and she met him in Cripple Creek. She was a delightful person and loved my father deeply. He found that Gold—and the world was mine! I went to a great university and had the power of knowledge.

I married the nicest girl I ever met. She's a doll. I have two sons in college and two little girls I adopted. I live in a beautiful home, and I'm the luckiest guy in the world. You see, I saw the people cry that day—I sent thousands of people to institutions. Yes, I saw the bad, and the good looked so very good to me.

When I was asked to talk today, I was thinking in my own mind, "Well, what could I talk about." I go to work every day in the busiest court in Colorado. I have over 100 employees in connection with my office. The first cases are the giving up of babies for adoption. There used to be 20 or 30 girls a month, but not anymore. There are over 100 girls per month who appear before me. Little kids who come to a far western city and cry in a judge's office as they give up their babies. I clear titles to people. Everything is being taken down by a court reporter.—"Remember, little girl, you'll never be able to change your mind. You will never be able to find out where your baby goes." The little girl breaks down. There were 30,000 little girls who appeared before me to give up babies. You wonder why we're not a little kinder to each other. Everybody wanted to adopt a baby. Everybody wanted a blue-eyed curly haired youngster,—but some babies were not that way. Some were dark, some defective, and no one wanted them.

When I go to the State Children's Home the children run up and grab me and say, "Why didn't I get adopted, Judge?" You realize there is not much equality in the world. It seems to me it is the inequality of the world that creates charity. When you have so many good things given to you they belong to the world. Certainly it belongs to the child that we deal with in juvenile courts. I knew the doctor at the State Home who put up a sign over the nursery for unwanted children: "These babies are to be loved every half hour." No, I don't believe in equality.

The next cases are the juvenile delinquents. You know we put out an awful lot of "bunk" about delinquency. I have heard over 38,000 kids in trouble, and for years they told me that there was no such thing as a "bad boy." Sometimes I think "They're meaner than Hell"—I say that affectionately.

Do you ever realize what a juvenile delinquent looks like? Do you realize that he is trained, ordinarily, by the greatest expert in the world? If you think you are good in your job, you should see the real experts on the other side of the fence. Teaching them every vile trick in the trade. After 15 years of training there is nothing easy about that youngster. He is the meanest kid in town! It takes a lot of good probation officers, a lot of dedicated people, great policemen, teachers, good parole officers and great facilities to fight crime.

Sometimes I think we over-simplify the business of fighting crime. We give the impression to people that we deal with simple problems and we have a simple solution on how to handle that problem. I never found them that way. I found them the most difficult children you could possibly deal with, and believe me it takes a great deal of help, money, intelligence and brains to fight what crime does to the American people.

I find from my own experience, whenever you simplify crime, whenever you simplify deliquency—by giving the impression to people that there is nothing really serious about our problem, that there is no such thing as a bad boy, you never get very far. I think you should actually get out to the people and explain what crime does to people, the broken homes, the cost from the standpoint of morality, from the standpoint of money and finance. No, I don't think we should over-simplify this, I think that we should actually bring the facts to the people so they will know that there is nothing simple about crime.

There is a great feeling at the present time that judges should throw people in jail. Everyone is demanding of the judge—"get tough" and it makes a very popular appeal. Another simplification! I have had to send thousands of people to institutions and jails in the last 35 years. I am ashamed of myself—what I did to them. No, my kids don't go to college —they go to penitentiaries. Then I meet them later on in the Big House. I wonder if I was at fault in what happened to them.

Disregarding the morality of the situation, every time I send a boy to the Training School it costs the taxpayers more than $7,000. Five thousand dollars for one little fellow for one year in a training school. You can send them to college cheaper than that! Sometimes it is said it does not really cost more than $2,000 or $3,000, but when you consider the improvements, the interest on the money, the depreciation, the appropriation from the Legislature, I don't think there are any children in any state institution who cost less than $7,000. However, that is not all. It would be alright, if you solved the problem, but so many times they graduate to reformatories, and then on to penitentiaries. According to the FBI, it costs more than $40,000 to send a man to the penitentiary. Yet, on the other hand, someone will come out in the paper and say, "The way to solve crime is to throw them in jail—publicize them." Believe me, we create monsters!

Don't get the impression that I am overly lenient in connection with my work. I realize there are some people who have to be confined. I am writing a book now, "These Will Kill." These are the sociopaths I have dealt with. It is surprising how accurate I am. It is not a question of getting tough or easy. It is a question of common sense.

For hundreds of years we have studied the problems of crime and delinquency. We come up with many solutions. One of the finest approaches was the classical approach. This was advocated by Cesare Becaria many, many years ago. In his book, "Crime and Punishment," published in 1764, he proposed an antidote to the arbitrary imposition of penalties according to the whim of individual judges of the day. Becaria, like his contemporaries, had embraced the doctrine of free will and its corollary, that each individual is morally responsible for his act. Thus, the punishment should fit the crime. That is, to be appropriate to the moral guilt, whether the criminal was rich or poor. Assuming that everyone prefers pleasure to pain, Becaria said that no one would engage in criminal acts unless he anticipated that the pleasurable consequences would out-weigh the painful ones. Therefore, the logical way to prevent crime would be to impose penalties painful enough to deter it. The degree of punishment must be severe enough to out-weigh the pleasurable effect of crime. Now, you understand that there was a lot of common sense in this theory. I don't think we can arbitrarily say that punishment does not deter. I think it all depends on the circumstances.

However, as time went on, there were many theories and many approaches to the problems of crime and the causes of crime. Lombroso, around 1900, felt that the emphasis should be shifted from the criminal act to the criminal himself, that he could predict crime by the shape of the head, etc. Again, this was part of the neo-classical school. If the person had protruding ears, abundant hair, low brow, broad cheekbones, and so forth, it was a prediction of crime. There were many theories given forth on the problem of crime. Sometimes they blamed it on the nerve centers and glands. Sigmund Freud didn't think anyone was responsible for his misdeeds.

When it all comes down to the basic causes of crime, you see there is a lot of truth in all of this. We have our psychological approaches, our sociological approaches, our physiological approaches. Maybe we should research more in the field of anthropology. The main thing is this, if you study these great authors and these books, over the years, you look at the various plans presented to the public on the causes and cures of crime, and you find there is an element of truth in most of them. From my own experience, I have never gone along with the idea of getting tough—that this solves the problems of crime. The danger, of course, is the danger of over-simplicity.

If I could point with pride and say that the children I sent to the Training School became good citizens, then I would know possibly that this was the better approach. But, I am very sorry, I cannot. The rate of recidivism in the institution to the penitentiary was appalling, and over the 35 years I have been on the bench, I have felt there must be a better way of solving this problem. No, I don't think it is a matter of simplicity.

The only true answer I have ever found was to have dedicated probation officers, good policemen, good parole officers, good social workers, good teachers and good parents. Nine out of ten of the boys and girls I placed on probation did not repeat. They were not lost causes. They were not sent to institutions. And I felt very glad that I could help them with their problems. I am glad I did not waste the taxpayers' money by sending thousands of youngsters to jail. No, I don't think the solution is to lock people up, or get tough. In the first place, we cannot afford it. I would break the city and state by locking up everyone who comes before me. On the other hand, a judge who turns everyone loose is also a serious problem, the same as the judge who locks everyone up in jail or in an institution.

Denver has been good to me. This year they gave me over a million dollars to enlarge the Juvenile Hall. It is one of the finest detention homes in the world. I know, because one boy had been in eleven detention homes. We call him the "Duncan Hines" of detention. He said it was the best! I go out there every day. I am very proud. I feel like the superintendent of schools, and I learn a lot. I was out there not long ago, and I said to one boy, "What's wrong with the boy in the corner?" He said, "he's a psycho-ceramic." I knew I shouldn't ask, but I did. I said, "What's a psycho-ceramic?" He said, "Judge, that's a crack-pot."

In the afternoon you listen to the family fights, the neglect, and you look at all those people who used to love each other—now they hate each other in the courtroom. One man said, "Judge, I always pay my alimony right on the dot." I said, "Why are you so prompt?" He said, "Judge, I didn't want that woman to repossess me." And I looked at her and I could get the point.

Toward the end of the day you shut the door. Your secretary knocks on the door and says, "Judge, somebody wants to get married." You think "What for?" And you go out at night and talk about child welfare. You wonder whether you really know much about it. I think the only ones who know much about children are the ones who don't have any. Aren't they sharp? It's amazing what simple solutions they have. I would be an expert, —but I have four children. We hear a lot of these great experts who expound in this field, and it seems so very simple. I heard a man get up the other day. He said, "You should never spank a child when you are angry." Now let's figure that out. Can you imagine spanking a kid when you weren't angry?

I think there is a little bit of good and a little bit of bad in everybody. We are part sinner and part saint, and wholly human. I know that is true of my life and I am sure it is true of your life. I have good days, and I have bad days. I have evil thoughts at times, sometimes I enjoy them. Don't you, really? I know I am married to such a nice girl, but I am seldom home. She is the most wonderful cook I ever saw, but I eat most of my dinners in churches. I have eaten more meat loaf than anyone in America. I am the King of the Meat Loafers—and ham and glue and raisins. You see, friends, you have evil thoughts too!

I have been a judge now for 35 years, and I have never pointed a finger at anyone. People always look good to me, and I took conduct as it was. But now I am worried. I think America is going downhill morally. Maybe we have too much. Buy now—pay later. Buy now—pay later. That's good for business, but it is very bad for people. And good guys are not winning anymore. It's hard to be a judge and have the little boy come up before you and say, "Judge, what do you mean—crime doesn't pay? It's paying a lot of people, and I'm going to knock over a store and get mine some day."

As I look back, I find in my home town there were 50 policemen who went to jail. It was the only town in America where a kid could play cops

182

and robbers all by himself. But I won't take the entire blame. I see the shaving of points in basketball—the highway scandal, the green-felt jungle of Las Vegas—trouble in New Orleans—and Billy Sol Estes—and trouble in Philadelphia, and I realize the good guys aren't winning anymore. It seems to me that the most important thing for America is "Let's make decency popular." It's good to be a good guy, and it's bad to be a bad guy. I like what Robert Frost had to say:

"I don't want my society to be homogenized, I want the cream to rise to the top."

I like that old-fashioned Dad. I like that shiny blue-serge suit—it looks like shining armor. The wise-guy in grey flannel is the Ugly American, and he walks the streets of my home town.

But, I'm not entirely discouraged, because I deal with young people, and I find more decency among young people than I ever found among the adults. I travel all over the United States. I go to many highschools. I go to many colleges, and I have never seen such a surge for decency. No, I am not discouraged. Everyone points a finger at the teenager and the young people, but if you go out to the Boy Scout Troop with me and see them stand up and say "On my Honor I will do my best," you go over to the YMCA—"Old MacDonald had a farm"—there is something very wonderful about young people. Yes, I find a great inspiration and great decency among them.

I go out to the highschools and I have never seen such a surge for decency. In the first place, they are better educated than we ever were. The means of communication around the world are tremendous. There is radio and television in darkest Africa. And you go out to the colleges, and they are extremely well-educated and very intelligent. You see the College Bowl program on Sunday afternoon. This is not unusual. You try to compete with these young people and you realize the tremendous surge that is sweeping the country. I find more religion in our schools today than I have ever found before. It seems to me this is the survival of America. Now, if the older people would only understand and follow them, I think it would be a great thing. We have great heroes among the young people, and I think we should dramatize these great heroes. I like this moral-rearmament. If you want your town to be a decent town, keep it at a high moral, spiritual and cultural level.

As I look back over the years in dealing with thousands of people in trouble, I have often wondered if I had some magic way of solving their problems. *My* job is to help people—and *our* job is to help people. And as I turn back the clock in my own life, I know I always wanted wealth and I always wanted health. But now I know what I want. I have found the secret of working with people, and it's not an easy thing to do. Yes, everybody wanted the judge to punish people. Everybody wanted the judge to get tough. I was never very successful that way. I think we should carry on the philosophy of the juvenile court—The People In the INTEREST of The Child.

And, after all these years, I feel that I have found the secret of solving problems and helping people. And the most important thing in my life—I want PEACE OF MIND! I want to *like* this fellow! I want to get up in the morning and look in the mirror and say: "Judge, you're not such a bad person." And it dawns on me that this is the most important thing in anybody's life. You ask for a solution of what a judge should do—I say this: Make that person feel important, because everybody needs that—it is his life. The most important thing in your life is that you love yourself. This is not a matter of conceit. The conceited man hates himself. But the most obvious signs of a deliquent child is that he doesn't like himself—he hates himself! There are many reasons for that. Maybe he has been told what a bum he was all of his life. Maybe he came from a poor environment and lousy parents. But believe me, the most successful thing I have ever done with a child is not to send them to an institution.

We have forestry camps as part of the philosophy of the Juvenile Court. We have them up in the Rocky Mountains in these small camps, where we teach them how to live gracefully under great leadership. Where we teach them how to climb that mountain. Where they will learn how to create with their hands and live well. Even food has a lot to do with juvenile delinquency. A good share of the delinquents today are under-nourished. Especially the girls. They go without breakfast so they will get thin. Instead of that they eat the "Jitterbug Diet" of candy and soda pop and potato chips—then they get sloppy. But up there in those forestry camps it's amazing to see them change. When they develop self-esteem—when they learn how to create—when they learn how to climb that mountain! Even their facial expressions change. And I believe I have found the secret of success in working with people in trouble. I have never seen anything quite as successful as those forestry camps.

And, it's more interesting, possibly, even with girls, because girls are much more serious delinquents than boys. A girl has to like herself.

> "Love to a man is a thing apart—
> 'tis woman's whole existence."

And when the little girls come up before me, the most serious delinquents of a big town, they look like alley cats. To see them walk across the floor with big bouffants, crying mascara, coming out of hotel rooms—the most depressed girls I have ever seen. And everybody says, "Judge, what you should do is to confine them—to lock them up." No, friends, the greatest success I have ever had with those girls, as part of the terms of their probation, they should go to a charm school. Fifteen weeks in a charm school to learn how to be lovely.

"There are no ugly women—there are only those women who don't know how to be pretty."

And I say to them: "Little girl, I'll teach you how to fix your hair, fix your makeup, to wear a dress properly, to get your shoulders back and walk across the stage—Isn't she a lovely person?" Every six months we have a charm school style show. And to see those little dolls walking across the stage is the greatest thrill on earth, because they learned how to like themselves. And when you feel good—when you feel pretty—when you feel intelligent—don't worry about getting into trouble. What's the comparison between punishment and rehabilitation? Draw your own conclusions. Should I lock them up—or should I help them? And then when you start believing in yourself—and everybody has to believe in themself—you start giving to other people. I know one of the greatest educators I have ever known—Dr. Ralph Pitts at East High School. He knew he was a great educator. When he walked down the halls of East High School he walked tall. And when you went into his classroom you had a thirst for knowledge.

"Those who desire to kindle others—must himself glow"

And, Dr. Pitts glowed. And I think that's what everybody needs. And, yet it's a hard job to like yourself. It's one of the most difficult things you can encounter, because we're not very charitable with ourselves. But if you only have a little faith in yourself, there is nothing you can't accomplish. You'll never be a good mother and a good father unless you know you are a good mother and a good father. And, then when you like yourself, you give to other people. You can't give what you haven't got. It doesn't come from a vacuum. It must come from within.

In working with a family of a delinquent you not only have to work with the child, but you have to work with the parents. The child is not in a vacuum either. You can't send him back to a lousy home and say, "Now you be a good boy, and when you make a mistake, Johnny, I'll be able to send you to an institution." It's intellectual dishonesty. But, if we could only teach the families to love each other.

A lot of people talk to me about delinquency, and they say, "Judge, how will I make sure that my boy or girl will not get in trouble?" I could talk to you all day about it, but you say, "Judge, name one thing I could do." I say this to you—Love your wife—and that's not easy! Love your husband —and that's harder! And yet it's the most important thing in life. Love is not a physical thing—it's an ethereal quality between man and woman. "I love her not only for what she is—but for what I am when I'm with her." When you feel that way about your wife or your husband, isn't that a wonderful feeling?

I don't think we should call it "The Wedding"—we should call it the "Commencement." It seems so strange that we have an idea that we fall in love—we get married—and then we relax. You do so at your peril! Love requires a continuous effort. It requires intelligence and hard work. But, when you go through that feeling of great love, you will find the greatest happiness you will ever know. And you will know what it means to those children. No matter how tough the world might be—they can come home and say, "I'm safe, my father and mother love each other."

We also have to teach parents the importance of discipline. Whenever you talk about discipline, it sounds like you want to beat somebody up, but discipline is a way of life. To become a disciple—I think our main job as parents is to teach a child to do without you, so that he will walk strong—this is a mean old tough world—don't let that little girl or that little boy go out into the world without a rehearsal—without strength. You won't be with him too long, and you teach him how to use his head and his hands so he will be properly prepared. This is the greatest form of love for a child. How do you hate a child? Do you say, "Get out of my life—I hate you." When you really love a child you teach him to be strong.

I met a fellow the other day and he said, "Phil, remember the baby I adopted?" You could imagine—after 35,000 babies. But I did remember. I remember when the mother cried that day, and I knew that baby went to him. And, it wasn't easy. He didn't have too much money. But, what he did for that child! He said, "Judge, my son was offered scholarships to three of the greatest universities in America. He graduated Phi Beta Kappa this year from Stanford. He led the class—he was No. 1 in the class—and a great athlete." He said, "Judge, that was the baby." You see, there was a "Forest King"—and I was so glad I was part of that.

> "A tree that never had a fight
> The Sun and Sky and Air and Light,
> Who lived out in the open plains,
> And always got its share of rain,
> Never became a Forest King—
> But lived and died a scrubby thing."

All my life I have dealt with scrubby things. It's wonderful to see a Forest King. Yes, we have to teach that to people. Not just to punish people, but to teach them to be strong.

As part of this business of rehabilitation, which I think is so much better than penalty, is to teach them a religious concept of human life. That God walks with us and talks with us. I used to think God was some kind of a celestial bell-hop. When I got in trouble I would ring the bell and say, "God, I need your service." But not anymore. God wants me to be a fighter.

Every Friday night I take out about fifty of the meanest kids in town. I said, "Fellows, lock up your bicycles," and everybody laughed. And I said, "What are you laughing about?", and they said, "Judge, anybody who would steal a bike in Denver is right here." And then I took them to a prize fight, and a little Mexican kid was going to fight. He was a good Catholic and he crossed himself before he fought. So, I turned to the priest and I say, "Father, will that help that guy?" He said, "It will if he can fight."

Yes, we'll have to learn how to fight. I went out to the Martin Plant the other day and I saw the big missile up in the air, and I thought—it's the most complicated thing in the world. And then it dawned on me. It was very simple in comparison to me. What made me laugh? What made me cry? It was that little boy in the classroom—that's your son—that's the little guy in the courtroom. And to me the greatest thrill is to help people.

"What you are, God gave you;
What you become, you give to God!"

It's the divine excitement of saying, "Let's get well—let's get well."

Corrective Treatment vs. Punitive Justice? There are so many who want to punish—but in thirty-five years in dealing with people in trouble, I know that corrective treatment is the greatest solution to help problem people and to build a strong nation.

Dr. Robert E. Kay

Dr. Robert E. Kay, Medical Director and Chief Psychiatrist, Center for Child Guidance, Philadelphia, gave the Jennings Scholar Lecture on May 1, 1971, at Bowling Green State University.

Dr. Kay's B.A. and M.D. degrees are from Brown University and Tufts University Medical School, respectively. From 1958–1961 he was a resident in psychiatry at Walter Reed General Hospital.

Dr. Kay has served as a psychiatrist at county and community mental health centers and at army hospitals. He is presently serving the Chester County Mental Health Clinic. From 1965–1967 he was a child psychiatrist for the Devereux Foundation, Devon, Pennsylvania.

Among his publications are "Our American Educational System" and "Helping a Child Learn to Read at Home," both in *Clinical Pediatrics*, the former in the September 1969 issue and the latter in the August 1970 issue. He also contributes to the *American Journal of Psychiatry*.

"THE CHILD, THE SCHOOL, AND THE UNPREDICTABLE FUTURE"

I promised myself sometime ago that I would never again give a lecture because we know that of all forms of human communication, the lecture method is the least effective. Under ideal circumstances, 15 percent of the information may get communicated.

Recently I heard Charles Silberman talk, and he told about the time that he was preparing to testify to the Senators down in Washington. He had received six calls from one of the Senators' assistants to remind him that, while he was welcome to submit as much written testimony as he cared to, he should please hold his spoken remarks to 15 minutes because the Senators begin fidgeting after that. I think there's a message here for all of us.

I'm talking to you as an outsider with all the hazards that implies. Outsiders never completely understand what another profession is all about, but we can be useful because human institutions and bureaucracies are particularly inept in the processes of self-criticism, self-renewal, and adaptation to changing conditions. There is a strong tendency on the part of any bureaucracy to want to maintain the system and preserve job security; this is very understandable, but it does prevent adaptation to the new demands of a complex society.

I'm a little apprehensive about talking to teachers; picking on education and blaming the schools for all of our national problems is one of the great American spectator sports. The result is that, while teachers tend to be self-critical, they also become rather defensive to any suggestions from outsiders. I can certainly understand why.

Inevitably, I think we will raise more questions today than give answers, because answers are very difficult to come by. But I get involved in this because I am very unhappy about the course our society is taking. I think we are in serious trouble, and there is reason to believe that our survival as a great nation is somewhat in doubt. One of the reasons that we are having so much trouble solving our problems is that we just don't seem to have developed enough people who are willing to get involved, who get concerned about what is going on beyond their own narrow community and families.

We have an amazing level of apathy and un-involvement, and the extent of this is indicated by two statistics: One is that 94 percent of the people do not know a single thing that their Congressman stands for. This, to me, is incredible; to know nothing about the individual who has such a major influence on our lives! We also know that 53 percent of American adults have never read a book from cover to cover.

One of the results of this apathy and the sense of powerlessness that accompanies it is the election of much incompetent leadership at all levels of government. I'm afraid we have to face the fact that most of our leaders don't really seem to know very much about what they are doing, and they certainly are not coming to grips with many of the problems in our very complex world.

Every system that we have developed for the betterment of mankind is in serious trouble, whether we are talking about the legal, the family, the church, the medical, the psychiatric, the government, the welfare, or the educational system. Every one is showing many stresses and strains and is proving itself much less effective than we have imagined.

Maybe I am unduly pessimistic, but we took a survey among junior-high school students in a wealthy Presbyterian church. We asked the kids what life would be like in 1985. More than 55 percent of them assumed there would be no life on Earth in just 15 years! So, if I'm pessimistic, I guess I come by it honestly.

We are finding out that all of us in "people-work" are much less effective than we had hoped, considering the efforts that we expend. For the fact is that people object to being changed by other people. You will resist my ideas if you feel I am trying to impose them on you, and even questions are seen as threatening. People need to learn, but they learn best when they have considerable control over the circumstances of learning.

You know very well how difficult it is to teach anybody anything unless we teach to the concerns of the individual. This is called affective education and is concerned with his self-image, where he fits, his hopes, his fears, his wishes, his curiosities, his needs and his perceptions. But so often in school, where we have a structured, graded curriculum, the major concern is to get through, to pass the test, to psych-out the teacher, to pretend that you know what you really may not know, and then forget the material quickly after the examination. I was an "A" student in algebra and forgot it very quickly because algebra was just not speaking to a need of mine.

When we talk about learning, we have to recognize the fact that man is a learning animal. We are learning constantly from the day of birth, and it is widely recognized now that the most complicated thing that the human being ever learns is how to speak the English language. He does this at home, in his own way, in his own time, with very little, if any, formal instruction. Any judgment that we make about subsequent learning needs to be weighed against the child's capacities to learn the English language. He learns for reasons of curiosity, mastery, competence, to achieve power and growth.

We know that kids come to kindergarten very enthusiastic; they're bright-eyed and full of questions. Then something seems to go wrong. At least it goes wrong from a psychiatric point of view, for learning becomes a painful chore and hard work; it becomes something the child does by virtue of the carrot or the stick. And we seem to be stuck with this incredible idea: that learning, to be good or effective, has to be painful.

The result is—and I realize that what I am saying is not applicable to all schools nor applicable to every teacher nor applicable to every child all the time—that we take kids, who at age four and five are very active, involved learners, and we often turn them off; they become passive receptacles to be filled with our curriculum.

Learning starts out as something you do for yourself, and very shortly it becomes something that somebody does *to* you. Though we try to tell them differently, we *tend* to teach children that learning is something that requires a teacher in order to be effective. Sometimes that is true, but obviously not always.

Then in school control and efficiency become the order of the day, and teachers are asked to control what no human being should be asked to control: normal human behavior. You should not be asked to control the normal tendencies of the human being, which are to socialize and move around. This is most unfortunate, but I realize the problems that you must have, in terms of both the community's expectations of teachers and the administrators', and how you get judged on this issue of orderliness.

The results all too often are varying degrees of frustration, resistance, negativism, anxiety, alienation, boredom, confusion, and learning blocks, which afflict a very high percent of the kids in school. All of this has been much better said in John Holt's *How Children Fail.*

It's not only the kids who are unhappy and nervous. I find schools generally to be tense and unhappy places where the goal of everyone is how to get through the day—more so than in any other job that I've seen. Teachers feel as hemmed-in and restricted as the students by the rules, the regulations, and the paperwork, although Holt, in his recent book, *What Do I Do Monday,* shows that you may actually have a great deal more freedom to innovate in your classroom than you may suspect.

This sense of powerlessness seems to pervade almost every level of the school. My favorite story about the rules and regulations concerns my 12-year-old son in junior high school, who likes to go a few minutes early and sometimes likes to stay a few minutes late. He put it in a nutshell when he said, "Daddy, when I go early, they won't let me in; when I'm there, they won't let me out; and when I want to stay, they make me go home." That's called powerlessness!

I'm not going to be able to spend any time discussing the role of education in society; it's a very long, interesting, and somewhat complicated issue. Silberman, in his *Crisis in the Classroom* goes into it and, if you do nothing else but leaf through his book as a result of this lecture, I think our time together will have been well spent. He points out that in 1900 only six percent of the country graduated from high school. The United States was run by dropouts and seemed to muddle along.

Now we've become what is known as the Credential Society. The schools have allowed themselves to be used as the sorting mechanism which puts labels on people that lets society decide who is going to get the rewards and who is going to be labeled reject. My favorite story about credentializing is about a law school down in Washington which decided its graduates were no longer Bachelors of Law; they were Doctors of Law. They were then automatically entitled to $1,000 a year more when working for the Federal Government because they had doctoral degrees instead of bachelor's degrees, although they knew nothing more. Being at the point where one's educational level may, in fact, be more important than what he can actually do is my definition of craziness.

The school has helped to integrate various ethnic, political, and religious groups into the American mainstream, and it was very useful in preparing people for living in an industrial society. But the problem is that we are now living in a postindustrial or super-industrial age as illustrated by Alvin Toffler in *Future Shock*. He says that everything is changing and changing rapidly. Every institution is under challenge and not only from the radical young. We're developing multiple lifestyles manifested by communes, drugs, astrology, and the liberation movement, including something called "insane-lib"—who are some of our dissatisfied customers. And, of course, we have the problems of technological change. Now all this means that we're going to have to start asking a lot of questions, and I think it's safe to say that more of our problems come from our inability to ask the right questions than from our failure to know the pat answers.

It may be much more important to develop people who know how to ask the right kinds of questions, for when you know how to ask the right questions—the relevant, the substantial, the appropriate ones—you've learned how to learn, and then you are in a position to learn anything you want to learn anytime in the future when you are going to need it.

This, I think, is a very central issue in education. I hope we have the courage to allow children to ask questions in the social and the political areas because this can be painful. Children ask very difficult and embarrassing questions, and we must be prepared to cope with them. But if we assume that the purpose of education should be to provide children with the means to meet the future, then we ask, of course, how we prepare them to cope with change, with unpredictability, with stress, with doubt, and with uncertainty and challenge.

We're at the point of asking, "What do we teach beyond the basic learning and communicating skills? What do we teach that stands any chance at all of being useful in the future? Which millionth of the available information do we pick out to feed the children?"

Is Holt correct when he says that the major difference between the poor student and the good one is that the poor student forgets right away, whereas the good one is careful to wait until after the examination?

Do any of us still believe that studying the products of disciplined thinking leads to disciplined thinking—the old faculty psychology concept that we somehow exercise the brain? I'm afraid there is a very little evidence for that. These are the questions that are being asked. And what is the obsession of the school system with the concept of memory?

Memory is one of the weakest of all human faculties, and yet it is the prime one that the school system exercises. We're reaching a point of information accumulation where it may be as important to forget irrelevant information as it is to remember.

Are we really helping the cause of self-esteem and pride, mastery, competence, appreciation of the self when we attach labels or "failure" or "special" to people at a very early age? Is it really useful to label little kids whose potential is neither determined nor developed? I'm not arguing that there are not differences in capacities between children, but is it right to judge a child on his performance in a few specific cognitive areas when he may have many other skills which we never evaluate?

Should we continue to keep everybody stuffed in buildings when the whole world is educational? I might add here, though I am not quite advocating it, that there is talk in our area about abolishing the compulsory attendance laws. Every time that has been tried experimentally, the attendance and the achievement rates go up, and the vandalism rate goes down. School is a natural meeting place for children; children do want to learn. Teachers are, by and large, attractive to kids—much more so when some of the coercion is taken out of the system.

Question: Is learning really dependent on control and quiet and grading? When we learn to play bridge, drive a car, and learn the language of our jobs, we usually do so without grades or control. Can we trust children more than we do without denying the role of the adult as potential instigator, catalyst, promoter of learning, and definer of relevance? Even in Ivan Illich's most radical proposals the teachers remain absolutely central to the educational process but in a very different role. Can we trust children' As Rogers points out: "The basic nature of the human being when functioning freely is constructive and trustworthy." There is no evidence for the existence of an aggressive drive or instinct. Man is a socially cooperative creature who can be frightened or hurt very easily and then act very badly.

Rogers goes on: "All of us have a basic need to grow that does not have to be imposed." It is there already, and each person has a built-in desire to be the best person it is possible for him to become.

Can we trust children to direct and control their own learning to a much higher degree? We know that achievement level is most highly correlated with the degree of control that a child feels he has over his own existence, and, typically, I think this is the major difference between the middle-class child and the lower-class child; the former feels he has a greater impact on his environment, that his messages are correctly read more of the time and has a greater influence on the responses of his parents. Certainly there is reason to believe from a wide range of studies that giving children a reasonable degree of choice and maneuverability in the school stiuation more often than not resuslts in a more enthusiastic and higher-achieving child. This is why reinforcement techniques tend to help and why teaching machines can be very useful. Though teaching machines are not particularly my thing, they are useful because they give the child some control over what happens to him, and they allow him to put his own mark on just when and where he gets involved.

Is it possible to evaluate and feed back notations about performance without putting labels on students? Yes, it certainly is, and it should be done. Silberman and most other reformers, while they may oppose grades, are much in favor of evaluation. And there are very few jobs that I know of where we have to study alone and solve problems on our own. When I run into trouble, I immediately go to somebody else; I don't spend hours by myself trying to figure out what to do next. On my job we call this team-work; in school it is called cheating.

Most of the people in my profession would very much support the concept of the tutoring of younger children by older children or paired learning. If I were to make one recommendation, it would be the pairing of older children with younger children. I know many of you are doing it already. I have never heard an educator say it does not work beautifully. It would undercut an awful lot of the problems that we see in the school.

Is it necessary to try to make everybody look, behave, and sound alike, or can we, once again, tolerate individuality and ethnicity? This is what our country was founded on, and I think this is what we are getting back to, whether we like it or not.

The ultimate question, of course, is what sort of people we want to produce in a highly interdependent society where we have to recognize that what happens in the ghetto of Cleveland is eventually going to have an impact on us. Is it enough to merely produce millions of competitive and obedient consumers who define themselves in terms of status, prestige, positions, and wealth while we ignore the poverty, the starvation, the disease, and the despair of millions that threatens to made a mockery of our democracy and of our affluence?

Despite much that has been written about the mass-man in the mass - culture, it is increasingly evident that we are developing a nation of 200 million egos. Everybody wants to be recognized as an individual, sometimes quite greedily and obnoxiously. This is a very recent and unique development in mankind's history.

Individualism is in the air; it may be self destructive, but it is pushing on. The old world of obedient conformity and tightly structured social hierarchies and even of the large bureaucracies, may be very rapidly dying out. I think we are going to have to make peace with that fact.

And there is strong reason to suspect that the compulsory attendance laws and the traditional curriculum with its lesson plans, fixed schedules, tests, grades, and normal curves is in very serious trouble indeed. They may no longer be meeting the needs of the individual or the society. We may have the traditional curriculum for a long time to come, and I'm sure many of you support it. But, I think it's safe to say that it may be on its way out. For the emphasis is away from the teacher as a dispenser of information and towards the promotion of self-initiated learning that will help children remain very active and effective seekers who will keep on learning for the rest of their lives.

I am reminded of a graduation card: "Congratulations! Now you can stop learning and start earning."

That world is gone forever. I suspect that we are going to have to encourage the development of responsible, autonomous, self-governing, and self-disciplined people, because democracy ultimately depends on self-discipline and cooperation much more than on obedience.

We need to develop independent human beings responsible to the needs of others who have been encouraged through their involvement in the outside world to believe that they can have an impact and an influence on their world and the leaders. I think that we're going to have to develop masses of people who are willing to get involved, and I think the school system could have a very definite role to play in that.

It's beginning to look as if keeping children isolated and powerless and separated from the real world and feeding each other's immaturity with drugs and astrology and antagonistic behavior is increasingly inappropriate.

I think we have a dangerous tendency in America to put children off with groups of children, away from the real world of the adults. Children can go for eighteen years without ever knowing an adult who wasn't specifically designed as a child-care professional. This is an incredible state of affairs, and I think we've got to get children out into the real world at least part of the time. Let them get hooked on us, and maybe we can cut into the drug problem. I think we need to give them more responsibility of a different sort; let them have more choices and take the consequences.

Silberman points out that nothing could be more wildly impractical than an education to prepare children for specific vocations or to facilitate their adjustment to the world as it is. I'd like to say that the world as it is does not exist; and the world to come will never be.

To be practical, an education should prepare children for work that does not yet exist and whose nature cannot even be imagined. This can be done only by teaching them how to learn, by giving them the kind of intellectual discipline that will enable them to apply man's accumulated wisdom to problems as they arise—the kind of wisdom that will enable them to recognize new problems as they arise.

Chase points out that the qualities essential to employability and productivity are coming closer and closer to the characteristics that we have long attributed to the educated person, which means that we have to turn out people with a desire to learn, to keep on learning, and to educate themselves and their neighbors.

To educate one's self means that a person has both the desire and the capacity to learn for himself, to dig out what he needs to know, as well as the capacity to judge what is worth learning. It means that one learns to think for himself so that he is dependent on neither the facts nor the opinions of others; that he uses that capacity to learn about his own place in nature, his own place in the universe.

One is supposed to come to a conclusion with some practical suggestions. I don't really have that many. The most practical suggestion I have is an appeal to read deeply, to think deeply about education and its role in society, and to become aware, as I am just beginning to become aware, of the very complex role in which education finds itself and the problems of trying to satisfy the competing demands of various groups.

I really feel that this is a very serious problem, indeed. Your role is a very difficult one. I'd like to see a lot more public debate, and perhaps you can do your part in stimulating discussions around these various issues —particularly the grading system and the issues of relevance in the curriculum. I hope many of you can stimulate your superintendents to look into the so-called open classrooms that you have heard described. The teachers say that they work harder, but they are very enthusiastic and are much less exhausted at the end of the day.

There are public schools developing in this country where neither teacher nor student wants to go home at the end of the day—and that's a very nice feeling, I am sure.

I think that teachers, like all other professionals, need to be constantly up-dating their skills, getting involved in in-service training. From a psychiatric point of view, I think the problems of the future are not production and the development of material goods, but the problem of human interaction and social behavior. I hope the school can find ways of going much further in promoting an understanding of how people operate in a wide variety of situations by allowing children many more opportunities to interact with others of different ages.

I think, finally, that as many educators are pointing out, the time has come for rather large-scale reforms away from teaching and judging and towards the development of what could be called learning communities.

I hope very much that you will be able to find a way to become a part of that process.

Dr. Harvey Wheeler

Dr. Harvey Wheeler, a Senior Fellow at the Center for the Study of Democratic Institutions in Santa Barbara, California, presented the Jennings Scholar Lecture, on May 29, 1971, at Bowling Green State University.

Dr. Wheeler came to the Center in 1960 from Washington and Lee University, where he had been a professor of political science.

His A.B. and M.A. degrees are from Indiana University and his Ph.D. from Harvard.

After serving in military government in the European theater during World War II, he taught political science at Harvard and at John Hopkins University.

In addition to monographs on political science and political theory in numerous academic and polemic journals, Dr. Wheeler is the coauthor, with the late Eugene Burdick, of the novel *Fail-Safe.*

In 1968, the *Encyclopaedia Britannica* included Dr. Wheeler's major essay on contemporary and future political concerns in their publication *Democracy in a Revolutionary Era.* Also published in 1968 was an anthology *Alternatives to Violence,* which includes "Moral Equivalent to Riots" and "The Strategic Calculators" by Dr. Wheeler.

POLITICS OF REVOLUTION

It's an intimidating experience to be at Bowling Green. To talk to teachers in the field of education, about which I know nothing, is even worse. So that's a kind of warning.

First let me say a few things about what I think is common knowledge. They say that we are entering the post industrial wars. I hear that story all the time. I guess that's a polite way of saying that we are entering the post capitalist wars because we don't like to say the word too loudly sometimes. They tell us that the scientific revolution is a new phase we've got. I suppose most of you have read that article on biological revolution that was in Time Magazine a few weeks ago. If you didn't read it, I hope you will run right out as soon as you get out of here and get hold of it, because it is really a remarkably good survey article. In fact, it is better than you could get if you knew all there is to know about biology and went through all the biological journals and got all the latest journals to find out what is happening in chromosomes and genetics and so on. Actually the article contains more up-to-date information about the biological revolution than you could get any place else.

That kind of writing is an indication of some of the things that we mean. But beyond that we know that they are going to be able to make synthetic life. I read just last week that we can discover in advance what sex a newborn baby is going to be. They can make a little injection and take a little bit of fluid out and figure out in advance what the sex is going to be. Then in about a year or so they will be able to do a little genetic engineering and see that you get a boy or a girl. Now that's a real startling thing because that means that we're all going to have to decide what we're going to do one way or the other about this kind of capacity. Are we going to be an individual choice so that every parent-to-be can decide if they want a boy or girl or what mix? What do you think you would do? Suppose 75 percent of the people decide to have boys, and the next generation has a three to one ratio? What would you do with a population like that? What kind of new problems would that bring. It's a public policy though, to let the people have their choice. Suppose you decide, "Well, I don't think I want to take what I get!" What would be the right mix for the population? Would it be 50–50, or do you think that we could overbalance it a little bit? We already have about 52 percent females and 48 percent males. How do you decide questions like that? And this is just the beginning one. They tell us that longevity is going to be stepped up maybe 50, maybe 60 to 70 years in not too long a time. Who is going to get longevity? At first it will probably be so expensive. You may have to have a transfusion type thing, blood washings, or you may get a kidney disease. That's terribly expensive. Sometimes it takes about $25,000 a year to keep a person under dialysis or a kidney-washing machine.

Suppose that breakthrough comes along. What are you going to do about the problem of scarcity? If you had, let's say, a choice between an extra 50 years or an extra $150,000, which would you take? What would most people take? If you have a society in which that kind of choice is available, who's going to get the 50 years or the 75? How are you going to distribute it? The struggle for time would probably take the place of the struggle for money wouldn't it? Especially since you're going to get older. When you're 20, you'd much rather have a few more years than $150,000. Then maybe later on you'd change your mind. But how are you going to distribute a thing like that? Think of power struggle in such a society. What would be the causes of death? Automobiles would still kill people off. My guess is that murder would become the main cause of death, because you see what a generation gap we have now. There's no room at the top, and so you go through a period of say 40 years and nobody dies off. You give the guys who are at the top another 50 years, and you have to stand there marking time until you're around 75 even to become a junior executive. What kind of future is that? So that's why I figure that murder will be the primary cause of death.

In a sense you could say that, while the flow of capital will be an extremely important factor throughout time, (it always has been) the flow of scientific innovations seems to me to be the thing that will be the critical factor in this new world that we are entering right now.

Suppose we want to change the shape of what's going to happen. We want to have control over whether or not we made a major advancement of the people or space ships. This field of science policy is a brand new field, and it is almost impossible to throw it into our legislature, because Congressmen don't know enough about things like technical scientific research. So one of the things that would have to come out would be some kind of new legislative program of advising (Putting together legislation) that would allow us to cope with these scientific problems that are going to be so critical in the future. So, as I look into the scientific revolution that we are going through, it seems to me that it involves a kind of reversal in that in the past, the role of the executive has been the critical one and the scientists have engineered more or less at his service. Increasingly today, it seems to me that the tables have been turned. The difference is something like the difference between the relationship in theory and practice today. In the old days, the practitioner was on top and the theoretician was on tap. Today, increasingly the theoretician is on top and the practitioner is on tap. The technical aspects are superior to the recent developments in theory. So that's the basic issue, it seems to me, of the post industrial war. We're into an era in which the more scientific aspects of our society will increasingly take the place of the more traditional business-orientated aspects that we grew up with. Well, that's enough to make a revolution of the critical kind.

Suppose that is the case? What does that mean for education? Do we tell our children that they should get an education and possibly go on to high school and college to improve their condition in life economically? Is that any longer the way we teach children? Do we feel that there is a kind of dollar sign value on a college degree? That if you have one you make more money in the end? I know that has been said in the newspapers. Is that the way you motivate children? I don't know. I assume that it has happened throughout the elementary school system, secondary schools, and even in college. So the question is: Is it true? Has it ever been true? Most of the families that I'm familiar with indicate that education doesn't have much relationship to the act of earning power. A kind of selective process goes on. People who are brought up in upper-class homes tend to end up in the colleges. They seem to get the better jobs and so it looks as if there is a correlation between higher education and higher earnings.

Until after World War II, it didn't made a great deal of difference because there weren't a great many people going to college. But after World War II, almost everybody who wanted better things had better go to college. Then people began to expect a real return from their college educations in financial terms, but they didn't get it because there weren't any more jobs after people got out of college than there were before. But do they still teach people to go to college in order to get a better job? My guess is that it never was true.

Suppose, even though it never was true, we are entering into a scientific revolution world. What are some of the characteristics of that world? One of the things that we are told about is the workless world and a four-day work week. That's undoubtedly going to be started everywhere. It's going to be in Washington very soon. How long before it will be a three-day work week? Technically you know it is possible to place into the computer almost every routine operation. That means that all office jobs as well as production and factory jobs theoretically can disappear. In an automated factory, ovens run down a line almost a half a mile long. All ovens work 24 hours a day and are attended by one man. He rides a bicycle up and down the rows between the ovens, and that's all there is to do except set the dials. Is that something like the work-world of the future? Everyone tells us that.

If you educated people in the past for earning a living and that was the purpose of the primary, secondary and college education, why are you doing that in a world in which the problem of earning a living takes up only a small proportion of time? You probably should have been educating them for different purposes in the first place.

We talk about the population explosion, and if you look at it very closely you can see that there just won't be enough to go around. Everyone will have a declining standard of living. It's already started, hasn't it? Haven't we been in kind of a declining standard of living for about three or four years? On the one hand, you can do more for everybody, and no work is attached to it. On the other hand, scientists come along and say, "You'll never live to get it, and, besides, even if you do it will be awful. You will have to consume refuse instead of food. You'll probably have a new muta-

203

tion in man. We won't be able to survive in the garbage atmosphere. Some kind of mutation, like a worm or something like that." You've got to start with a zero population growth movement right now. That's upsetting, isn't it? You're not going to have kids: you're going to adopt them. You're going to the slums, the bad areas, the ghettos, and adopt you 2.4 allotment instead of adding. And then you're going beyond that. That's called the sterlization movement. It's a strange new world, isn't it? But you go on beyond that zero population growth, and reduce the population. In the end that's the only thing that will save us. How many people will the American environment support in relatively decent circumstances? It won't support around 200 million. It will only support around 150 million. But there are 250 million all ready to come along. What are you going to do about it? So we are going to have to talk about negatives, how to reduce the population by some kind of birth control method.

To what extent do the educational systems of the country give any kind of preparation about environmental issues? I don't know to what extent it's taking place in the primary schools and the high schools. It is taking place in the colleges. A new part of the University of Wisconsin's educational system is being devoted entirely to the ecology area. A part of the University of Michigan's system is being established entirely with environmental orientation. Evergreen University in Washington State is going to be part of that. Part of the Washington State system has an entire new area on ecology.

A new college in Maryland is going to an environmental college. It seems that almost every university that doesn't have a college for ecology is getting a new ecology program. Most of them are not very good. They're something to advertise in the catalog and get the state legislature to give them more money for. What will ecology mean for education in the lower grades? I assume that with this ecological orientation the quality of life will be stressed instead of the quantity. We live in a quantitated society, don't we? What effect would a qualitated society with a different kind of foundation or orientation have on the students? What effect would that have on the roles of primary, secondary, and college education institutions?

What should society learn? What should society be teaching itself? It will have to teach itself some new subjects. How will it do it? Will it have a new method? What is the content or the substance for the education of this new society? I don't know. I think it is going to have to be some form of politics, and not politics on how to get elected before an election. Politics in processing, in maintaining a community. That's what by and large, we normally mean in politics. We must develop highly dedicated people for a new society, a society that is post industrious and I think probably post prosperous, a learning society rather than an earning society.